SOCIAL INVESTIGATION AND RURAL ENGLAND 1870–1914

Mark Freeman

THE ROYAL HISTORICAL SOCIETY
THE BOYDELL PRESS

First published 2003

A Royal Historical Society publication
Published by The Boydell Press
an imprint of Boydell & Brewer Ltd
PO Box 9, Woodbridge, Suffolk IP12 3DF, UK
and of Boydell & Brewer Inc.
PO Box 41026, Rochester, NY 14604–4126, USA
website: www.boydell.co.uk

ISBN 0 86193 257 9

ISSN 0269–2244

A catalogue record for this book is available
from the British Library

Library of Congress Cataloging-in-Publication Data
Freeman, Mark, 1974–
    Social investigation and rural England, 1870–1914 / Mark Freeman.
        p. cm. – (Royal Historical Society studies in history. New series)
    Includes bibliographical references and index.
    ISBN 0–86193–257–9 (Hardback : alk. paper)
    1. Social surveys – England – History – 19th century. 2. Social
surveys – England – History – 20th century.   3. England – Rural
conditions – 19th century.   4. England – Rural conditions –
20th century.
I. Title. II. Series.
    HN398.E5 F74 2003
    300'.723 – dc21   2002010794

This book is printed on acid-free paper

Printed in Great Britain by
St Edmundsbury Press Ltd, Bury St Edmunds, Suffolk

ROYAL HISTORICAL SOCIETY

STUDIES IN HISTORY

New Series

SOCIAL INVESTIGATION AND RURAL ENGLAND 1870–1914

Contents

FOR MY MOTHER AND FATHER
CATHERINE AND ALEC FREEMAN

List of Tables

Publication of this volume was aided by a grant from the Scouloudi Foundation, in association with the Institute of Historical Research.

Acknowledgements

This book began as a PhD thesis in the Department of Economic and Social History at the University of Glasgow. The research was supported by a Snell-Newlands Research Scholarship and was supervised by Anne Crowther, to whom my greatest thanks are owed. I would also like to thank the examiners of the thesis, Rick Trainor and Eileen Yeo, together with Susan Cohen, David Eastwood, Bridget Fowler, Eleanor Gordon and Peter Hennock, who have all made helpful and constructive suggestions at various times. I am also grateful to Mike French for his encouragement and support both during and since my PhD research. Christine Linehan has assisted in many ways with the preparation of the manuscript. During the course of the research Pauline McCormack and Ewan MacLean assisted me with many computing-related difficulties. I was able to work on revisions to the thesis during my tenure of a Tawney Fellowship at the Institute of Historical Research, supported by the Economic History Society; and I am also grateful to the Joseph Rowntree Charitable Trust for supporting a research fellowship at the University of York, and to colleagues in the Department of History there, especially Bill Sheils, Jim Walvin and Allen Warren.

I would like to record my thanks to John Moore of Glasgow University Library, and to the staff of the British Library, the Mitchell Library in Glasgow, the National Library of Scotland, the Borthwick Institute of Historical Research in York, the Norfolk Record Office, the House of Lords Record Office, the British Library of Political and Economic Science and the University of London Library. I am particularly grateful for communications from Philip Saunders of the Cambridgeshire Record Office, John d'Arcy of the Wiltshire Record Office and Mr B. Carpenter of the Devon Record Office. Some portions of chapter 3 appeared in *Social History* xxvi (2001), 209–16; I thank the publishers, Taylor and Francis (http://www.tandf.co.uk), for their permission to reproduce them here.

I have incurred many personal debts during the period spent writing this book, of which only very few may be recorded here. I am particularly grateful to those with whom I worked for a number of years in Glasgow, and who have assisted me in numerous ways, especially Ian Anderson, Matt Bevis, Fiona Dobbie, Matt Egan, Rosemary Elliot, David Hopkin, Catriona Macdonald, Krista Maglen, Lily Mo, Debbie Nicholson, Megan Smitley, Nicola Sneddon and Paula Summerly. In addition, I would like to acknowledge the friendship of Niall Barr, Fiona Black, Zoe Bliss, Christine and Lucy Cheepen, Giles Cooke, Rowin Cross, Susan Currie, Fiona Dalrymple, Gavin Deas, Anna Evangelidis, Steve Fisher, Paul Foot, David and Tamsin Gammie, David Gwynne, Joseph McHugh, Damon Miller, André Reibig, Alessandro Usai,

Jacob Sharpe, David Walker, Hadrian and Joanna Wise, Matthew Woodward and Andrew Young. My final thanks must be reserved for my parents, Alec and Catherine Freeman, to whom the book is dedicated. Although all those mentioned here have assisted me in many ways during the course of writing this book, any errors of fact or interpretation are entirely my own.

Mark Freeman
Glasgow
October 2002

Abbreviations

BL	British Library
COS	Charity Organisation Society
ELRL	English Land Restoration League
MAFF	Ministry of Agriculture, Fisheries and Food
NALU	National Agricultural Labourers' Union
NAPSS	National Association for the Promotion of Social Science
NRO	Norfolk Record Office
RASE	Royal Agricultural Society of England
RC	Royal Commission
SC	Select Committee

Introduction

This book examines a large and diverse group of social investigators in rural England between 1870 and 1914.[1] The historiography of social investigation in Britain in this period has focused mainly on the pioneering social surveys of Charles Booth in London and Seebohm Rowntree in York, with many backward glances towards Henry Mayhew and his descriptions of metropolitan trades and low-life. All three have attracted book-length studies.[2] The role of Arthur Bowley, the academic mathematician who pioneered the sample survey of poverty, has also been discussed;[3] and Roger Davidson has analysed the collection of labour statistics by the Board of Trade under the direction of Hubert Llewellyn Smith.[4] Other historians have examined the development of social science and statistics in the mid-nineteenth century, focusing on early social surveys and bodies such as the National Association for the Promotion of Social Science.[5] Others have concentrated on the role of official inquiries such as royal commissions, the number of which peaked in the mid-nineteenth century, and whose published output in the form of 'blue

---

1 Scotland and Wales lie outside the scope of this book, and are referred to only incidentally.
2 Asa Briggs, *Social thought and social action: a study of the work of Seebohm Rowntree*, London 1961; T. S. Simey and M. B. Simey, *Charles Booth: social scientist*, London 1960; Anne Humpherys, *Travels in the poor man's country: the work of Henry Mayhew*, Firle 1977, and *Henry Mayhew*, Boston, Mass. 1984; Rosemary O'Day and David Englander, *Mr Charles Booth's inquiry: Life and labour of the people in London reconsidered*, London 1993; David Englander and Rosemary O'Day (eds), *Retrieved riches: social investigation in Britain, 1840–1914*, Aldershot 1995.
3 E. P. Hennock, 'The measurement of urban poverty: from the metropolis to the nation, 1880–1920', *Economic History Review* 2nd ser. xl (1987), 219–27, and 'Concepts of poverty in the British social surveys from Charles Booth to Arthur Bowley', in Martin Bulmer, Kevin Bales and K. K. Sklar (eds), *The social survey in historical perspective, 1880–1940*, Cambridge 1991, 189–216.
4 Roger Davidson, *Whitehall and the labour problem in late-Victorian and Edwardian Britain: a study in official statistics and social control*, London 1982, and 'Llewellyn Smith, the Labour Department and government growth, 1886–1909', in Gillian Sutherland (ed.), *Studies in the growth of nineteenth-century government*, London 1972, 227–62.
5 Eileen Janes Yeo, *The contest for social science: relations and representations of gender and class*, London 1996; Lawrence Goldman, 'A peculiarity of the English? The Social Science Association and the absence of sociology in nineteenth-century Britain', *Past and Present* cxiv (1987), 133–71, and 'The origins of British "social science": political economy, natural science and statistics, 1830–1835', *Historical Journal* xxvi (1983), 587–616; Michael J. Cullen, *The statistical movement in early Victorian Britain: the foundations of empirical social research*, Hassocks 1975; T. S. Ashton, *Economic and social investigations in Manchester: a centenary history of the Manchester Statistical Society* (1st edn 1934), Brighton 1977.

books' has been seen as an important feature of state formation in Britain;[6] however, the historiography of the official inquiry remains deficient, and governmental investigations are often not fully incorporated into histories of social inquiry.[7] Historians have been reluctant to examine contemporaneous attempts to document and enumerate rural poverty, partly because Mayhew, Booth, Rowntree and Bowley are all known for their surveys of urban areas. There were, however, many investigations of rural life. For example, Mayhew's investigations in London formed only one of three series of articles that appeared in the *Morning Chronicle*; another dealt with rural districts.[8] Mayhew's investigative skills and descriptive ability have ensured that his articles have been remembered while those of his colleagues have been largely forgotten, forming a useful source for social historians of rural England but not considered as significant social investigations in themselves. More important, perhaps, Booth and Rowntree both carried out studies of rural life, and Bowley was interested in problems of rural economics and demography as well as urban poverty.[9] E. H. Hunt has pointed out that agriculture 'was more frequently and more thoroughly investigated than any other nineteenth-century occupation':[10] if nothing else, the sheer volume of work on rural areas deserves the historian's attention. Although the proportion of the English population living in rural districts, and the numbers engaged in agriculture, were declining throughout most of the period covered by this book, agricultural workers still formed the largest single occupational group recorded in every census until 1901. Moreover, as many solutions to the problems of urban England were sought throughout this period in a return to the moral values and social relationships associated with rural life, it is important to

6   Hugh McDowall Clokie and J. William Robinson, *Royal commissions of inquiry: the significance of investigations in British politics*, London 1937; T. J. Cartwright, *Royal commissions and departmental committees in Britain: a case-study in institutional adaptiveness and public participation in government*, London 1975, ch. iii; Philip Corrigan and Derek Sayer, *The great arch: English state formation as cultural revolution*, Oxford 1985, ch. vi; Charles J. Hanser, *Guide to decision: the royal commission*, Totowa, NJ 1965.

7   P. W. J. Bartrip has described Englander and O'Day, *Retrieved riches*, as 'a history of social investigation with the government left out': *Urban History* xxv (1998), 130; cf. Brian Harrison, *Peaceable kingdom: stability and change in modern Britain*, Oxford 1982, ch. vi, and Hennock, 'Measurement', 216–19, which discusses the Board of Trade inquiries of the 1900s in the context of Rowntree and Bowley.

8   See P. E. Razzell and R. W. Wainwright (eds), *The Victorian working class: selections from letters to the* Morning Chronicle, London 1973; J. Ginswick (ed.), *Labour and the poor in England and Wales, 1849–1851: the letters to the* Morning Chronicle *from the correspondents in the manufacturing and mining districts, the towns of Liverpool and Birmingham, and the rural districts*, London 1983.

9   Charles Booth, *The aged poor in England and Wales*, London 1894, pt iv; B. Seebohm Rowntree, *Land and labour: lessons from Belgium*, London 1910; B. Seebohm Rowntree and May Kendall, *How the labourer lives: a study of the rural labour problem*, London 1913; A. L. Bowley, 'Rural population in England and Wales: a study of the changes of density, occupations and ages', *Journal of the Royal Statistical Society* lxvii (1913–14), 597–652.

10   E. H. Hunt, *Regional wage variations in Britain, 1850–1914*, Oxford 1973, 66.

understand the preoccupations and methods of inquiry that were brought to bear on the rural areas in which many of the same problems of poverty, ignorance and discord were identified. One urban historian has asked rhetorically 'what should they know of towns and cities who only towns and cities know?';[11] and investigators of the period agreed. Thus Seebohm Rowntree insisted in 1914 that '[r]ural and urban conditions are too intimately related for a general and permanent improvement to take place in the one that is not rapidly reflected in the other'.[12]

Not only has the history of social investigation concentrated on urban inquiries, but it has also been largely restricted to the history of the quantitative social survey. Charles Booth is usually regarded as the founding father of this form of social study, although most historians nod in the direction of the statistical societies of the 1830s as forerunners in the tradition and some have seen Mayhew's survey of *London labour and the London poor* as part of its pre-history.[13] The early historiography of sociological method was concerned to celebrate the development of positivistic social research, and to legitimate the quantitative social survey at the expense of the descriptive study of working-class life. Thus A. F. Wells, a historian of social surveys writing in 1935, denied Mayhew a place in his canon of investigators on the grounds that his method was 'essentially non-statistical: it is rather the concrete descriptive method of a journalist or novelist. His spiritual relatives are Dickens and Defoe'.[14] Wells claimed that quantitative survey work was required to substantiate the (admittedly sometimes useful) accounts of men like Mayhew, and that 'the journalistic method when used by itself is unsafe, even dangerous'.[15] Many other historians of sociology have followed Wells's lead in criticising 'the unrepresentative character of [Mayhew's] material and the unreliability of his conclusions'.[16] In these teleological versions of the development of social inquiry the descriptive accounts of 'social explorers' are relegated to an inferior subdivision of social investigation, comprising entertaining and possibly influential, but ultimately suspect and non-verifiable descriptions of working-class life. The association of investigators such as Mayhew, James Greenwood and Jack London with working-class

11 P. J. Waller, *Town, city and nation: England, 1850–1914*, Oxford 1983, 185
12 B. Seebohm Rowntree, *The labourer and the land*, London 1914, 5.
13 Ashton, *Economic and social investigations*; Raymond A. Kent, *A history of British empirical sociology*, Aldershot 1981, 17–26, 43–52; Yeo, *Contest*, chs i–iii; Englander and O'Day, *Retrieved riches*, 5, 7–10.
14 A. F. Wells, *The local social survey in Great Britain*, London 1935, 14.
15 Ibid. 14 n. 1.
16 David Englander, 'Comparisons and contrasts: Henry Mayhew and Charles Booth as social investigators', in Englander and O'Day, *Retrieved riches*, 105, citing among others Ruth Glass, 'Urban sociology in Great Britain: a trend report', *Current Sociology* iv (1955), 43; F. B. Smith, 'Mayhew's convict', *Victorian Studies* xxii (1979), 431–48; Gertrude Himmelfarb, *The idea of poverty: England in the early industrial age*, London 1984, 212–370. See also Catherine Marsh, *The survey method: the contribution of surveys to sociological explanation*, London 1982, 12–13.

fiction has to an extent compounded this exclusion from the history of social inquiry, by focusing on language and representation rather the implications of the methods adopted.[17] Similarly, the two best known authors of rural non-fiction of this period, Richard Jefferies and George Sturt, although often cited by rural and agricultural historians, have generally been examined in their literary contexts rather than as social investigators as such.[18] The linguistic turn, by emphasising the status of sources as texts, has facilitated more integrated analysis of the systematic social inquiry with the descriptive account: Karen Sayer, for example, has examined representations of rural labouring women in a variety of nineteenth-century sources ranging from reports of parliamentary commissions to novels and poems, while Alun Howkins has traced the changing representations of the agricultural labourer through a similar variety of published source material.[19] This book engages with as diverse a range of sources, although the central purpose is the analysis of the construction of knowledge rather than modes of representation. It thus adopts a broad definition of social inquiry, incorporating participant observation accounts such as those written by George Sturt and Richard Jefferies as well as official inquiries and quantitative social surveys. It is worth pointing out that although these participant observation studies have been denied a place in the accepted genealogy of sociological method in Britain, they nevertheless had their descendants in much sociological inquiry carried out later in the twentieth century.[20]

The value of the cultural study of working-class life, based on the personal experience of the investigator and adopting a descriptive and often anecdotal approach, has been reasserted by Ross McKibbin, who has examined the work of Florence Bell, Helen Bosanquet and Martha Loane in predominantly

[17] Peter Keating (ed.), *Into unknown England, 1866–1913: selections from the social explorers*, Manchester 1976, and *The working classes in Victorian fiction*, London 1971, 32–43 and passim; Victor E. Neuberg, 'The literature of the streets', in H. J. Dyos and Michael Wolff (eds), *The Victorian city: images and realities*, London 1973, ii. 191–209; Himmelfarb, *Idea of poverty*, 468–71; Judith Walkowitz, 'The Indian woman, the flower girl and the Jew: photo-journalism in Edwardian London', *Victorian Studies* xlii (1998), 3–46; cf. Mark Freeman, ' "Journeys into poverty kingdom": complete participation and the British vagrant, 1866–1914', *History Workshop Journal* lii (2001), 99–121.

[18] F. R. Leavis and Denys Thompson, *Culture and environment: the training of critical awareness*, London 1930; John Fraser, 'George Sturt ("George Bourne") and rural labouring life', unpubl. PhD diss. Minnesota 1961; Philip Drew, 'Richard Jefferies and the English countryside', *Victorian Studies* xi (1967), 181–206; W. J. Keith, *The rural tradition: William Cobbett, Gilbert White and other non-fiction prose writers of the English countryside*, Toronto 1975; David Gervais, 'Late witness: George Sturt and village England', *Cambridge Quarterly* xxx (1991), 21–44.

[19] Karen Sayer, *Women of the fields: representations of rural women in the nineteenth century*, Manchester 1995; Alun Howkins, 'From Hodge to Lob: reconstructing the English farm labourer, 1870–1914', in Malcolm Chase and Ian Dyck (eds), *Living and learning: essays in honour of J. F. C. Harrison*, Aldershot 1996, 218–35.

[20] Freeman, ' "Journeys" ', 101–4, 115–16.

urban areas,[21] while a number of historians have considered the role of women in social investigation, focusing on Booth's collaborators Beatrice Webb and Clara Collett[22] and Edwardian investigators including Loane and Olive Malvery.[23] Although not engaged in social survey work, it should not be assumed that these investigators lacked an awareness of methodological issues, even if they were clearly unable to provide the sort of quantitative data on which Booth's and Rowntree's surveys rested. Indeed, a number of historians, unwilling entirely to dismiss the 'journalistic method', have credited Mayhew with a number of methodological and conceptual advances, validating in some respects his status as a systematic social investigator.[24] On the other hand, inquiries which have been viewed as important landmarks in the development of quantitative social research themselves embraced a variety of approaches. Thus David Englander has used Booth's unpublished notebooks to argue that his London survey was by no means as reductively quantitative in its conception as the seventeen published volumes would suggest.[25] Clearly the historian must look to different sources depending on the information being sought. Sarah Williams, for example, in a study of working-class religion, explains the futility of relying on Booth's survey of 'religious influences' in London for an assessment of the 'meanings' of popular religious customs and rituals to those who participated in them.[26] Similarly, the method of cross-examination used by the official inquiry may have represented an authoritative gathering of factual data, the evidence from which is an invaluable source for all kinds of historians, but it was an inherently socially restrictive method, producing findings open to contestation from other quarters, and could reveal only certain aspects of working-class life. Thus Brian Harrison argues that the official inquiry 'could never produce the wealth of information collected by investigators who "dropped out" and engaged in participant observation' such as Jack London and George Orwell,[27] while Mayhew's achievement lay in a 'vivid resurrection' of the lives of the London street-folk with whom he enjoyed personal contact and a measure of

---

21 Ross McKibbin, *The ideologies of class: social relations in Britain, 1880–1950*, Oxford 1990, 169–96.
22 See, for example, Rosemary O'Day, 'Before the Webbs: Beatrice Potter's early investigations for Charles Booth's inquiry', *History* lxxviii (1993), 218–42, and 'Women and social investigation: Clara Collett and Beatrice Potter', in Englander and O'Day, *Retrieved riches*, 165–200.
23 Walkowitz, 'Indian woman'; Freeman, ' "Journeys" '; Susan Cohen, 'The life and works of M. Loane', unpubl. MPhil diss. Middlesex 1997, and 'Miss Loane, Florence Nightingale and district nursing in late Victorian Britain', *Nursing History Review* v (1997), 83–103.
24 E. P. Thompson and Eileen Yeo (eds), *The unknown Mayhew: selections from the Morning Chronicle, 1849–1850*, London 1971; Humpherys, *Travels*, 87–94; Kent, *History*, 43–52.
25 Englander, 'Comparisons and contrasts', 132–4.
26 Sarah C. Williams, 'The problem of belief: the place of oral history in the study of popular religion', *Oral History* xxiv/2 (1996), 27–34.
27 Harrison, *Peaceable kingdom*, 288.

empathy.[28] Raphael Samuel also counterposed the official inquiry with Mayhew's survey, pointing to the latter as an example of a historical document dealing with the lives of a group of people who would be hidden from the view of the social historian working with traditional source material.[29]

Samuel was one of the most influential practitioners of the new social history, which encouraged historians to take more account of the first-hand testimony of social observers and of working-class informants themselves, and to examine more closely the social biases reflected in the documentary evidence that survives from the past. In a key essay that signposted this new history, written in 1975, Samuel asserted that '[i]t is remarkable how much history has been written from the vantage point of those who have had the charge of running – or attempting to run – other people's lives, and how little from the life experience of the people themselves'.[30] Thus social historians needed to move beyond their traditional source base, which delivered a distorted view of working-class experience. In particular, Samuel argued, blue books are

> invidious, because they encourage the historian to rely on second- and third-hand opinion – heavily class biased – whose worth he cannot begin to assess unless he has primary material to use as a yardstick. Poverty inquiries . . . are in many ways the most treacherous to use: their question and answer form and the fact that the witnesses were outsiders – sanitary reformers, temperance advocates, chief constables, chairmen of boards of guardians, philanthropists, clergymen, 'lady' visitors – make it questionable whether they should be treated as primary sources at all (except for the appendices). There is an enormous amount of value to be gleaned from the Blue Books, but only if the historian works against the grain of the material, refusing to accept the witnesses' categories as his own, ruthlessly winnowing out opinion and harvesting the residue of fact however small.[31]

Samuel compared the typical historian of working-class life, reliant on the evidence of blue books, to the nineteenth-century administrator who based his actions on the same evidence: 'His vocation, as an historian, places him far above the madding crowd; he surveys them, retrospectively, from a height, as objects of reform rather than as the active agents – or subjects – of change.'[32] The quantitative social survey as pioneered in the nineteenth century can be considered in the same way: Eileen Yeo has pointed out that the word 'survey', signifying a view from above, is suggestive of an approach that elevated the investigator methodologically and culturally above the

---

[28] Ibid. 307.
[29] Raphael Samuel (ed.), *Village life and labour* (1st edn 1975), London 1982, p. xvii.
[30] Ibid. p. xiii.
[31] Ibid. p. xvi.
[32] Ibid. pp. xvi–xvii.

subjects of his inquiry.[33] To emphasise this symbolically, Bertrand Taithe highlights Mayhew's observations of London made from a balloon, arguing that this physical bird's-eye view inadvertently analogised the cultural distance between the readers of Mayhew's work and those who were described in it, facilitating a 'scientization or objectivization' of the lives of the poor.[34] Another journalist, writing in a rural context and employing appropriate metaphorical devices, explained that '[y]ou cannot judge of a country from a balloon; you must walk over the ridges and along the furrows'.[35] By contrast, the investigation that took an intensive approach, examining in depth the ridges and furrows but not generalising outwards to the field as a whole, was open to the charge that the subjects of inquiry were unrepresentative and perhaps atypical. In effect, the impartial investigator had to be aware of the 'conflicting vantage points' enjoyed by different participants in the life of the community under investigation, and mould his or her approach accordingly.[36]

The social location of accurate and unbiased knowledge of working-class life was the subject of fierce contestation throughout the nineteenth and early twentieth centuries. In this context Catherine Marsh has developed a helpful model to chart the changing strategies of social investigators in this period.[37] She argues that the 'informant' method of inquiry was developed in the nineteenth century, became the mainstay of parliamentary investigations, and was epitomised by Booth's London survey, which involved interviewing school attendance officers to obtain their opinions of the population among which they worked. It was characterised by a reluctance to consult at first hand the subjects of inquiry. The changing economic and political position of the English working classes – manifested, for example, in the concession of a wider electoral franchise and the growth of trade unionism – as well as the different kinds of information that were increasingly sought, especially more detailed knowledge of the working-class domestic economy, encouraged the development of the 'respondent' inquiry, which entailed more direct consultation of the people about whom information was wanted. For Marsh, Rowntree's survey of York, first published in 1901, the result of a house-to-house investigation of all working-class households in the city, reflected this transition. The model is useful in contrasting two different approaches, and explains a growing willingness among social investigators to consult the subjects of inquiry directly. The transition was not simple, however, and the model downplays the degree of conflict that accompanied

33 Yeo, Contest, 27.
34 Bertrand Taithe (ed.), The essential Mayhew: representing and communicating the poor, London 1996, 16–17.
35 Daily News, 30 Mar. 1872, 3.
36 Yeo, Contest, 86.
37 Catherine Marsh, 'Informants, respondents and citizens', in Martin Bulmer (ed.), Essays on the history of British sociological research, Cambridge 1985, 206–27.

it. This book will show that, throughout the period under consideration, disagreement among social investigators of rural life coalesced around issues of standpoint epistemology arising from the adoption of the informant or respondent methods, and that these methodological contests both reflected and in turn impinged upon the social and political conflicts surrounding English rural life. Inquiries that primarily employed the informant method were charged with elitism and class prejudice, while respondent inquiries were accused of unrepresentativeness and of manifesting overtly political designs. To complicate matters, even among those who used the informant method, controversy surrounded the choice of suitable informant; and ironically the assessment of an informant's authority was often based on the closeness of his personal contact with the working-class population. In this context the distinction between the two methods is blurred. Moreover, Marsh's account is restricted to the canon of social investigations that have become the widely accepted antecedents of modern empirical sociology, and does not consider the kind of qualitative account that this book incorporates into the canon of social inquiry. In some respects the inclusion of such material in the model would strengthen her case for transition, as the participant observation study of working-class life and culture, which was developing during this period, necessarily entailed the sensitive employment of a respondent method of inquiry. In any case, it will become clear that intensive cultural investigation generated its own methodological debates, many of which have since been echoed among sociologists, oral historians and theorists of the interview method.[38]

Marsh recognises that the development of a respondent method did not necessarily equate to the democratisation of the agendas or procedures of social inquiry: 'The respondents . . . were still at the powerless end of the relationship between researcher and researched: the researcher asked the questions, the respondent provided the answers.'[39] However, powerlessness did not necessarily entail passivity, and careful deployment of the available evidence enables the historian to assess the responses of the subjects of inquiry to those who sought to investigate them. Thus in her book on *The contest for social science*, Eileen Yeo attempts 'to keep the activity of less powerful groups in focus whether they act as producers of knowledge, or as objects of scrutiny, or as clients of policy or as parties to negotiated outcomes which they affect but do not decisively influence'.[40] Social inquiry always entails a process of interaction between different social actors, with often divergent social outlooks, and represents the result of a dialogue between researcher and researched. Moreover, the dialogue does not end with the

---

[38] For participant observation see Freeman, ' "Journeys" '; Danny L. Jorgensen, *Participant observation: a methodology for human studies*, London 1989; for oral history see Paul Thompson, *The voice of the past: oral history* (1st edn 1978), Oxford 2000, 222–45.
[39] Marsh, 'Informants', 215.
[40] Yeo, *Contest*, p. xvii.

dissemination of the results. Bertrand Taithe has analysed in some detail the correspondence received by Henry Mayhew following the publication of his reports on London, and asserts that '[w]orking-class readers of *London labour and the London poor* knew the book for what it was: a struggle and a drama . . . the result of a Socratian intercourse'.[41] The interactions that generated these contested documents can be overlooked by accounts that concentrate on language and representation to the exclusion of the social realities that lay behind them. Thus, for example, Karen Sayer's analysis of representations of female labourers in the nineteeth century, while a valuable deconstruction of the content of the texts she examines, tells us little about the genesis of the texts themselves.[42] This book attempts to follow the processes of social investigation from their initiation through their operation and into their readership, aiming to present a more complete picture of the construction and contestation of social knowledge and cultural understanding of rural labouring life in the period.

This approach fulfils some of the conditions set out by Adrian Wilson in an essay on the methodology of the social historian published in 1993. Arguing that the 'foundations of an integrated historiography' are to be found in the study of 'the genesis of documents',[43] and instancing the work of Lawrence Goldman and Edward Higgs on the nineteenth-century General Register Office as exemplars of such historiography, Wilson suggests that official publications 'need to be seen not just as convenient bodies of evidence but rather as reflections and instruments of a new kind of State'.[44] This approach transcends Samuel's exhortation to dissect these bodies of evidence with care, and suggests that through a careful examination of how such documents came to be produced – surviving for the historian as effects of the past society in which they were generated – 'a distinctive transection of the society we are studying' can be achieved.[45] It also transcends the focus on language and discourse encouraged by the linguistic turn by insisting on the social realities that lay behind the genesis of the documents under consideration:

the study of document-genesis takes as its explanatory object not the mere existence of a given document or genre, but rather its very *content*. For example, this includes the origin of key items of vocabulary (thus incorporating a

41 Taithe, *Essential Mayhew*, 21.
42 Cf. Sayer, *Women*, 33–5, 67–9, on the appointment of official investigators.
43 Adrian Wilson, 'Foundations of an integrated historiography', in Adrian Wilson (ed.), *Rethinking social history: English society, 1570–1920, and its interpretation*, Manchester 1993, 315. Italicised in the original.
44 Ibid. 320–1. See also Lawrence Goldman, 'Statistics and the science of society in early Victorian Britain: an intellectual context for the General Register Office', *Social History of Medicine* iv (1991), 415–34; Edward Higgs, 'Disease, febrile poisons, and statistics: the census as a medical survey', ibid. 465–78.
45 Wilson, 'Foundations', 323.

central lesson of the 'linguistic turn') and the influence of conventions of content (which connects the theme of content with that of genre). Moreover, a reconstruction of the genesis of content embraces the *boundaries* of that content: its outlines, its limits, the relation between what it includes and what it excludes. . . . By attending to the genesis of content we can not only tackle but also exploit the uneven reflections of gender, class, age, power on the surface of the documents.[46]

Although Wilson cites the study of official publications as one avenue of future research, the benefits of such an approach also apply to the other manifestations of the passion for social investigation that overtook British society in the nineteenth century. Whether this passion resulted in the preparation of careful statistical surveys of specific social problems, widespread but unsystematic surveys of social conditions, or detailed analyses of single villages or even individuals, the creation of these sources involved a series of real and dynamic social processes. Thus an analysis of the dialogues and conflicts that generated the reports of social investigators can open the door to a more integrated understanding of the societies in which they operated.

The conflicts had some peculiarly rural dimensions. A substantial literature details specific moments of rural class conflict in the nineteenth century, in particular the 'Captain Swing' riots of the early 1830s and the agricultural trade unionism of the 1870s,[47] while other historians including David Jones and Alun Howkins have provided particularly valuable evidence of a continuous undercurrent of social protest, especially in East Anglia but also in many other areas of England and Wales, before and after 1872.[48] Even where rural discontent was not manifested in specific instances of protest, it both reflected and reinforced a cultural distance between economic and social actors in rural communities. Contemporaries were conscious of the apparent results of a decline in the 'face-to-face' social relationships associated with pre-industrial society and the pre-enclosure countryside. A combination of improved educational opportunities, the establishment of institutions of working-class self-representation and the indirect influence of urban political radicalism encouraged agricultural labourers to contextualise their economic and social position within wider political discourses, while employers of labour generated resentment through the construction of

[46] Ibid. 321. Original emphases.
[47] See, for example, Andrew Charlesworth (ed.), *An atlas of rural protest in England and Wales, 1548–1900*, London 1983; E. P. Thompson and George Rudé, *Captain Swing* (1st edn 1969), Harmondsworth 1973; Barry Reay, *The last rising of the agricultural labourers: rural life and protest in nineteenth-century England*, Oxford 1990; J. P. D. Dunbabin, *Rural discontent in nineteenth-century Britain*, London 1974; Pamela Horn, *Joseph Arch, 1826–1919: the farm workers' leader*, Kineton 1971.
[48] David Jones, 'Thomas Campbell Foster and the rural labourer: incendiarism in East Anglia in the 1840s', *Social History* i (1976), 5–43; Alun Howkins, *Poor labouring men: rural radicalism in Norfolk, 1870–1923*, London 1985; Mick Reed and Roger Wells (eds), *Class, conflict and protest in the English countryside, 1700–1880*, London 1990.

cultural affinities with the village gentry, cemented on a practical level by conspicuous consumption and withdrawal from active farm labour.[49] As Howard Newby has suggested (again from an East Anglian perspective), '[t]here is a good deal of evidence to show that farmer and worker became a great deal more remote from each other, socially and culturally, and that the apparent peace and tranquillity which descended on rural England after the "Captain Swing" disturbances was almost everywhere superficial and ephemeral'.[50] The experience of protest challenged conceptions of rural paternalism, while the growth of religious Nonconformity, especially village Methodism, brought a more egalitarian religious influence to many English villages and challenged the place of the Church of England parson within the paternalist hierarchy. Nevertheless, despite these challenges to the traditional model of the rural community, throughout this period ruralism was identified as a curative for the ills of industrial England, and groups ranging across the political spectrum projected their visions of national salvation onto the land.[51] Thus any sense of agricultural or rural malaise was frequently overlaid by a series of fantasies of the English countryside rooted in a modified pastoral tradition. In particular, the 'reconstruction' of the labourer and the 'discovery' of rural England provoked a reappraisal of rural vernacular culture that culminated in the invasion of the countryside by folklore and folk song collectors concerned to document vanishing ways of life and to revalidate the culture of the 'folk' at the expense of the debased mass culture of urban England.[52] As Alun Howkins has explained, 'for all groups, in different ways, the land, "peasant proprietorship," even country life itself, were coming to represent order, stability and naturalness . . . the country and country people were seen as the essence of England, uncontaminated by racial degeneration and the false values of cosmopolitan urban life'.[53]

It was within these complex and frequently contradictory discourses surrounding rural life that the work of social investigation in the countryside was carried out. The conflicts inherent in the processes of inquiry need to be understood against the backdrop of concerns about agricultural trade unionism, the rural franchise, rural depopulation and the land question, not

49 Richard Jefferies, *Hodge and his masters*, London 1880, passim.
50 Howard Newby, *The deferential worker: a study of farm workers in East Anglia*, London 1977, 28.
51 See, especially, Jan Marsh, *Back to the land: the pastoral impulse in England, from 1880 to 1914*, London 1982. For an earlier period see Malcolm Chase, *The people's farm: English radical agrarianism, 1775–1840*, Oxford 1988.
52 Howkins, 'From Hodge to Lob', and 'The discovery of rural England', in Robert Colls and Philip Dodd (eds), *Englishness: politics and culture, 1880–1920*, Beckenham 1986, 62–88; Georgina Boyes, *The imagined village: culture, ideology and the English folk revival*, Manchester 1993; Mark Freeman, 'Folklore collection and social investigation in late-nineteenth and early-twentieth century England', in David Hopkin (ed.), *Folklore and the historian*, London (forthcoming).
53 Howkins, 'Discovery', 69.

to mention the basic facts relating to labourers' remuneration and housing. This book, therefore, opens with an account of the development of social investigative techniques in the hundred years before 1872, establishing the main currents of inquiry and the main issues that were repeatedly identified, as well as tracing perceptions of the labourer and the countryside in a period of rapid urbanisation. Two chapters then proceed chronologically, charting the investigative responses to the upheavals of the 1870s and the very different concerns of the 1880s, and then the effects of the panic over rural depopulation in the 1890s. The Edwardian period is covered in three chapters, the first an examination of the application of quantitative social survey methodology to the investigation of rural communities, the next describing approaches to qualitative cultural inquiry, and the final substantive chapter illustrating the continuing contestability of assessments of agricultural wages, labourers' housing and the land question. Four different groups of investigations, essentially, are identified: firstly, the official or governmental inquiry, published in 'blue book' form and intended to draw guidelines for future legislative or other activity; secondly, the newspaper investigation, carried out by special correspondent journalists, sent out from London or other urban centres to explore the condition of the countryside and report back, in much the same way as an official investigator but usually with a freer brief and a wider choice of methodology; thirdly, the systematic sociological survey of material conditions, developed in response to urban social concerns, whose application in rural theatres of inquiry posed specific methodological and ideological questions; and finally the cultural study of rural life, usually carried out by a resident of the district being described, adopting an approach that was essentially (and usually unashamedly) descriptive, anecdotal and impressionistic. These were different forms of social inquiry, but ultimately all formed a part of the same project of conveying information about life in rural England and suggesting remedies for its problems; and in doing so they helped to shape the ways in which rural society was understood by contemporaries and has since been interpreted by historians.

1

From Arthur Young to Canon Girdlestone: Approaches to Social Inquiry in the English Countryside before 1872

The inquiry into the number and condition of the people, the analysis of the social structure and the descriptive account of working-class life all have a long history in Britain and elsewhere; historians have traced this history as far back as Domesday Book and beyond.[1] Notable investigators who might be said to form the prehistory of the social survey include Gregory King, whose 'Scheme of the income and expense of the several families of England', published in 1696 but referring to 1688, and other works have been widely used by historians of early modern England;[2] Daniel Defoe, whose *Tour through the whole island of Great Britain* (1724–6), which, although not necessarily a work of social exploration in the modern sense of the term, has been described as 'an account of a journey during which the range and variety of human life is displayed';[3] and Joseph Massie, a political economist and commercial historian who published an *Estimate of the social structure and income* for the years 1759–60.[4] The initiation of the national census under the shadow of the population debates of the late eighteenth century and its subsequent development have also attracted much historical scholarship.[5] These early inquiries dealt with both urban and rural communities; however, in the second half of the eighteenth century a number of investigators began to apply their energies specifically to the English countryside. Thus when Marie Jahoda, Paul Lazarsfeld and Hans Zeisel traced the history of 'sociography' for their influential study of the Austrian village of Marienthal in 1933, the

1 Bulmer and others, *The social survey*, 1, 5–7; Kent, *History*, 12–13; Englander and O'Day, *Retrieved riches*, 3–4.
2 G. S. Holmes, 'Gregory King and the social structure of pre-industrial England', *Transactions of the Royal Historical Society* 5th ser. xxvii (1977), 41–68; Peter Laslett, *The world we have lost* (1st edn 1965), London 1971, 31ff, 57–9 and passim.
3 Daniel Defoe, *A tour through the whole island of Great Britain* (1st edn 1724–6), Harmondsworth 1971; Kent, *History*, 37.
4 Peter Mathias, 'The social structure in the eighteenth century: a calculation by Joseph Massie', *Economic History Review* 2nd ser. x (1957), 30–45.
5 D. V. Glass, *Numbering the people: the eighteenth-century population controversy and the development of census and vital statistics in Britain*, Farnborough 1973; Edward Higgs, *A clearer sense of the census: Victorian censuses and historical research*, London 1996, and 'Disease, febrile poisons, and statistics'; Richard Lawton (ed.), *The census and social structure: an interpretative guide to nineteenth-century censuses for England and Wales*, London 1978.

earliest investigators they mentioned were all primarily concerned with rural life. In particular, Arthur Young was identified as an early forerunner of the social-scientific inquirer, and although Jahoda and the others recognised that his large body of work consisted of 'more socio-economic travelogues than systematic investigations', they none the less believed that Young's output contained valuable sociographic data.[6] Similarly, David Davies's inquiry into agricultural domestic budgets, a venture which pioneered the use of the questionnaire, was considered an important development; while Frederick Eden's investigation into *The state of the poor*, for these sociologists, 'marked another step forward in survey methodology' with its employment of an interviewer.[7] By contrast, more recent histories have ignored this legacy of rural social inquiry: Raymond Kent, for example, in his *History of British empirical sociology*, published in 1981, although he has a full history of early social inquiry and social exploration embracing King, Defoe and Sir John Sinclair, fails to mention Young and his contemporaries at all, and nowhere deals with the influential reports of the Board of Agriculture on agricultural conditions during and after the Napoleonic wars. However, it is important to be aware of these early surveys, because they were considered important by investigators of rural life in the later Victorian and Edwardian period, who often represented themselves as operating within the same tradition of social inquiry.

Arthur Young was a practical farmer and prolific agricultural journalist whose career spanned the investigation of agriculture both for independent publication and for the Board of Agriculture.[8] An active agricultural experimenter and promoter of scientific approaches to farming, he carried out a number of agricultural tours, first published in the late 1760s, which concentrated on the practice and profitability of farming innovations across the country; one historian has suggested that the tours 'may claim to be the first real attempts at a general survey of agricultural practice'.[9] There followed Young's independent serial publication, the *Annals of Agriculture*, which appeared between 1784 and 1815, and he became secretary to the Board of Agriculture on its establishment in 1793, a position he held until his death in 1820. Young was more interested in agricultural practice than in the rural population as such, although later in his life he was concerned to describe and assess the impact on the rural labouring classes of the enclosure movement to which he had previously given his wholehearted support. Young has been viewed by some historians as a proto-sociologist, although others have

---

[6] Marie Jahoda, Paul F. Lazarsfeld and Hans Zeisel, *Marienthal: the sociography of an unemployed community* (1st German edn 1933), London 1972, 101.
[7] Ibid. 102.
[8] For a full account of Young and some of his contemporaries see John G. Gazley, *The life of Arthur Young, 1741–1820*, Philadelphia 1973; for Young in his own words see M. Betham-Edwards (ed.), *The autobiography of Arthur Young, with selections from his correspondence*, London 1898. See also G. E. Mingay (ed.), *Arthur Young and his times*, London 1975.
[9] G. E. Fussell, 'English agriculture from Arthur Young to William Cobbett', *Economic History Review* 1st ser. vi (1936), 216.

dismissed the accuracy and value of his reports, preferring to take their evidence from some of his less well-known contemporaries. For example, William Marshall was engaged in similar work, and, as G. E. Mingay has pointed out,[10] has been viewed as a more reliable authority for the historian of late eighteenth-century agriculture than Young because of his concentration on presenting a general picture of agriculture rather than on describing innovations, which were by their nature atypical; he also had what some commentators have seen as an advantage over Young in that he lived in the midst of his informants rather than touring around the country. Between 1787 and 1798 Marshall produced a twelve-volume series on *The rural economy of Norfolk, Yorkshire, Gloucestershire, the midland counties and the southern counties*, the result of living for a year or two in each of the areas described. G. D. Amery has described Marshall's writings as 'more exclusively agricultural and perhaps more sound than those of Young',[11] but both men advocated an essentially scientific approach to social inquiry, and found themselves in agreement over many issues, notably in their support for a general enclosure act.

Although Young and Marshall began work as independent investigators, both were associated with the Board of Agriculture. The board was the brain-child of Sir John Sinclair, who had organised the *Statistical account of Scotland*, a twenty-one-volume survey published in the 1790s based on a questionnaire sent to local ministers, and whose financial acumen and contacts enabled him to persuade William Pitt to award a government grant to run the board.[12] The board had a semi-official status, supported by government funds but operating essentially as a 'closed corporation';[13] the bulk of its members were landlords and bishops, while Arthur Young acted as secretary. The twentieth-century sociologist T. H. Marshall later described the impressive range of the board's activities:

> The board collected statistical and other information, promoted scientific research and disseminated knowledge, all with the object of stimulating and improving British agriculture. Thus it agitated for the compulsory commutation of tithes and the enclosure of waste lands; it established an experimental farm and organized the first British agricultural show; and it encouraged Joseph Elkington's work on drainage, Sir Humphrey Davy's studies in agricultural chemistry, J. L. McAdam, the road maker, and Andrew Meikle, the inventor of the threshing machine.[14]

---

10 Mingay, *Arthur Young*, 3–4, 16ff.

11 *Encyclopaedia of the social sciences* (1st edn 1930–5), London 1962, x. 159.

12 Rosalind Mitchison, 'The old Board of Agriculture, 1793–1822', *English Historical Review* lxxiv (1959), 41–2, and *Agricultural Sir John: the life of Sir John Sinclair of Ulbster, 1754–1835*, London 1962, chs x–xi.

13 Mitchison, 'Old Board of Agriculture', 43.

14 *Encyclopaedia of the social sciences*, xiv. 63.

The board's scientific disposition was also reflected in the presence of Thomas Coke of Norfolk, which 'mark[ed] the new farming at its height'.[15] G. E. Fussell remarked that the 'growth of the scientific outlook encouraged experimental work and the writing of descriptions of experiments';[16] it also encouraged a more scientific approach to the work of agricultural and social investigation. The board commissioned a series of reports on the agriculture of each English county, and although these were often unsuccessful in that they suffered, like Young's tours, from 'an overweighting with individual detail' and were uneven in their coverage and trustworthiness,[17] some of them at least represented a valuable addition to the existing stock of knowledge on the English countryside. The county reports, each published under the title *General view of the agriculture of . . .*, could never, as had been the original intention, be grouped together into a single nationwide survey, although William Marshall published a more manageable five-volume summary between 1808 and 1815.[18] The reports generally employed the method of despatching an external investigator to the county in question – Young was responsible for six of the reports and Marshall wrote the volume on the central highlands of Scotland – and allowing local residents to correct and amend the first draft. Although this was not dissimilar to methods of social inquiry employed over a century later, it did not in this case result in a coherent series of county reports, and their value to the historian is limited as a result.

Young and the board's other investigators tended to use an informant method of inquiry, basing their reports almost entirely on the consultation of rural elites, as Mingay has explained:

> The method he adopted for his two major tours, those in the north and the east, as for later ones [for the Board of Agriculture], was to advertise his journey in advance and collect letters of introduction and information about which estates and farms were worth visiting. At each stop he detailed notes of crops, livestock, practices, costs and profits, preferably direct from the landlord or farmer himself; these notes he printed almost verbatim, occasionally with criticisms of a severe kind. . . . Young relied exclusively on personal information from the leading proprietors and farmers of the district; he had no faith in the wisdom of small farmers, whom he constantly characterised as ignorant and prejudiced . . . when he travelled it was usually in company with other experts of the farming fraternity. . . . Young's method of collecting information was perfectly proper for his purpose [of describing agricultural innovations], and was the only feasible way of going about it.[19]

---

15 Mitchison, 'Old Board of Agriculture', 43.
16 Fussell, 'English agriculture', 219.
17 Mitchison, 'Old Board of Agriculture', 49–51.
18 William Marshall, *The review and abstract of the county reports to the Board of Agriculture* (1st edn 1808–15), Newton Abbot 1969.
19 Mingay, *Arthur Young*, 15–16.

Young, then, however sympathetic to the plight of the rural poor,[20] adopted an approach firmly grounded in the informant method of inquiry, and was followed by contemporaries such as Marshall who, whatever their personal disagreements with Young, were engaged essentially in the same project of documenting the changing conditions of English agriculture from the point of view of the practical farmer. Other investigators in the late eighteenth century, however, took a different approach, reflecting the different concerns with which they approached their inquiries. Sometimes these approaches exhibit the kinds of contestation that were to become more readily discernible in the second half of the nineteenth century. David Davies, for example – whose *The case of labourers in husbandry*, published in 1795 (but based on research carried out in 1787), described the conditions of his own parish of Barkham in Berkshire – gathered a series of family budgets which he used to show that the weekly wage received by most labourers was insufficient to meet the basic needs of an average-sized family, and that hence a large proportion of his parishioners were thrown onto poor relief. Davies's book was addressed to the Board of Agriculture, established two years earlier, and effectively constituted a plea for the needs of the labourer to be foregrounded in the board's activities: 'In every nation the welfare and contentment of the lower denominations of people are objects of great importance, and deserving continual attention . . . of all the denominations of people in a state, the labourers in husbandry are by far the most valuable.'[21]

Davies, concerned with the lived experience of the rural labouring classes rather than the mechanisms of agricultural improvement, did not achieve the prominence of Young or Marshall, but because of his field of concern he clearly prefigures some of the sociological investigators of the subsequent century. In his employment of direct consultation of labouring families to ascertain the details of their domestic circumstances he was followed by the more ambitious and somewhat better known Frederick Morton Eden, whose *The state of the poor* appeared in 1797 and who worked with what one commentator has called 'the beginnings of a scientific technique'.[22] The nature of Eden's research – like Davies, he collected domestic budgets, although his geographical spread was much wider and, as we have seen, he employed an interviewer to gather his data – meant that much of the information was collected at first hand from the working-class subjects of the inquiry. Appearing more than fifty years before Frederic Le Play's influential study of thirty-six budgets, *Les Ouvriers européens* (1855), Eden's contribution

---

[20] Gazley, *Arthur Young*, ch. viii, has an account of Young's support for a general enclosure act and the provision of allotments as remedies for the agricultural distress at the turn of the century.
[21] Quoted in Wilhelm Hasbach, A *history of the English agricultural labourer* (1st German edn 1894), London 1908, 395–6.
[22] *Encyclopaedia of the social sciences*, vi. 73.

has been a useful source for historians of eighteenth-century consumption.[23] With more than a hundred budgets, his work can claim to have been a reasonably extensive study of working-class life, and it was used by social investigators over a century later as an illustration of how social conditions had changed since the late eighteenth century.[24] Eden's portrait of the English poor involved first-hand consultation with labouring families, but the agenda it followed was dominated by contemporary debates on poor relief expenditure, and he blamed many of the problems of the poor on personal improvidence rather than low wages. As such one historian has placed him in an interim category, as representing 'the ruthless new husbandry of Arthur Young against the newer humanitarianism of Davies and [the anti-slavery campaigner and advocate of an agricultural minimum wage Samuel] Whitbread'.[25] Nevertheless, despite the moral judgmentalism in which Eden engaged, his interest in issues of consumption, anticipating the widespread collection of domestic budgets that would characterise much social investigation a century later, suggested that some elements of a respondent approach might be necessary for the effective investigation of the life of the labouring classes; and he is therefore a significant figure in the development of British social research.

Whatever the main interests of these early investigators, and whatever moral preoccupations motivated them, they all adopted a methodology that could to some degree be considered scientific. Although the Board of Agriculture, which epitomised this scientific disposition among prominent agriculturists, met its demise in 1822, its impact on the scientific investigation of agriculture and rural social conditions outlasted it. Agricultural distress during the Napoleonic wars and the aftermath of the new corn law provoked more inquiries at governmental level, which echoed the passion among members of the board for careful and detailed investigation. The board's own inquiries in 1815 and 1816 drew attention to the high rents which farmers could not meet, while as Rowland Prothero (later Lord Ernle) noted in his history of English farming, during the two decades following the war '[t]he attention of Parliament was continually called to the distress of the landed interests', resulting in the appointment of select committes on agriculture in 1820, 1821, 1822, 1833 and 1836.[26] All classes of the agricultural community suffered in the post-war years – in one footnote Prothero listed fourteen publications that appeared between 1813 and 1820 detailing evidence of widespread distress[27] – and the falling real wages of agricultural labourers, subsidised in many cases by the parish, were eventually addressed by the poor

---

[23] See, for example, John Burnett, *Plenty and want: a social history of diet in England, from 1815 to the present day*, London 1966, 2–3, 22.

[24] Helen Bosanquet, 'Wages and housekeeping', in C. S. Loch (ed.), *Methods of social advance: short studies in social practice by various authors*, London 1904, 139.

[25] *Encyclopaedia of the social sciences*, v. 397.

[26] Rowland E. Prothero, *English farming past and present*, London 1912, 324.

[27] Ibid. 319 n. 2.

law reforms of the 1830s. However, accounts of rural distress, whether 'scientific' or otherwise, did not focus on the privations of the landless workers, whose access to the mechanisms of social investigation was limited and whose condition was interpreted largely in terms of its impact on the institutions concerned with poor relief. It was left to campaigning journalists, most notably William Cobbett, to highlight the sufferings of the labourers, and to challenge (in Cobbett's case, somewhat unconvincingly) the findings of new manifestations of social inquiry, in particular the national census.[28] Cobbett's *Rural rides*, originally published in the *Political Register* during the first half of the 1820s, were commenced in 1821 as part of an agricultural campaign against what he saw as the obstruction of the cause of agrarian reform by the farming classes (to which Cobbett himself at times belonged). The *Political Register* was antagonistic to the most widespread diagnoses of the problems of rural society of the period, and represented an attempt to state the labourers' case with a stridency that was arguably necessary given their lack of alternative means of public self-expression. Adopting a 'populist' approach that involved 'hearing what gentlemen, farmers, tradesmen, journeymen, labourers, women, girls, boys, and all have to say',[29] Cobbett claimed to redress the balance in the dominant forms of rural social inquiry and to speak for the lowest classes who, in Ian Dyck's words, did not 'have many friends and supporters to articulate their experiences and aspirations'.[30] (Nevertheless, even Cobbett often recorded only his visual impressions of the labourers he encountered: for example, their clothes, cleanliness or physical characteristics.)[31] Cobbett's large output has attracted a range of biographers and historians, and need not be discussed in detail here;[32] but he deserves notice as a prominent, if hardly representative, example of an investigator who sought to bring the poor man's experience and culture within the scope of social inquiry.

Although many of the early social investigators to come to prominence in the eighteenth and early nineteenth centuries were mainly concerned with rural life, it was to urban Britain that most investigative energy was turned from the 1830s, and the problems associated with the rapid and unregulated growth of new urban industrial communities tended to marginalise the rural poverty that had stimulated Cobbett to his savage indictment of the post-war countryside. There were some notable outbreaks of rural discontent, particularly the Captain Swing riots in the early 1830s and the 'Battle of Bosenden Wood' of 1838, in which a small group of rioting Kentish labourers was

28 George Spater, *William Cobbett: the poor man's friend*, Cambridge 1982, ii. 442.
29 Quoted in Ian Dyck, *William Cobbett and rural popular culture*, Cambridge 1992, 12.
30 Ibid. 3.
31 See, for example, William Cobbett, *Rural rides* (1st edn 1830), Harmondsworth 1967, 74–5, 206, 140–1.
32 See, for example, G. D. H. Cole, *The life of William Cobbett*, London 1924; Spater, *William Cobbett*; Raymond Williams, *Cobbett*, Oxford 1983; Dyck, *William Cobbett*; Leonora Nattrass, *William Cobbett: the politics of style*, Cambridge 1995.

'massacred' by the 45th Infantry Regiment.[33] This rising prompted a barrister, Frederick Liardet, to undertake a detailed investigation of the circumstances of the labouring families of the region, in which Barry Reay has found useful evidence for his assessment of the economic and social condition of the local labouring population.[34] Chartism also reached the countryside at times;[35] but as one observer remembered in 1891,

> [f]rom about the year 1840 down to the great agricultural strike of 1870 [sic], the world heard little of the agricultural labourer. The interest of the philanthropical public now became concentrated on the artisan class, on the truck system, and on factory tyranny. But after these grievances had been redressed and political rights conferred upon town populations by the bill of 1867, the public had leisure to turn once more to the condition of the peasantry.[36]

This does not mean that social disruption was absent from the English countryside in this period: a number of historians have identified a continuing undercurrent of often very bitter protest which challenged the settled agrarian order and was manifested in various attempts at combination and in isolated acts of violence against property,[37] and the effects of this can be seen in the work of those social investigators who concerned themselves with country life in the period. However, in general the most notable investigations of working-class life focused on industrial towns, and those who pleaded for the recognition of rural problems were in a minority. The rise of the 'middle-class social survey' in the early Victorian period was a response to distress in urban communities, and the attentions of social investigators were focused on the evils of the factory system and the squalor and ignorance that prevailed in the new towns that had grown up to house the new generation of industrial workers; and it was these conditions that prompted the various contemporaneous developments in method and technique of social inquiry.

Eileen Yeo has explained that '[t]he years between 1832 and 1850 became an age of enthusiasm for the statistical idea and for investigations into the condition of the working class',[38] and she has traced the development of the use of statistics within the early social science movement. Groups such as

---

33 Reay, Last rising.
34 Ibid. See also idem, Microhistories: demography, society and culture in rural England, 1800–1930, Cambridge 1996.
35 See Dorothy Thompson, The Chartists: popular politics in the industrial revolution (1st edn 1984), Aldershot 1986, 173–9.
36 T. E. Kebbel, The old and the new English country life, London 1891, 160–1.
37 See, for example, David Jones, Crime, protest, community and police in nineteenth-century Britain, London 1982, chs ii–iii; Charlesworth, Atlas of rural protest; Reed and Wells, Class, conflict and protest; Barry Stapleton (ed.), Conflict and community in southern England: essays in the social history of rural and urban labour from medieval to modern times, Stroud 1992.
38 Yeo, Contest, 58.

local statistical societies (of which the Manchester Statistical Society was probably the most notable) and individuals including medical men like James Kay-Shuttleworth and investigative journalists like Henry Mayhew embarked on what Yeo elsewhere describes as a 'social scientific offensive',[39] a response to social distress and political challenge predicated on the hope that that the poor could be counted, subdivided and accordingly controlled through the application of specific remedies derived from comprehensive knowledge of the facts. Embedded within this movement was the contest that Yeo uses as the organising theme of her analysis. She argues that the social investigators of the period approached their work from a moral standpoint which emphasised the separate and alien nature of urban working-class life, to the extent that those under investigation were portrayed as degraded and at times as virtually subhuman.[40] Giving particularly detailed consideration to the Manchester Statistical Society and Kay-Shuttleworth, Yeo shows how the statistical approach to social inquiry enabled the investigator to bypass working-class culture and reduce the analysis of cultural meanings to the merely numerical. This was representative of a 'survey' attitude and symptomatic of the cultural distance between investigator and investigated:

> The devaluing way in which middle-class social investigators often constructed the poor did not come from or lead to mutual respect. Kay-Shuttleworth's adjectives of 'loathsome', 'noisome', 'squalid', 'disgusting', and 'revolting' to signify some of the customs of poor people, blocked the recognition of separate and valid cultures among the working classes. People 'rubbished' in this way were not likely to be regarded as having legitimate access to the arena of public speech, and their representation of their own experience was likely to be excluded from scientific space. . . . On the whole, the middle-class investigators had an affinity for statistics partly because they did not need to develop methods of inquiry and presentation which would allow cultural facts about meanings and values, habits and customs, to be expressed. The presence or absence of an activity or of membership in a school or church was a sufficient register of intellectual and moral condition. This kind of information could be expressed statistically.[41]

This attitude to 'social science', Yeo argues, dominated the investigation of the early Victorian urban poor. Only Henry Mayhew, who avoided marginalising the poor man's experience, expressed the cultural lives of the working classes without the adjectival damnation that accompanied Kay-Shuttleworth's poor. Identifying a 'Mayhew Moment',[42] Yeo suggests that Mayhew was fully aware of the conflicting perspectives of employer and

[39] Ibid. 242.
[40] Ibid. ch. iii.
[41] Ibid. 73.
[42] Idem, 'The social survey in social perspective', in Bulmer and others, *The social survey*, 53.

employee,[43] whereas other investigators of the period confined themselves within a middle-class agenda and allowed working-class informants little access to the shaping of public understanding of their own condition.

Although the agricultural labourer was not usually considered 'loathsome', 'squalid' or 'revolting' like his urban counterpart, he was nevertheless also encumbered with a series of unflattering representations which compounded his reputation for ignorance and backwardness. He was commonly stereotyped using the label 'Hodge',[44] a nickname which, as Jan Marsh has shown, was derived from 'Roger', and sounded like 'a cross between hedge (where he spent much of his time, especially in bad weather) and clod (the substance on his boots and in his brain)'.[45] Hodge was heir to the 'clown' that was in common usage in the literature of the eighteenth century as a derogatory synonym for the agricultural labourer,[46] and was characterised pithily (and, in this case, ironically) by one commentator as 'unimaginative, ill-clothed, ill-educated, ill-paid, ignorant of all that is taking place beyond his own village, dissatisfied with his position and yet without energy or effort to improve it'.[47] The limited education and narrow horizons of the agricultural labourer were ridiculed by urban and rural elites alike: one farmer thought that '[t]he very fact of [the labourer's] having so little to exercise his mental faculties is the secret of their being generally so uncultivated';[48] and another referred to 'the illogical mind of Hodge', whom he characterised memorably as being 'of strong faith and a gross feeder'.[49] At least prior to 1872, as Alun Howkins remarks, the labourer was 'seen as stupid but contented, the far end of a chain of paternalism';[50] in the words of a near-contemporary commentator, he was 'below the notice of history'.[51] He was an easy target for the ridicule of urban radicals, one metropolitan Chartist explaining how 'the squire is [the labourer's] King, the parson his deity and the tap-room his highest conception of earthly bliss'.[52] Representations like this could only discourage the social investigator from using the labourer as an informant in

43 Idem, *Contest*, 86.
44 For a more detailed examination of the Hodge stereotype and its implications see Howkins, 'From Hodge to Lob'; K. D. M. Snell, *Annals of the labouring poor: social change and agrarian England, 1660–1900* (1st edn 1985), Cambridge 1987, 5–14, 381–91; Marsh, *Back to the land*, ch. iv; Mark Freeman, 'The agricultural labourer and the Hodge stereotype, c. 1850–1914', *Agricultural History Review* xlix (2001), 172–86.
45 Marsh, *Back to the land*, 60.
46 Freeman, 'Agricultural labourer', 173.
47 J. Dent Dent [sic.], 'The present condition of the English agricultural labourer', *Journal of the Royal Agricultural Society of England* 2nd ser. vii (1871), 343–4.
48 Anon, *A farmer's views on the agricultural labour question, by one of them*, Norwich 1873, 21–2.
49 'A Wykehamist', *The agricultural labourer*, London 1873, 10.
50 Alun Howkins, *Reshaping rural England: a social history, 1850–1925*, London 1991, 186.
51 D. C. Pedder, *The secret of rural depopulation* (Fabian Tract cxviii), London 1904, 4.
52 Quoted in Howkins, *Reshaping rural England*, 133.

investigations into rural life. As Catherine Marsh has pointed out, referring to social investigation in both urban and rural areas,

> There were wide divergencies [sic] in the way these early investigators collected their data. One of the most important variations was whether or not they trusted the objects of their inquiry to speak for themselves. Many government officials equated the move towards collecting more systematic, reliable information with collecting it from more stout and reliable informants than from the poor themselves. Royal Commissions and parliamentary committees adopted the method of interrogating people who might be presumed to be experts, rather than taking their information from the horse's mouth.[53]

This tendency is illustrated in the rural context by the reports of the special assistant poor law commissioners, who in 1843 were sent across England to report on the employment of women and children in agriculture. As a widely used source of evidence on the condition of rural England in the mid-nineteenth century, the reports of this commission have been dissected by historians interested in the representations of the labouring poor that they contain.[54] The inquiry, as Karen Sayer points out, was a 'minor affair',[55] never actually discussed in parliament and overshadowed in public debate by the more sensational revelations of the conditions of women and children working in factories and mines. The assistant commissioners were limited to just thirty days in which to investigate the counties allotted to them, and this restricted the scope of their investigations.[56] The four commissioners – all barristers – generally had little contact with the labouring population. The one exception was Alfred Austin, who investigated Wiltshire, Somerset, Dorset and Devon: of the thirty-nine people he personally interviewed, four were labourers and twelve were labourers' wives. However, he also recorded written communications from fifteen people, including six vicars or curates, three medical officers of health, a farmer, a manufacturer and the clerk of St Thomas's poor law union in Exeter.[57] Written evidence was by its nature likely to come from the literate classes; this method entailed a built-in bias against the labouring classes. Sir Francis Doyle, who was sent to Yorkshire and Northumberland, took evidence from sixty-eight people, of whom forty-two can be identified; these included nineteen vicars or curates, a churchwarden, a medical man, four farmers and three stewards or land agents. Fourteen of his informants were concerned in some way with the administration of poor relief.[58] As Stephen Denison, the commissioner for Suffolk,

---

53 Marsh, *Survey method*, 18.
54 See, especially, Sayer, *Women*, 34–9, 79–81.
55 Ibid. 35.
56 *Reports of special assistant poor law commissioners on the employment of women and children in agriculture*, PP 1843, C. 510, 1.
57 Ibid. appendices to Austin's report.
58 Ibid. appendices to Doyle's report.

Norfolk and Lincolnshire, pointed out, the short time available for the inquiry meant that the commissioners were obliged 'to ascertain rather the general opinion of those persons best qualified to form one, than to attempt to get at the truth by a personal investigation of the facts'.[59] Although, as Brian Harrison has suggested, '[s]ocial investigation in the 1840s had not become so sophisticated in technique nor (partly in consequence) so insulated from contact with the observed, as it became later',[60] this rural inquiry was one which clearly concentrated on the information obtainable from rural elites.

This strategy was also followed by James Caird, whose agricultural tour, carried out for *The Times* in the wake of the repeal of the corn law in 1846, was reprinted as *English agriculture in 1850–51*, which has become a standard source for agricultural historians. Caird's importance lies not only in his authorship of one of the classic nineteenth-century texts on English farming, but also in his role as an established authority on agricultural conditions whose influence stretched much later in the century until his death in 1892. Caird's approach involved very little direct contact with the labouring classes, partly because of what one commentator fifty years later remembered as his concentration 'on the condition of farm-buildings, on the methods of tillage pursued, on the character of the implements and machinery employed, on the breeds of sheep and other kinds of live-stock raised, on the degree of knowledge, ability, and enterprise displayed by owner and cultivator'.[61] The articles were cumbersomely entitled 'Relations between landlord and tenant in the agricultural districts of England'; in this context labour was examined as frequently in terms of its cost and availability as in its impact on the bulk of the rural population. Caird, describing his own approach, explained that his information was obtained 'by personal inquiry and inspection, principally by walking or riding carefully over individual farms, in different districts of each county, accompanied by the farmers, – by traversing estates with the landlord or his agent, – and by seeking access to the best and most trustworthy sources of local information'.[62] On only one occasion did he record consulting a labourer, when in Wiltshire he commented on a labouring family's consumption patterns, information which was unlikely to be obtainable from other sources.[63] The home life of a labouring family was not accessible to their employers, although in Derbyshire Caird obtained detailed dietary information by interviewing a farmer, some of whose men boarded in the farmhouse:[64] labourers who 'lived-in' were more accessible to the investigator

59 Ibid. 215.
60 Harrison, *Peaceable kingdom*, 307. A 'few' labourers has given evidence before the SC on the Poor Law Amendment Act, which reported in 1837: Howkins, *Reshaping rural England*, 63–4.
61 *Economic Journal* xiii (1903), 207.
62 James Caird, *English agriculture in 1850–51* (1st edn 1852), London 1968, p. xxxiv.
63 Ibid. 84–5.
64 Ibid. 395.

than were those who had a purely economic relationship with their employers.

If Caird was primarily interested in the condition of agriculture rather than the rural population, the investigators who, between 1849 and 1851, carried out the rural counterpart of Henry Mayhew's better known London inquiry for the *Morning Chronicle*, announced the very different object of their survey in their title 'Labour and the poor'. Alexander Mackay and Charles Shirley Brooks toured the rural districts, producing what Anne Digby has called 'a uniquely detailed picture of rural poverty',[65] covering twenty-eight English counties and extending their investigations to rural industries as well as agriculture.[66] Despite their concern for the condition of the rural working-class population, they spent only a short time in each place they visited, and as Peter Razzell has explained, they generally employed the informant method of inquiry, using key resident witnesses as short cuts to social knowledge.[67] Given the time constraints on the publication of their results, this was to an extent unavoidable, and they did attempt in some cases to interview labourers, but, unlike Mayhew, they never really sought to overcome the barriers of class, status and gender to communicate meaningfully with the labouring population. Indeed, they subscribed to much of the underlying basis of the Hodge stereotype, finding in the labourer an unhelpful and at times resentful informant:

> When you accost him, if he is not insolent – which he seldom is – he is timid and shrinking, his whole manner showing that feels himself at a distance from you greater than should separate any two classes of men. He is often doubtful when you address, and suspicious when you question him; he is seemingly oppressed with the interview while it lasts, and obviously relieved when it is over.[68]

Elsewhere they characterised the labourer as a 'physical scandal, a moral enigma, an intellectual cataleptic'.[69] As K. D. M. Snell has shown, this kind of representation of the agricultural labourer reflected 'social ignorance and class isolation',[70] and effectively set an agenda for social inquiry that understood the needs of the 'labouring poor' within a middle-class interpretive framework. This agenda has often been followed by historians who have conducted the 'standard of living debate' in terms of real wages and other indicators which were not necessarily prioritised by those whose standard of living is under discussion.

---

[65] Anne Digby, 'The rural poor', in G. E. Mingay (ed.), *The Victorian countryside*, London 1981, ii. 591.
[66] Ginswick, *Labour and the poor*, i, p. xiii.
[67] Razzell and Wainwright, *Victorian working class*, p. xviii.
[68] Quoted in Snell, *Annals*, 6–7.
[69] Ibid. 7.
[70] Ibid. 5. See also Freeman, 'Agricultural labourer', 175.

Snell's account of the rural working-class standard of living draws on testimony from within the world of the agricultural labourers themselves, especially letters sent home by emigrants, which express the areas in which they felt their condition had been improved by the move overseas. He also uses the interviews with south-western agricultural labourers recorded in Alexander Somerville's *The whistler at the plough*, first published as a series of articles in the Cobdenite press, which 'may indicate at times the ignorance of their class, which the common stereotype of "Hodge" celebrated', but which also 'demonstrate also an intense bitterness and class animosity, which that stereotype . . . served conveniently both to conceal and discount'.[71] These interviews, as Snell shows, 'provide a good indication of the range of [labourers'] discontents: for example, the game laws, low wages, pretentious living standards of the farmers, or the bad diet and difficulty in keeping their families alive',[72] and perhaps above all the workings of the new poor law. Somerville based much of his analysis of the problems of rural Britain on what he learned from farmers and, to a lesser extent, landowners, but, although there is no particular reason to trust the veracity of his account more than that of any other investigative journalist, his inquiries do reveal the working-class side of a contest that in this period was otherwise heavily weighted in favour of rural elites. Although his main concerns were to press for security of farm tenure and to campaign for free trade in corn, Somerville was no less passionate in his denunciations of the workhouse system, especially the incarceration of the aged;[73] and he illustrated the resentment among the labouring classes of the ostentatious lifestyles of local elites. One labourer on the duke of Wellington's land told him that while his earnings were 8s. a week, and he existed almost wholly on bread, lard and salt, and was unable to buy clothes for himself or his family,[74] the duke and his friends 'all go to London to spend their money; they only come hereabout for their pleasure for a week or a month – or not much more – sometimes for a day only, to look at us, and they be off again to London'.[75] Somerville and other radical critics of English landlordism, as Alun Howkins has suggested, did internalise some features of the Hodge stereotype,[76] and Somerville was not averse to delivering unfavourable indictments of the agricultural labourer – remarking, for example, that the labourers were 'a redundant population of loose moral habits, of vicious prejudices, of confirmed idleness . . . a people rapidly sinking deteriorating every year in physical comfort'[77] – and criticised what he saw as the ill-conceived uprisings at Bosenden Wood and elsewhere

[71] Snell, *Annals*, 383–4.
[72] Ibid. 386.
[73] Alexander Somerville, *The whistler at the plough* (1st edn 1852), ed. K. D. M. Snell, London 1989, pp. xiv–xv, 256–65 and passim.
[74] Ibid. 118–20.
[75] Ibid. 118.
[76] Howkins, 'From Hodge to Lob', 220.
[77] Somerville, *Whistler at the plough*, 73.

in the 1830s, as well as confirming the findings of the 1843 commissioners as to the injurious effects of the annual influx of hop-pickers into the country-side on the thrift and sexual morality of its inhabitants.[78] Nevertheless, he spoke to a labourer who had undergone imprisonment for his part in the Captain Swing riots;[79] and attended a meeting of labourers held at Upavon in Wiltshire in 1845, to discuss the corn law question.[80] From this meeting – which was also reported in the local press – the investigator was able to learn something of the discontents among the labourers as they themselves expressed them, and was able to convey the rural working-class side of the corn law debate to a wider public. Although Somerville was writing to advance a particular political position, he employed the strategies and the language of the social investigator and delivered a detailed if declamatory account of the English countryside to his readers.

The investigation of rural life was particularly reliant on the work of the roving correspondent such as the investigative journalist or the official assis-tant commissioner. Rural social problems were isolated and information had to be gathered across a wide geographical area in which transportation was evidently more difficult than within or between towns and cities. The result of this practical necessity, it might be argued, encouraged investigators and their readers to construct the countryside as different: as the location of a significantly different set of social conditions and cultural forms that were less easily assimilated by the investigator than those which prevailed in urban England. Karen Sayer has taken this view, arguing that the employment of assistant commissioners (in this case by the Royal Commission on Labour in the 1890s) showed that '[t]he countryside required special investigation, as if it was a foreign land'.[81] It was at any rate peculiarly susceptible to the type of journalism characterised by 'miscellaneous articles, half news and half comment, and often with an allowable colouring of fiction to the facts set forth', 'a hybrid between the news-column and the leading article', as described (and praised) in 1887 by H. R. Fox Bourne, who traced its history back to Defoe and listed journalists as diverse as Mayhew and Caird as its mid nineteenth-century exemplars.[82] The exploratory tradition which can be traced through Young's and Cobbett's tours through to Caird and the *Morning Chronicle* and beyond became the site of contests over the location of social knowledge no less intense than those discerned by Yeo in the activities of the statistical societies and men like Kay-Shuttleworth.

Nobody could have been more aware of these contests than Thomas Campbell Foster, whose articles on East Anglian social conditions in 1844

78 Ibid. 269–72.
79 Ibid. 261–5.
80 Ibid. 381–7.
81 Sayer, *Women*, 137.
82 H. R. Fox Bourne, *English newspapers: chapters in the history of journalism*, London 1887, ii. 379–80.

have been likened by David Jones to Mayhew's series on London.[83] Foster had made his name through his coverage of the south Wales 'Rebecca' riots in *The Times*,[84] and was commissioned by the same newspaper to investigate the condition of the agricultural labourer in Norfolk and Suffolk at a time of widespread localised social protest, of which incendiarism was the dominant manifestation. His method, at each centre from which he conducted his investigations, was to request information, either in written form or through an interview, from various local authorities including clergymen, farmers, landowners and tradesmen; but he also consulted the labourers at first hand.[85] Jones suggests that he may have visited as many as a hundred labourers' cottages during his East Anglian tour;[86] and in south Wales he attended secret meetings of 'Rebecca' rioters.[87] Although, like Mayhew, Foster was a journalist essentially employing a descriptive method, Jones has called his approach 'avowedly scientific',[88] paralleling the reclamation of Mayhew as part of the history of 'scientific' social investigation. Foster found himself at the cutting edge of the conflicts that shaped the construction and dissemination of social knowledge of rural labouring life in the mid-nineteenth century. Moreover, although Foster was portraying a rural region at a time of atypically overt protest, he was just one of many special correspondent journalists who were exploring rural England in this period. There were many tours of inquiry organised by local newspapers, and it is probable that those known to historians represent only a small proportion of the total investigative attention directed towards the agricultural labourer in the mid-nineteenth century. Examples of such activity include an investigation of rural housing for the *Norfolk News* in the early 1860s, which came to the attention of contributors to metropolitan journals;[89] and the work of William Alexander, whose articles on rural life for the Aberdeen press were rediscovered and partially republished in the 1990s.[90] Other inquiries were initiated by the specialist agricultural press; and even the *Gardeners' Chronicle* carried a series of pieces on 'The agricultural labourer'.[91] All this work was representative of the development of an inquisitive spirit, in the countryside as well as in the towns, and it illustrates how the employment of the methods and spirit of social inquiry

83 Jones, 'Thomas Campbell Foster', 6, and also *Crime, protest, community and police*, ch. ii.
84 Pat Molloy, *And they blessed Rebecca: an account of the Welsh toll-gate riots, 1839–1844*, Llandysul 1983, 98–104; David Williams, *The Rebecca riots: a study in agrarian discontent* (1st edn 1955), Cardiff 1968; David Jones, *Rebecca's children: a study of rural society, crime and protest*, Oxford 1989, 96–7, 225, 330ff.
85 Jones, 'Thomas Campbell Foster', 21–2.
86 Ibid. 22.
87 Williams, *Rebecca riots*, 226–7.
88 Jones, 'Thomas Campbell Foster', 22.
89 Richard Heath, *The English peasant: studies historical, local and biographic*, London 1893, 69–70; John Burnett, *A social history of housing, 1815–1985* (1st edn 1978), London 1986, 29.
90 William Alexander, *Rural life in Victorian Aberdeenshire*, ed. Ian Carter, Edinburgh 1992.
91 Cited in the *Journal of the Statistical Society of London* xxiv (1861), 413–14.

were diffusing among a wide range of social investigators and, just as important, a wide range of readers.

The importance of the rural special correspondent journalist also reflected the limited engagement of the new mid nineteenth-century social-scientific elite with the social problems of rural England. The *Transactions* of the National Association for the Promotion of Social Science (NAPSS) before 1872 contain little on the subject of the agricultural labourer, and what little discussion did occur was carried on only by a dedicated group of enthusiasts. Similarly, little work was carried out in rural areas by the statistical societies, although one exception was a survey carried out by the Manchester Statistical Society in three Rutland parishes and read before the Statistical Section of the British Association in 1839, mainly for the purposes of comparing town and country conditions; while a clergyman, Edward Stanley, undertook a detailed survey of the parish of Alderly in 1836.[92] More significant in an agricultural context was the private body which assumed many of the functions of the old Board of Agriculture: the Royal Agricultural Society of England (RASE). The RASE, established in 1838 as the English Agricultural Society, promoted agricultural experimentation and investigation, and, along with the Rothamsted Experimental Station (founded in 1843) and Cirencester Agricultural College (1845), has been credited with an important role in the background to the age of scientific 'high farming'.[93] The RASE can be viewed as a rural counterpart to the statistical societies that were flourishing in the mid-nineteenth century: like the Manchester Statistical Society, it was established on the basis of a 'wise exclusion of politics',[94] and it was involved in a wide series of inquiries, illustrating the scientific disposition that characterised a large section of a farming community enjoying what historians have termed its 'golden age'. If the NAPSS meetings attained the status of a 'social parliament', bringing together social reformers in 'a type of research institute' whose proceedings were fully reported in the national press,[95] the RASE's agricultural shows, similarly peripatetic, served for the agricultural community as a forum for the 'interchange of ideas and opinion', which were in turn disseminated through the agricultural press to a national audience.[96] Events like this, mirrored at the local and regional level by chambers of agriculture and farmers' clubs, helped to cement a shared social and cultural identity. Although social issues were rarely at the centre of its deliberations, the RASE's *Journal* and other sections of the agricultural press came later in the

[92] Ashton, *Economic and social investigations*, 23–5, 32.
[93] J. D. Chambers and G. E. Mingay, *The agricultural revolution, 1750–1880*, London 1966, 170ff.
[94] Prothero, *English farming*, 359.
[95] Goldman, 'Peculiarity', 138.
[96] Nicholas Goddard, *Harvests of change: the Royal Agricultural Society of England, 1838–1988*, London 1988, 43, 71 (quoted), 77. For an earlier account of the RASE see J. A. Scott Watson, *The history of the Royal Agricultural Society of England, 1839–1939*, London 1939.

nineteenth century to provide the farming community with a vehicle of self-defence against the charges levelled against it by agricultural trade unions and their supporters. The motto of the RASE was 'Practice with Science', and it was in its preoccupation with scientific improvements that the society was most representative of the mid-Victorian concern for the collection of factual information on which to base future reforms. In the case of agriculture, this passion for statistical data eventually resulted, four decades after the demise of the old Board of Agriculture, in the first systematic and continuous collection of agricultural statistics at a governmental level in the form of the 'agricultural census', first taken (amid some opposition) by the Board of Trade in 1866. One Ministry of Agriculture statistician, celebrating the centenary of the 'agricultural census', considered this development a resumption of the Domesday Book,[97] and if this exaggerates its impact, it does emphasise the importance attached in the nineteenth century to the progressive implementation of regularised systems of gathering 'scientific' data about the state of the countryside.

Those who were in a position to supply information about the English countryside were often very different from those who might be expected to assist an urban investigator. In particular, the rural clergy formed an important group of informants, relying on their position as residents in rural communities for their knowledge and for their status as authorities. Nowhere was this more true than in Scotland, where local ministers had been the main informants consulted in the compilation of Sir John Sinclair's *Statistical account*, an inquiry that was repeated in the 1840s. Ministers frequently contributed to the perception of the rural population as ignorant and backward. The Revd James Begg, for example, contributed a series of papers to the NAPSS *Transactions*, mostly dealing with poor housing and the bothy system; he argued that the country was rapidly becoming 'more degraded and debased than the cities themselves'.[98] A glance through the *Transactions* reveals the persistent involvement of Scottish divines in the work of social inquiry and social reform. Thus the Revd Nash Stephenson commented on the evils of the statute fair;[99] the Revd John Montgomery of Inverleithen discussed rural overcrowding;[100] the Revd Peter Hope described the economic and social gulf

---

[97] A. H. J. Baines of the Ministry of Agriculture, Fisheries and Food (MAFF) Statistics Division, in MAFF and Department of Agriculture and Fisheries for Scotland, *A century of agricultural statistics: Great Britain, 1866–1966*, London 1968, 1.

[98] Revd James Begg, 'Houses of the working classes of Scotland: the bothy system', NAPSS *Transactions* (1858), 624.

[99] Revd Nash Stevenson, 'On statute fairs: their evils and remedy', NAPSS *Transactions* (1858), 624–31, and 'On the rise and progress of the movement for the abolition of statutes, mops, or feeing markets', NAPSS *Transactions* (1860), 797–805.

[100] Revd John Montgomery, 'On overcrowded villages', NAPSS *Transactions* (1860), 787–90.

between the farmers and labourers;[101] and the Revd Thomas Hutton contributed a well-known paper on agricultural gangs.[102] The preponderance of such sources of information is not surprising. Clergymen were not a particularly well-represented group within the association's membership;[103] but for the purposes of passing comment on rural society for the benefit of the urban elite represented by the NAPSS, they were in an almost unique position. Whereas urban life could be described by investigators such as Louisa Twining, secretary of the Workhouse Visiting Society,[104] and others whose involvement in organised philanthropy gave them valuable insights into the social problems of the metropolis and other large towns, there was on the whole less organised charity in the countryside, and social knowledge had to be derived from elsewhere. Because the labouring population did not usually fall within the remit of inquiries carried out under the auspices of the RASE, and was only of marginal interest to the urban statistical societies and the 'social parliament', clergymen with a reforming agenda tended to look elsewhere for an outlet for their views.

Pamphleteering engaged the attentions of many such clergymen. One persistent clerical pamphleteer and advocate of improved sanitary conditions was Henry Moule, vicar of Fordington, a suburb of Dorchester, who counted Thomas Hardy among his friends and who, among many other accomplishments, was the inventor of the dry earth system of sewage disposal, to which he devoted much of his literary output.[105] Moule was responsible for a series of published letters on sanitary and social conditions, addressed to Prince Albert as president of the council of the duchy of Cornwall, which owned his parish, in the early 1850s. These letters graphically described the open sewers, filth, overcrowding and poverty of his parish, and related these problems very closely to the moral condition of the labouring inhabitants.[106] The close proximity of the population made moral contamination inevitable: 'in streets, into which, with the exception of the few who go there on errands of mercy, or the many with purposes of vice, scarcely any one above the labourer or mechanic ever enters, children, from their earliest infancy, are in conse-

---

101 Revd Peter Hope, 'On the right condition of an agricultural community', NAPSS *Transactions* (1860), 791–7.
102 Revd Thomas Hutton, 'Agricultural gangs, their influence upon the morals and the education of the young', NAPSS *Transactions* (1864), 650–5.
103 Yeo, *Contest*, 152–5.
104 Louisa Twining, 'Workhouses', NAPSS *Transactions* (1857), 571–4, and 'The Workhouse Visiting Society', NAPSS *Transactions* (1858), 666–72.
105 See, for example, Henry Moule, *The impossibility overcome, or the inoffensive, safe, and economical disposal of the refuse of towns and villages*, London 1870; Robert Gittings, *Young Thomas Hardy*, London 1975, 36–7, 53–4.
106 Henry Moule, *Four letters to His Royal Highness Prince Albert, as president of the council of the duchy of Cornwall, on the dwellings and condition of eleven hundred of the working classes and poor of Fordington*, London 1854, and *Eight letters to His Royal Highness the Prince Albert, as president of the council of the duchy of Cornwall*, London 1855.

quence familiarised with sin'.[107] Similar evidence for squalid conditions, from the other end of England, was adduced by W. S. Gilly, vicar of Norham in Northumberland, whose pamphlet on *The peasantry of the border*, first published in 1841, claimed that of eighty-three tenements in Norham which had changed hands during the previous two years, fifty-four were 'deficient in all that is necessary to convenience and cleanliness'.[108] Thus, in a period when the poor sanitation and immorality of the slums of London and other large cities were being sensationally revealed by urban social explorers,[109] many of the same themes were being addressed from a rural perspective, often employing similar imagery. The hidden poverty of rural England was contrasted with the visible destitution of the metropolis, just as slum journalists pleaded for as much attention to be given to the population of London as was given to the poor in Britain's imperial outposts. Thus, whereas in 1870 the social explorer Thomas Archer hoped for a time

> when we shall be as thoroughly informed about the dwellers in the poverty-stricken districts of Westminster, Southwark, Spitalfields, and Whitechapel, as we are in respect of the natives of those countries to which so much missionary enterprise has been devoted ever since the establishment of a society for the purpose of converting the more remote heathen,[110]

Henry Moule exhorted his readers to take account of the distress of their own localities before subscribing to metropolitan charities: 'Numbers will . . . collect for the London City Mission Society, or contribute to its funds, who will make no attempt to rescue from ignorance or unbelief the many or the few in their own town or village.'[111]

Most of these clerical commentators on rural life were anxious to describe the immorality and heathenism of the labouring population.[112] Many intervened in the debates on some of the supposedly immoral customs that still prevailed in the nineteenth-century countryside. Moule, for example, protested successfully against the moral evils connected with the race meetings at Dorchester;[113] while Gilly regretted the moral consequences of the

---

107 Idem, *Four letters*, 17.
108 W. S. Gilly, *The peasantry of the border: an appeal on their behalf* (1st edn 1842), ed. R. H. Campbell, Edinburgh 1973, 14.
109 To take almost random examples: Hector Gavin, *Sanitary ramblings, being sketches and illustrations of Bethnal Green*, London 1848; Thomas Archer, *The pauper, the thief and the convict: sketches of some of their homes, haunts and habits*, London 1865; Revd James Yeames, *Life in London alleys, with reminiscences of Mary McCarthy and her work*, London 1877; Hugh Shimmin, *The courts and alleys of Liverpool described from personal inspection*, Liverpool 1864.
110 Thomas Archer, *The terrible sights of London, and labours of love in the midst of them*, London 1870, 99.
111 Henry Moule, *Our home heathen: how can the Church of England get at them?*, London 1868, 16.
112 John Eddowes, *The agricultural labourer as he really is, or village morals in 1854: a pamphlet for the present day*, Driffield 1854, 16; Moule, *Our home heathen*, 6, 16.
113 *Dictionary of national biography*.

frequent movement of Northumberland hinds from village to village.[114] Parsons often followed the fashion for stereotyping the labourer as ignorant and helpless: for example, an unnamed clergyman from the south of England remarked on how '[a] singular feebleness seems to pervade everything [in the countryside] . . . the land and the productions of it have the same feeble character, as well as the labourers and the mechanics'.[115] However, it could be argued that the parson's regular visitation of labourers' homes gave him a significant advantage as a commentator on rural life: thus John Eddowes, vicar of Garton-upon-the-Wolds in Yorkshire, spelt out his credentials as an authority on the agricultural labourer by remarking that '[t]hey who have not occasion to go in and out among the poorer families in country districts, seldom arrive at a correct conception of their social and spiritual condition'.[116] Indeed, this personal contact was a prerequisite for the promotion of a more active religious life among the rural population that was a goal of the more evangelical mid nineteenth-century country parsons. As Brian Heeney has shown, an undercurrent of priestly humanitarianism was present even during the pre-evangelical period in which the predominant 'ideal of clerical detachment' found itself personified by the Trollopian 'gentleman-cleric'; and under the influence of an impressive array of pastoral theologians many mid nineteenth-century country parsons 'forged links with their people', just as 'many ritualist slum priests became identified with the London poor'.[117] The country parson's self-identification with his labouring neighbours often encouraged him in advocacy on their behalf, as in the case of Henry Moule; at the same time, the experience of visiting rural working-class homes and attempting to guide the moral life of their parishioners led many clergymen to the recognition that the achievement of a genuine cultural understanding of and empathy with the rural labouring population was a both necessary and difficult precondition for the effective reform of rural life.

Evangelical parsons were hampered in this project by the legacy of the austerity and unworldliness that had characterised the clergy in the earlier nineteenth century. As Heeney suggests, '[t]he demand for detachment from the world and withdrawal from any aspect of life deemed "worldly" . . . meant that clergymen found it difficult, in most cases impossible, to know intimately the affairs of their parishioners, [and] to identify with their secular lives'.[118] The effacement of this unworldliness could be achieved only through active immersion in the social life of the parish. One of those who followed this strategy was Charles Kingsley, vicar of Eversley in Hampshire and a popular

114 See, especially, his condemnation of the practice of 'flitting' in Gilly, Peasantry of the border, 12.

115 Quoted in E. W. Moore, An address on the condition of the agricultural labourer and his cottage home, delivered at a meeting of the Oxford Farmers' Club, London 1864, 33.

116 Eddowes, Agricultural labourer, 5.

117 Brian Heeney, 'On being a mid-Victorian clergyman', Journal of Religious History vii (1973), 215, 220, 213.

118 Ibid. 224.

social novelist, whose local involvement extended to many areas of the economic and social life of the parish: among other ventures, he was responsible for the establishment of clubs, schools, mothers' meetings, loan funds, a lending library, night classes and village lectures.[119] His approach was guided by the precepts of the emerging social-scientific movement: he shared the belief that accurate social knowledge was a prerequisite for effective social reform, and in the words of an early biographer, he aimed 'to guide these [reformatory] tendencies [in men] by stating forcibly the data of the problem'.[120] However, he also preached the necessity of the achievement of more intimate communication with the working-class population, and along with Frederick Denison Maurice and other members of the Christian Social Union he devoted much thought to the development of schemes of domestic visitation of the poor and the adoption of strategies to overcome the social barriers he encountered in his daily intercourse. Kingsley was aware of 'that very inward gulf' which existed between members of the different classes of the countryside and which it was the task of the visitor to bridge,[121] and became himself 'a most regular and conscientious visitor . . . personally intimate with every soul in his parish'.[122] Through this more intimate knowledge of the poor information could be obtained which transcended the simple catalogue of insanitary evils drawn up by other social investigators; and the experience of domestic visitation became a significant counterpart to the new social-scientific understandings of rural poverty as the century progressed. The task of establishing interpersonal relationships with the poor was, arguably, easier for the parish priest than, say, in institutions such as the prison, hospital or workhouse, as J. S. Brewer explained:

> In parishes, gradations of rank shade off the differences between one class and another: the clergyman is seen in free intercourse with all. He is seen in daily and familiar communion with people of every grade; he is the poor man's advocate with his superior, and the interpreter of his superior to the inferior.[123]

This kind of assessment, however positive, reflects another significant barrier to the achievement of a genuine cultural understanding of rural working-class life, a barrier derived from an impetus in some ways contradictory to that which generated the Hodge stereotype. Whereas on the one hand the conditions of urban industrial England pushed the no less serious problems associated with rural life into the background, on the other hand they encouraged the generation of images of rurality which presented an optimistic alternative

---

119 Charles William Stubbs, *Charles Kingsley and the Christian social movement*, London 1899, ch. ii.
120 Ibid. 69–70.
121 Idem, 'The country parish', in [F. D. Maurice (ed.),] *Lectures to ladies on practical subjects*, Cambridge 1855, 63.
122 Stubbs, *Charles Kingsley*, 51.
123 J. S. Brewer, 'Workhouse visiting', in [Maurice], *Lectures to ladies*, 270.

to the debasement of urban life. Conceptualising rural poverty was still diffi-cult: even Hodge was a fairly harmless figure, amusingly ignorant rather than a political or social danger; while an alternative series of constructions repre-sented the rural population as an altogether superior breed, very different from the faceless mass that inhabited England's towns. Thus Anne Digby has argued that, for all the detail of the *Morning Chronicle* survey and other mid-century ventures, rural poverty 'remained substantially hidden, and even in its more obvious manifestations it bore a quaint rusticity which induced nostalgia in observers rather than remedial activity'.[124] The literary output of country writers such as Mary Russell Mitford of Berkshire and Thomas Miller of Nottinghamshire reinforced the pastoral image of the countryside through a focus on characters – for example Miller's Butcher Heron the poacher and old Abraham the woodman[125] – who represented the exotic (and untypical) side of country life and were designed to appeal to an urban readership. Miller's publishers reserved an important role for the illustrator, and his books are full of charming rustic portraits: a pretty milkmaid carrying her stool, a hay-cart surrounded by hard-working but cheerful harvesters, and other ruralist imagery.[126] Similarly, Miss Mitford's 'sketches of rural character and scenery', appearing in the widely read and influential *Our village* series, featured love tales, comic narratives and rich descriptions of the Berkshire landscape. Although appearing around the time of Captain Swing and other outbreaks of rural discontent, conflict was almost entirely written out of Mitford's work, although on on one occasion she gave a somewhat exagger-ated account of the fear that descended on the respectable inhabitants of the village during an outbreak of incendiarism.[127] Her rustic neighbours enjoyed an outdoor life that allowed for the full development of character and indi-viduality, and bred a population far superior to that found in the towns: 'in every condition of life goodness and happiness may be found by those who seek them, and never more surely than in the fresh air, the shade, and the sunshine of nature'.[128] Mitford's sketches generated a ruralist sentimentality that was widely diffused through the rural literature of the nineteenth century and beyond. The investigator had to penetrate the veil of benign rusticity if he was to present an accurate picture of labouring life, as the literary tradition had no place for the sort of squalor that W. S. Gilly and Henry Moule described. Thus John Eddowes argued in 1854 that the picture of country life drawn from reality was very different from the 'fancy-sketch' offered in other accounts,[129] while twenty years later another commentator, in the *Cornhill*,

124 Digby, 'Rural poor', 591.
125 Thomas Miller, *Rural sketches*, London 1839, 109–22, 150–7.
126 Idem, *English country life*, London 1859, 118, 288.
127 Mary Russell Mitford, *Our village: sketches of rural character and scenery* (1st edn 1824–32), London 1863, ii. 318–24.
128 Ibid. i, p. v.
129 Eddowes, *Agricultural labourer*, 6.

remarked on the differences between the popular conception of a rural summer and the harsher realities of winter:

> To those who think it is such pleasant and picturesque employment, that the labourer's life is an idyll, only needing to be translated into words, we would recommend that they should go, not only on some fine summer's evening when the heat of day is declining . . . but with Roger on a foggy November morning, to spread rotten muck over the heavy clay land; not only to 'hear the milk sing in the pail, with buzzings of the honied hours', but to milk those same cows at four o'clock in winter, when the frost is on the grass, and a keen north wind blowing across the pastures.[130]

It became increasingly common for investigators to insist that roses, honey-suckles and other visually attractive features of the rural environment were deceptive in concealing the 'misery, poverty, and abject dependence' of labouring families from the view of the outsider.[131]

Rural poverty, then, was hidden both geographically from the investigator and ideologically, behind a series of pastoral conceptions of the countryside that accorded rurality a status superior to that of urban cultural life. The physical surroundings of the rural community, allied to the paternalistic social structure that supposedly continued to function, overlaid rural destitution with a partially redemptive quaintness. On a more practical level for the social investigator, this paternalism was also replicated in the structure of agricultural labourers' remuneration, and was thus ideologically embedded in one of the fundamental tasks of social inquiry, the accurate assessment of how much the labourer actually earned. E. H. Hunt has pointed out that 'farm wages were more often and more competently investigated than earnings in any other occupation'.[132] This investigative activity drew attention to the regional diversity of agricultural wages, illustrated in James Caird's famous map, published in *English agriculture in 1850–51*, which showed how wages were significantly higher in the mainly pastoral counties of the north of England than in the arable south, a theme emphasised by many rural historians.[133] More contestably, the labourer's wage was normally augmented by a one-off payment at harvest time – itself often a cause of social conflict in rural communities[134] – and often by additional earnings from piece-work. On top of this, payments in kind often formed a substantial proportion of agricultural earnings: the labourer may have had cottage accommodation free or at a

---

130 *Cornhill* xxix (1874), 693.
131 Edward Girdlestone, 'Landowners, land and those who till it', *Fraser's Magazine* lxxviii (1868), 734.
132 Hunt, *Regional wage variations*, 5.
133 Ibid. 61–4; Chambers and Mingay, *Agricultural revolution*, 136–42, 190; Alan Armstrong, *Farmworkers: a social and economic history, 1770–1980*, London 1988, 66, 85, 91, based on sources including Caird, *English agriculture*.
134 David Hoseason Morgan, *Harvesters and harvesting, 1840–1900: a study of the rural proletariat*, London 1982.

non-economic rent, he might be given an allotment, free milk, free food for a pig or poultry, free potatoes or meat, or perhaps free or subsidised fuel. Naturally enough, when investigators sought to ascertain the cash equivalents of non-wage payments, they found that different informants valued them very differently: as J. P. D. Dunbabin has remarked, 'it is not surprising that whenever the question of agricultural wages was ventilated, it always occasioned heated disputes as to their real value'.[135] One contemporary despaired that

> the practice of payment in kind, with all its perplexing ramifications, opposes an obstacle to the inquirer which it is impossible to overcome without a patient and minute investigation of the system in all its phases – a task, it is needless to add, which the constant work of several years would be no more than sufficient to execute.[136]

The ideological significance of payments in kind, as one of the structures which cemented the paternalistic social relations of the countryside, gave them an added importance to social investigators, who approached the practice – and, consequently, the valuation of such payments – from a range of political perspectives. According to the stance of the investigator, the perquisite system could be interpreted as anything from beneficent through benign to pernicious and degrading. For the radical critic, payment in kind, and especially the provision of tied cottages, was symptomatic of an anachronistic feudalism that denied the labourer the economic independence that was necessary for his personal and social elevation; while the conservative defender of the system would emphasise the linkages between payment in kind and the persistence of face-to-face charitable relationships in the countryside that prevented the labourer from falling into the kind of degradation that was all too common in the urban industrial environment. Thus while the kind of evidence that Snell adduces in his commentary on the rural standard of living testifies to many labourers' dislike of payments in kind, especially the provision of non-marketable corn or 'grist',[137] others interpreted the practice in a wider context of social harmony. Thus one observer remarked in 1855: 'To preserve unbroken, a connexion, during many years, between the employers and the employed is a worthy object, one which we contemplate with deep satisfaction, as indicating something excellent in both parties; kindness and beneficence on the part of the farmer, contentment and gratitude on the part of his dependent.'[138]

The disputed valuation of the labourer's earnings became a central feature of social investigation in the countryside in the 1860s, a period during which

---

135 Dunbabin, *Rural discontent*, 66.
136 T. E. Kebbel, *The agricultural labourer: a short summary of his position*, London 1870, 222–3.
137 Snell, *Annals*, 386, citing Heath, *English peasant*, 126.
138 Martin Doyle, *The agricultural labourer, viewed in his moral, intellectual and physical conditions*, London 1855, 68.

the stirrings of conflict were increasingly felt, and which can be seen as an overture to the more explosive contests of the 1870s. The efforts of campaigning journalists, parsons and pamphleteers to bring to public attention the problems of the rural areas were beginning to bear fruit and, as noted above, once the steady reform of the conditions of urban artisan labour had been set in train, the focus of many reformers' attentions shifted onto the plight of the rural poor. The most notable result of this was the appointment in 1867 of the Royal Commission on the Employment of Children, Young Persons and Women in Agriculture, which, despite the specificity of its brief, was aptly described by one contemporary as 'nothing less than an inquiry into the whole condition of the agricultural peasantry'.[139] It was a much larger venture than the poor law commissioners' inquiry of 1843, but like its predecessor it entailed the despatching of assistant commissioners across Britain with orders to report on the vital issues of the day. The inquiry was prompted by the public outcry which followed the publication of Seymour Tremenheere's report on agricultural gangs in the same year,[140] and the problems of gang labour and education were the subject of the bulk of the report. The concern over gang labour resulted in the passage of the Gangs Act in 1867 which, together with the educational reforms of the early 1870s, effectively diminished the role of children's labour gangs in agriculture. The commission's report emphasised the adverse moral effects of the gang system; and the field-labouring woman in particular was represented as a particularly undesirable specimen of Victorian womanhood. Karen Sayer has analysed these representations in more detail.[141] Even more so than the commission of 1843, the 1867 inquiry was conducted within a consciously established methodological framework intended to exclude the rural labouring population from involvement in the representation and interpretation of its own condition and outlook.

This is made clear from an examination of the procedures used in the taking of evidence. The assistant commissioners were instructed to send out a printed circular of questions to 'the most competent persons you can meet with',[142] and to take information from all sectors of society in the areas for which they were responsible. They were reminded, however, of the potential untrustworthiness of information derived from the working classes: 'In receiving the statements of the labouring class you will, as far as possible, record them in their own language; and in case of doubt submit them to their employers, teachers, or others, for explanation or correction.'[143] In practice, the reports were primarily based on the evidence of elite informants,

139 Kebbel, *Agricultural labourer*, 1.
140 H. S. Tremenheere, *I was there: the memoirs of H. S. Tremenheere*, ed. E. L. Edmonds and O. P. Edmonds, Windsor 1965, 111.
141 Sayer, *Women*, 76–81.
142 *RC on the Employment of Children, Young Persons, and Women in Agriculture: first report of the commissioners*, PP 1867–8, C. 4068, 161.
143 Ibid.

especially the clergy, whose importance as a source of social knowledge for the English countryside was reinforced by this commission. The commissioners also focused on the evidence of landowners and those concerned with poor relief. For example, George Culley, reporting on Oxfordshire and Buckinghamshire in 1868 having centred his inquiries on the boards of guardians in each area he visited,[144] distributed his printed circular and received 168 completed responses, of which 75 were filled out by clergymen, 31 by landowners, 54 by 'occupiers of land' (of whom 49 were also poor law guardians) and 8 by 'other persons'.[145] Similarly, from Derbyshire and Hertfordshire, 57 were received, of which 13 came from clergymen, 18 from landowners or their agents, 23 from occupiers of land (again mostly also guardians) and 3 from others.[146] The importance of clerical and landowning informants is also evident in the Revd James Fraser's report on East Anglia, Sussex and Gloucestershire. Fraser, later bishop of Manchester and a sympathiser with agricultural trade unionism, used his fellow clerics as his main informant group.[147] He also held public meetings, arranged in each area by the clergyman or churchwarden, which were to be attended by 'the owners and occupiers of land, the clergy, the magistrates, the overseers and guardians of the poor, the medical and relieving officers, &c'.[148] Fraser, 'whose reports [as Alun Howkins notes] . . . are by far the most sympathetic to the workers',[149] attempted to take some information from labourers,[150] but it was not used in the compilation of his report. This investigative strategy resulted in a generally optimistic view of the condition and outlook of the labouring population, supplemented by some highly unflattering representations of particular subgroups, especially women working in gangs.

Public discussion of the position of the agricultural labourer coalesced around the reports of the 'employment commission', partly because of the effective work by independent journalists and propagandists in distributing its findings. Thomas Kebbel's *The agricultural labourer*, published in 1870, was written partly in fulfilment of his self-appointed task of spreading the commission's findings to a wider audience than would normally have the time or inclination to read parliamentary papers; while Charles Whitehead, whose *Agricultural labourers* appeared in the same year, was driven by a similar motivation. A literate population which might read a clergyman's pamphlet or a series of newspaper articles about the English rural population would be unappreciative of the small print and legalistic language of a government report.

---

144 Ibid. appendix to 1st report, 122.
145 *RC on the Employment of Children, Young Persons, and Women in Agriculture: second report of the commissioners*, PP 1868–9, C. 4202, 75.
146 Ibid. 106.
147 Ibid. 5–6.
148 Ibid. 4n.
149 Howkins, *Reshaping rural England*, 187–8.
150 *RC on the Employment of Children, Young Persons, and Women in Agriculture: second report*, 6.

As one contributor to the *Journal of the Royal Agricultural Society*, summarising the contents of H. M. Jenkins's official report on agricultural education, remarked some years later,

> if there is one thing which more than another the ordinary English reader dreads to tackle, it is the ponderous volumes issued in such variety by the Government printers for the instruction of our legislators, the blue covers and general aspects of which are in themselves sufficient to frighten away at first sight all but industrious students. The volumes in question are likely to remain sealed books to the majority of agricultural readers.[151]

Because the findings of the 1867 report were more comprehensive and more widely disseminated than those of 1843, the employment commission gained a higher profile and a wider influence than its predecessor. Following the commissioners, Kebbel dealt with women and children's work (especially gang labour), the public house, the hiring or statute fair, and education, in the context of the legislation of 1870. As Karen Sayer has explained, both Kebbel and Whitehead were 'actively engaged in the dissemination and universalisation of ideologically constructed "facts" in order to achieve "the gradual influence of public opinion" to improve rural conditions, and therefore English society as a whole'.[152]

They disseminated these 'facts' to advance an essentially optimistic assessment of the position of the agricultural labourer. In this they followed the commission's lead, although Kebbel, while recognising many of the drawbacks of the agricultural life,[153] asserted that even the commissioners' generally optimistic outlook was an understatement.[154] His analysis was based on the additional earnings available to the labourer in addition to his basic weekly wage; and he illustrated his case with examples of individual families with more than one earner. One man – according to information supplied by a farmer – while he received only £27 12s. in wages in a year, took home £38 17s. when harvest, haytime, piecework and other extra money payments were added; and he and his three sons earned a total of £103 9s. between them in the course of a year.[155] Kebbel conceded that in half of all agricultural families the chief male breadwinner did not receive enough in permanent wages to keep his family, and that many children's earnings did not cover the cost of their keep.[156] However, he emphasised four 'facts' which pointed to a generally encouraging outlook for the labourers: many families earned over £100 a year in total, and many more between £70 and £80; many had money in

---

151 Herbert J. Little, 'Report on agricultural education', *Journal of the Royal Agricultural Society of England* 2nd ser. xxi (1885), 127.
152 Sayer, *Women*, 120.
153 Kebbel, *Agricultural labourer*, 15–16.
154 Ibid. 23–4.
155 Ibid. 32.
156 Ibid. 17–18.

savings banks; their personal health and appearance were generally good; and they enjoyed considerable longevity.[157] Whitehead presented a similar case: the Devon labourer, he confidently asserted, although his wages were undoubtedly lower than in most of the rest of England, earned 11s. a week in money wages, 'which, in spite of all that has been alleged to the contrary, is fairly believed to be the minimum average wage, even in the western counties'.[158] A defender of the 'patriarchal system' that he believed still functioned in rural England,[159] Whitehead pointed to the many farmers who kept their men on full wages even at slack times of the year, and to the various benefits enjoyed by labourers such as free cottages, cheap flour and fuel, 'which are . . . in many cases forgotten by those who make the most of their unsatisfactory state'.[160]

One of those at whom Whitehead's accusation was implicitly pointed, especially in view of the use of Devon as his case study, was Canon Edward Girdlestone, vicar of Halberton in Devon, who in the 1860s became a well-known advocate of the labourers' cause, earning the sobriquet 'the agricultural labourers' friend'.[161] Soon after his arrival from a northern industrial parish, Girdlestone began attacking the local farmers for their treatment of their employees, and established a scheme of migration to high-wage areas, as a consequence of which some 500 Halbertonians moved to distant parts of the country. Girdlestone became notorious among the farming community, and contributed articles on the agricultural population to a number of influential periodicals, as well as stating the labourers' case to generally unsympathetic bodies such as the Church Congress; he was also an important early supporter of agricultural trade unionism. Girdlestone was certain that farmers' views of agricultural conditions should not be accepted. For example, in 1868 he disagreed publicly with the farmers' spokesman Clare Sewell Read, who had claimed that 'the main objects of unions was to do the least amount of work and receive the largest amount of pay'. To this Girdlestone replied that Read was 'not perhaps very likely to look with a favourable eye upon anything which has a tendency to make the agricultural labourers independent', adding that Read was probably a member of a chamber of agriculture himself, and arguing that, if other professions and sectors of the agricultural community had their unions, so the labourer should also have his.[162] On another occasion Read claimed that labourers' wages in his own county of Norfolk were were 12s. a week, or 13s. including harvest money, which

[157] Ibid. 223.
[158] Charles Whitehead, *Agricultural labourers*, London 1870, 7.
[159] Ibid. 10.
[160] Ibid. 9.
[161] P. J. Perry, 'Edward Girdlestone, 1805–84: a forgotten evangelical', *Journal of Religious History* ix (1977), 292.
[162] Girdlestone, 'Landowners', 745, and 'The agricultural labourer', *Macmillan's Magazine* xxvi (1872), 261.

Girdlestone disputed, pointing out that stoppages for wet weather would bring average earnings over a year down to below 12s. He remarked that 'Mr. Reade [sic], known in the House of Commons as the farmers' member, and himself a tenant farmer, is often looked up to as a great authority on the condition of the agricultural labourer. So he is no doubt from a farmer's point of view.'[163]

Girdlestone continually reiterated his denunciation of the payment of perquisites as part of the agricultural wage structure, and the high valuation given to such payments by farmers and their spokesmen. He demonstrated that perquisites were by no means universally available to labourers, and even where they were, many disadvantages were attached to them: for example, the free cider was 'very sour and often very weak', the fuel that was given had to be carried off by the labourers themselves, potato ground was charged at a high rate, and labourers in tied cottages were often forbidden to keep pigs or poultry.[164] Girdlestone kept up this assault into the 1870s, reminding his readers that the farmer 'not infrequently exaggerates the value of the so-called privileges, and also makes the wages he professes to give appear much larger than they really are, or even pays in kind of an inferior quality'.[165] He cited one Halberton farmer's estimate of his labourers' earnings, which were nominally 8s., but actually 10s. in cash, augmented by grist, pig ground and other perquisites which made the full value as much as 14s. As this farmer told a group of his peers in Halberton, this showed that '[t]he labourer was not . . . in the poverty-stricken and degraded state which had been represented' on occasions by the canon.[166] But as Girdlestone explained to the readers of *Fraser's Magazine*, such a calculation was unrealistic. The grist, itself an inferior and unsaleable by-product of arable agriculture, was given on terms frequently unfavourable to the labourers; and

> The wages of 8s. a week are calculated at 10s. a week by adding the receipts for over work, when a hard day's work has been already done, while on the other hand, no deduction is made for wet days with no work and no wages. . . . The convenience for a pig either means a stye which ought to be annexed to every cottage, or an occasional run for the pig in an adjoining field, which not one farmer in a thousand allows. These, together with other things, which are not named, and which in reality do not exist, are calculated from a farmer's point of view at 4s. a week!!![167]

Girdlestone's view did not go unchallenged. In his report on Devon for the employment commission, Assistant Commissioner Edwin Portman talked to the farmer who had made this statement, Mr Pearce of Uploman, who

---

163 Idem, 'Landowners', 732.
164 Ibid. 729, and 'The National Agricultural Labourers' Union', *Macmillan's Magazine* xxviii (1873), 442.
165 Idem, 'National Agricultural Labourers' Union', 441.
166 Idem, 'Landowners', 729 n. 1.
167 Ibid.

defended his argument against the canon's criticisms. He claimed that he used the same grist as the labourers himself, and reasserted his claims as to the value of wages. Nevertheless, Portman was able to use a rare piece of evidence from the labouring classes here: the wife of an Uploman labourer told him that her husband received only 9s., plus cider, and no other privileges at all.[168] Other critics of 'the agricultural labourers' friend' included Charles Whitehead, who believed that migration (as encouraged by Girdlestone) would 'embitter the relations between employer and employed, and . . . completely sever those ties which have existed in such peculiar force between farmers and their labourers'.[169] Even the *Daily News*, a newspaper of Liberal sympathies, remarked that '[t]he correspondents of the newspapers that represent the opinions and prejudices of farmers will angrily deny the correctness of [Girdlestone's] picture; and they will be partially justified'.[170]

In the years prior to the upheavals of 1872, then, the debate about the conditions of agricultural employment and remuneration, and other features of the agricultural labourer's life, was intensifying in the wake of new political challenges to the settled agrarian order and new emphases among social investigators of rural life. The wide regional variations in wages, conditions of work, housing and the structure of remuneration ensured that the perspectives of many investigators were unlikely to intersect, and allowed scope for sharply conflicting portrayals of rural social conditions. There could be no accurate single portrait of 'English agriculture' (let alone 'British agriculture') or of the rural labouring classes. As one observer in the 1880s remarked, '[y]ou might as wisely construct a harmonious theory of British agriculture from observations made in Russia and Spain as by tabulating scraps of information picked up in Devonshire and Norfolk, in Cumberland and the Isle of Ely. . . . Northamptonshire is not England any more than Norfolk is Wales'.[171] However, even when investigators visited the same region, the structure of agricultural employment and the state of community relations in rural England allowed a wide range of politically determined interpretations of the outlook for agriculture and the condition of the labourer. Given that the investigative impulse was at its strongest at times of social unrest and agricultural uncertainty or upheaval, the element of contestation in the productions of social investigation was intensified. In this context the investigator's point of access to the rural community was an essential determinant of the kinds of fact and opinion to which he would be exposed; and as we have seen this was a matter of which many investigators were aware. Even the output of resident investigators – in this period primarily but by no means exclusively the rural

---

[168] *RC on the Employment of Children, Young Persons, and Women in Agriculture: second report*, 34.

[169] Whitehead, *Agricultural labourers*, 9.

[170] Quoted in the *Journal of the Statistical Society of London* xxxii (1869), 117.

[171] Augustus Jessopp, *Arcady: for better for worse* (1st edn 1887), popular edn, London 1887, 199–200.

clergy – was subject to fundamental contradiction and challenge arising from issues of standpoint epistemology that were embedded within the social structure of rural communities. Overlaying the whole project of social inquiry were the competing constructions of the labourer and of the countryside which drove the ways in which rurality was interpreted. Yet whatever developments had occurred during the preceding century, within the whole arena of social inquiry, the agricultural labourer, although increasingly the main subject of investigation, remained a marginal figure in the project of the construction of social knowledge; and it was only in the wake of the new impetus given to rural trade unionism by the agricultural strikes of 1872 that the exclusion of the labourer from the processes of social inquiry began to come under widespread and sustained challenge.

2

Special Correspondents and Resident Investigators: The 'Revolt of the Field' and its Aftermath

Although the Warwickshire strike of 1872 and the subsequent formation of the National Agricultural Labourers' Union (NALU) are given an important place in virtually every account of English rural history, it is not always appreciated just how severe a jolt they gave to the complacency that characterised the prevailing view of rural life in the 'golden age' of agriculture.[1] A full decade and a half before the 'new unionism' came to the dockers and match-girls of the metropolis, Joseph Arch's agricultural workers' union seemed to shake the roots of one of the more apparently stable sectors of British society. For the first time since the Tolpuddle 'martyrdoms' of 1834, agricultural combination became a serious political issue, and although the union activities of the 1870s were not, on the whole, accompanied by the physical violence that characterised the 'Captain Swing' agitation or the incendiarism of the 1840s, they indicated the potential power to threaten the stability of the existing social order that lay in the hands of the agricultural labourers. David Jones has shown that 1872 represented only the most spectacular example of rural social protest and disorder, which at times during the previous forty years had reached levels that 'indicated that paternalism and deference were virtually fractured';[2] but in the early 1870s the agricultural labour problem, previously characterised by localised social protest and disorder, took its place, if temporarily, at the centre of the national political stage. The support of prominent churchmen including Edward Girdlestone and Bishop Fraser of Manchester, and the sympathetic stance of Liberal MPs such as A. J. Mundella, Bromley Davenport and Jesse Collings, gave the union an even higher public profile. The union interjected overt class conflict into a society that was still often conceived as paternalist and deferential, with the perceived backwardness and ignorance of the agricultural labourer at its base. The class dimension shattered the illusion of deference, and challenged the Hodge stereotype and its associated implications. Observers looked with disbelief at the political awakening of Hodge, one remembering later that '[i]t had seemed to us impossible that there should be

[1] Ernest Selley, *Village trade unions in two centuries*, London 1919; Reg Groves, *Sharpen the sickle! The history of the farm workers' union*, London 1949; Horn, *Joseph Arch*; Dunbabin, *Rural discontent*.
[2] David Jones, 'Rural crime and protest', in Mingay, *Victorian countryside*, ii. 567.

any stirring of the dry bones'.[3] As Alun Howkins has explained, '[b]y "interfering" in the sacred relationship between master and man the union hit at the core of the paternalist social structure'.[4] The apparent splintering of the social basis of agriculture, whether the direct result of Arch's union or symptomatic of more fundamental malfunctions of the social order, issued a new challenge to social investigators, for whom the assessment of social relationships in rural communities became as important as the transmission of information about social conditions in the countryside. This task entailed more intensive conflicts about the location of social knowledge within those communities.

The first national newspaper to respond actively to the Warwickshire strike was the Liberal *Daily News*, which sent Archibald Forbes to Wellesbourne, the centre of the union's activity, two weeks after *The Times* had first reported the strike, in March 1872.[5] Forbes was the paper's star reporter, fresh from his exploits describing the Franco-Prussian War, his articles on which had played a leading role in the rapid growth of the circulation and influence of the *Daily News*.[6] That such a celebrated correspondent should be sent reflects the perceived importance of the strike. Forbes, in the company of Arch, visited a number of villages, and attended several strikers' meetings. His articles generally expressed support for the labourers, and were later remembered with gratitude by Arch and other prominent unionists.[7] They initiated a fierce debate on the agricultural labour problem, and prompted other investigations of the rural labouring classes. Francis Heath, a civil servant in his late twenties, and later a campaigner for urban parklands and a prolific author of nature books,[8] made tours of inquiry in his native west country for the *Morning Advertiser*[9] in 1872 and 1873, on which he based two series of articles and two books, *The 'romance' of peasant life* (1872) and *The English peasantry* (1874); these were followed by *Peasant life in the west of England* (1880), in which Heath's own investigations were supplemented by information from correspondents. Heath's articles dealt with Devon, Dorset,

---

3   Quoted in Frances Evelyn Greville, countess of Warwick, 'Preface', to Joseph Arch, *Joseph Arch: the story of his life told by himself*, London 1898, p. xi.
4   Howkins, *Reshaping rural England*, 186.
5   Horn, *Joseph Arch*, 50ff.
6   The paper's circulation tripled to 150,000 in one week: R. J. Cruikshank, *Roaring century, 1846–1946*, London 1946, 168. There is a character sketch of Forbes in Joseph Hatton, *Journalistic London, being a series of sketches of famous pens and papers of the day*, London 1882, 58–62.
7   Arch, *Joseph Arch*, 83–4; Arthur Clayden, *The revolt of the field: a sketch of the rise and progress of the movement among the agricultural labourers known as the 'National Agricultural Labourers' Union'*, *with a reprint of the correspondence to the* Daily News *during a tour through Canada with Mr Arch*, London 1874, 8, 95.
8   See, for example, F. G. Heath, *Burnham Beeches*, London 1879; *The fern paradise: a plea for the culture of ferns*, London 1875; and *The fern world*, London 1877.
9   The *Morning Advertiser* was traditionally Liberal, although it had switched its allegiance in 1871 as a result of the Gladstone government's attacks on the brewing interest.

Somerset and Wiltshire, a region in which agricultural wages were even lower than in Warwickshire. When the labour unrest spread in 1874 to East Anglia, where the farmers initiated a large-scale lockout of agricultural labourers in another low-wage region, *The Times* sent its reporter Frederick Clifford, less sympathetic to the labourers' cause than Forbes or Heath, but nevertheless influenced by the developments in special correspondent methodology spawned by the 'Revolt of the Field'.

Both Forbes and Heath made a point of communicating at first hand with agricultural labourers and their families rather than relying on the evidence of informants. Forbes found that this yielded a different kind of information from that obtained by investigators using a more traditional informant base. In his first and second articles, he described his experiences boarding in a family home, including a rare example of a rural domestic budget, albeit a rough and ready one. Forbes explained that the family with whom he boarded numbered seven, earning a total of 15s. a week, eating for breakfast dry bread and poor tea, for dinner potatoes fried in scraps of bacon rind, and for supper bread and boiled potatoes, or on rare occasions a single herring divided among the seven.[10] Similarly, Heath used labourers and their families as his chief source of information. For example, John P. from Barnwell explained to Heath in 1872 that his earnings were only 5s. a week, out of which he paid £2 10s. a year for rent, 10s. a year for pig ground and 15s. for potato ground;[11] while near Minehead in 1873 Heath met a carter who earned 10s. a week with three or four pints of cider a day: this man paid £3 5s. a year in rent and 10s. on poor rates, school rates and gas rates, even though his cottage was not supplied with gas.[12] This kind of information, Heath pointed out, had not been generally available to the members of the employment commission or to James Caird, questioning the latter's reliance on informants with a dubious claim to be 'the best and most trustworthy sources of local information'.[13] The commission's information was 'principally gathered from Boards of Guardians, clergymen, agents, and individual farmers. The Commissioners did occasionally take evidence from the labourers and their wives, but it was the exception, and not the rule, for them to do so'.[14] Heath was forced to rely on evidence from this commission, from the reports of the assistant poor law commissioners of 1843, and from Caird's *English agriculture in 1850–51* to

10 *Daily News*, 27 Mar. 1872, 6; 28 Mar. 1872, 2. The budgetary information was also quoted in F. G. Heath, *The English peasantry*, London 1874, 2, and Forbes obtained similar information about a household in Cambridgeshire: *Daily News*, 5 Apr. 1872, 3.
11 Heath, *English peasantry*, 47–9, and *The 'romance' of peasant life in the west of England*, London 1872, 27–30.
12 Idem, *English peasantry*, 107–8. See also Burnett, *Social history of housing*, 121–2.
13 F. G. Heath, *Peasant life in the west of England*, London 1880, 10, quoting Caird, *English agriculture*, p. xxxiv.
14 *Morning Advertiser*, 21 July 1873, 6.

compile a survey of conditions before 1872;[15] but in his own investigations he 'rarely failed to question any labouring man or woman' whom he met on his travels.[16] He distrusted the evidence of farmers: in 1872, for example, he heard from farmers in northern Somerset that the agricultural labourers of the area were 'dissipated in their habits', but decided on personal inspection that this was untrue.[17]

Heath's explorations had a dual purpose, reflecting the social tensions which prompted them. Firstly, he was reporting to a metropolitan audience, with its own preconceptions about rural life and labour, on the realities of the rediscovered rural poverty. This role entailed an emphasis on the alienness of rural life, and an adoption of a self-consciously exploratory outlook. Karen Sayer has compared Heath to a 'colonial explorer', collecting information from 'a separate land that was remote . . . which was only just becoming civilised as social reformers began to explore its depths': 'the rural was a mini-empire within the borders of England, which had to be explored'.[18] The role gave scope for the kind of intrepidity displayed by metropolitan slum journalists, a tradition of social exploration of which Heath was certainly aware: indeed, during his tour of 1873, he visited a family of farmers known as the Devon 'savages',[19] which James Greenwood, the 'Amateur Casual', had also described.[20] As with Greenwood and other social explorers, the language of the ethnographer pervades Heath's account of his visit. Throughout their reports, Heath and other special correspondents employed literary strategies to convince the reader that they had 'been there', lifted the veil that covered rural labouring life, and seen what lay beneath.[21] Whereas metropolitan social explorers continually invoked the contrasts between wealth and poverty that could be experienced in London, the alienness of rural life was conveyed through a transparent counter-pastoral literary strategy, an incidental by-product of which was an enhancement of the reader's sense of the intensity of contact Heath had enjoyed with the rural population. Setting out with the declared intention of 'reveal[ing] to luxurious Londoners a state of things that is terrible in its reality of misery',[22] Heath showed his readers, who too often pictured the labourer 'in the fields under the blue canopy of heaven'[23] in 'rose-bound cottages',[24] that the 'romance' of rural working-class

---

15 Heath, *Peasant life*, 8.
16 Idem, *English peasantry*, 116.
17 Ibid. 85.
18 Sayer, *Women*, 121–2, citing Heath, *Peasant life*, 296–302, 376–9, 386.
19 *Morning Advertiser*, 12 Aug. 1873, 3; 14 Aug. 1873, 3.
20 James Greenwood, *In strange company, being the experiences of a roving correspondent*, London 1874, 109–22.
21 In a modern context see Clifford Geertz, *Works and lives: the anthropologist as author*, Cambridge 1988.
22 *Morning Advertiser*, 21 May 1872, 6.
23 Heath, *Romance*, 6–7.
24 Idem, *English peasantry*, 110; *Morning Advertiser*, 8 July 1873, 5.

life was a fiction. He drew on the contrast between the attractive cottage exteriors and the scenes of squalor and wretchedness that could be found within, and through this contrast conveyed aspects of the domestic life of the rural poor: according to one reviewer, almost as effectively as Dickens.[25] In so doing he awakened complacent Londoners to the condition of the agricultural labourers, who, he claimed, until his exposure of their grievances, had been '[s]cattered over the land in remote and outlying districts, away from the busy hum of busy city life': until now, they had 'lived and toiled . . . in a world apart'.[26]

The second purpose of Heath's inquiries was to bridge the social divide which, he argued, had made rural elites ignorant of the condition of the labourers in their midst. Indicting these elites on a charge of dereliction of their duty of social leadership in rural communities, he saw in special correspondent journalism a means of campaigning for the better recognition of the claims of the labouring classes. As an external investigator, he was in a position to view conditions more objectively than those who lived in the countryside themselves. His friend Canon Girdlestone pointed out that it could be an advantage not to be one of those 'who have lived all their lives in the country, and have in consequence been so long accustomed to the miserable plight of the peasantry as to take no heed of it';[27] and the *Somerset County Gazette*, one of a number of west country newspapers in which Heath's articles were reprinted, agreed:

> Human nature is in some things apt to be less affected by that which is nearest to it. The open sewer of a dirty village is seen by very different eyes by the dweller in a city in which sanitary measures are carried into perfection to those of him who has been bred and brought up in close proximity to the unconcealed abomination. . . . Familiarity breeds not only contempt, but obtusiveness; and many an evil is indebted for its long existence solely to the quiescence that consents to let things remain as they have always been.[28]

Heath himself put the point even more forcefully in 1873, in a passage that vividly demonstrates his perception of the role of the campaigning journalist:

> [The landowners and farmers in the west country] have lived hitherto, most of them, in a kind of close community, with the labourers as the pariahs or outcasts of their community. . . . All the wrong and injustice which have been dealt out to the poor labourers, and all the wretchedness and neglect from which they have suffered, have arisen from the fact that they have not hitherto been looked upon by the close communionists of the little villages and hamlets as human beings. . . . Look for a moment at yonder gate leading up to the splendid country mansion of Squire —. It is flung wide open to admit the

25 Heath, *English peasantry*, back matter.
26 Idem, *Romance*, 94.
27 Girdlestone, 'Agricultural labourer', 258.
28 Quoted in the *Morning Advertiser*, 4 June 1873, 5.

dashing equipage of the squire. The carriage is filled with handsomely-dressed ladies, and drawn by a pair of sleek, well-fed, well-groomed horses. It passes rapidly cottage after cottage, through the straggling street of the village, without one thought from those who are in it of 'the poverty, hunger and dirt' which find their home in these 'smiling' cottages, and of the poor heathens who dwell in them, – a crying reproach to a 'Christian' land which sends its charitable wealth to reform the blacks in foreign climes. But, thank Heaven! the great outside world has at length looked in upon these abodes of wretchedness and squalor, and has discovered that the poor peasant is one of God's human family; and with a power and an urgency which cannot be gainsaid it cries out through its minister, the Press, that these things shall no longer be.[29]

Heath claimed in 1880 that one duke, with substantial estates in the west country, 'admitted, to a mutual friend, that his first knowledge of the dilapidated condition of some of his own cottages, which he had not seen for many years, was derived from the perusal of the present writer's description of them'.[30] The duke then visited his cottages and quickly remedied the situation. Many landowners knew of their cottages only at second hand, receiving infrequent and inadequate reports on their condition from their agents,[31] and this ignorance emphasised the journalist's role in bridging the chasms within rural society.

Heath and Forbes both found that their method of inquiry provoked dissent. Having stated unequivocally the labourers' point of view, and having derived most of his information from labourers themselves or from those likely to be sympathetic to them, Forbes's articles sparked controversy in the *Daily News*. 'An East Essex farmer', for example, wrote to remind readers that the labourers' weekly earnings in Warwickshire were really higher than the 12s. claimed by Forbes and the union. In his area, ordinary money wages stood at 13s. a week, but with extras they amounted to up to 16s., and many families with supplementary earners received a total of between 25s. and 35s. a week.[32] In turn, the Essex farmer's assessment was contested by the Revd J. W. Leigh of Stoneleigh, a leading clerical supporter of Arch's union,[33] and by the political economist Henry Fawcett, who argued that it could not 'be ultimately advantageous either to farmers or landowners that land should be cultivated by under-paid and under-fed labourers'.[34] Others blamed the social upheavals on the decline of face-to-face social relations, one correspondent dating this to around 1840, while a Suffolk clergyman emphasised the village elites' own complicity in the demoralisation of the labourer: 'there is a bitter rankling in [the labourers'] minds that they have not been well treated by the

29 Ibid.
30 Heath, *Peasant life*, p. x.
31 Idem, *Romance*, 88.
32 *Daily News*, 30 Mar. 1872, 3. See also the letter from 'A farmer's boy', ibid. 13 Apr. 1872, 3.
33 Ibid. 2 Apr. 1872, 2.
34 Ibid. 1 Apr. 1872, 2.

employers', who had for many years ejected them from tied cottages and thrown them onto the poor law when they were old and sick.[35] Heath's articles also elicited a variety of responses. At Stoke-sub-Hamdon in Somerset in 1872, he spoke to some of the women and children employed in the local glove factory, finding that '[s]ome of them are able to earn . . . two or three shillings a week – for very excellent work a little more'.[36] Six days later, an indignant letter appeared in the *Morning Advertiser* from Richard Southcombe, the glove manufacturer, hotly disputing Heath's claims. In fact, he said, *children* earned between 2s. and 3s. a week, and 'a young person, who works a whole week' earned 7s. to 10s. and sometimes more, 'and when an agricultural labourer has a family of grown-up girls, each of them can, and does, earn very nearly as much as the father'.[37] Heath had stressed the worst aspects of life in Stoke-sub-Hamdon, and the manufacturer felt obliged to speak in his own defence.

The debate spread much further than the columns of the *Daily News* and *Morning Advertiser*, and a powerful defence of the rural paternalist tradition and the system of payment in kind was launched. Richard Jefferies, writing as a spokesman for the farming interest in *The Times*, indicted the labouring population with their ingratitude for the 'many great benefits which are bountifully supplied them' by their 'superiors' in rural communities;[38] and the editorial of the same day expressed sympathy with this conception of agricultural life: 'Every farm, and, to a great extent, every parish, is, for the Labourer, one household, and he has the gratuitous use of commmon advantages.'[39] Jefferies provoked a hostile response from a number of correspondents, including Canon Girdlestone,[40] who had spent many years trying to demonstrate the fiction of these 'common advantages'. A reply to Jefferies from 'the son of a Wiltshire labourer', detailing the poor quality of cottages, the high cost of both cottages and allotments, and the long hours worked in harvest time in return for the additional harvest payment, makes it clear that the conflict aroused extreme passions on both sides.[41] In that day's editorial, *The Times* remarked on the value of first-hand evidence such as that supplied by this correspondent, and announced that '[e]verybody and every class sees things from their own point of view – best, of course, what is nearest and most familiar'.[42] The schisms revealed in the pages of the newspaper as a result of the explosion of interest in the agricultural population suggested the necessity of further investigation; and the recognition of the differing testimony

---

35 Ibid. 3 Apr. 1872, 2.
36 *Morning Advertiser*, 27 May 1872, 5.
37 Ibid. 3 June 1872, 2.
38 *The Times*, 14 Nov. 1872, 8.
39 Ibid. 7.
40 Ibid. 27 Nov. 1872, 10.
41 Ibid. 25 Nov. 1872, 6.
42 Ibid. 9.

obtainable from different standpoints indicated serious methodological difficulties with which the social investigator of rural life would need to grapple.

When *The Times* sent its own correspondent, Frederick Clifford, to the scene of the East Anglian lockout of 1874, he demonstrated his awareness of these epistemological issues, and his tour provides many examples of the difficulties of obtaining an unbiased picture of conditions amongst the labourers. The lockout of union members had begun in April 1873, and had embittered whole communities in the eastern counties: Clifford believed that it had caused 'the rupture of intimate relations between employer and employer'[43] and that 'the day of paternal, perhaps even of friendly or cordial relations, had passed away during this six months' struggle'.[44] Clifford attended meetings of both farmers and labourers, and was willing to criticise both sides; he was well aware that information about labouring life varied according to who gave it.[45] However, on the question of agricultural earnings, he tended to trust the word of the farmer ahead of his employees, finding that labourers would often tell the investigator their nominal weekly wages, exclusive of all extras, as one way of 'enlisting sympathy'.[46] He agreed with many farmers that agricultural labourers often did not know what their earnings were, living as they did from hand to mouth and never taking the trouble to calculate their average earnings.[47] He undertook a detailed analysis of all extra payments and perquisites available to the labourer, including harvest-work, piece-work, allotment produce, cheap cottages, gardens, pigs and gleaning.[48] In addition, he remarked on the informal benefits available to the labourers, including assistance from farmers' and clergymen's wives in times of illness, the borrowing of wagons from farmers, and other services 'which can be estimated by no money value'.[49]

Clifford also contributed to the defence of the farmer that was mounted in the *Journal of the Royal Agricultural Society*. Pointing out that many farmers kept old and infirm hands on their payroll when they were unable to work,[50] Clifford argued that although the labourers were deserving of sympathy, 'our sympathy ought to be an intelligent one, based upon a correct appreciation of the difficulties of those for whom they work'.[51] Others concentrated on what they saw as the understatement by labourers of their earnings. Herbert Little of Wisbech, writing in 1878, took as his example 'John Jones', a Fenland labourer he claimed to know, who,

---

43 Frederick Clifford, *The agricultural lock-out of 1874, with notes upon farming and farm-labour in the eastern counties*, London 1875, 53.
44 Ibid. 140.
45 Ibid. 72–3.
46 Ibid. 180.
47 Ibid. 75–6.
48 Ibid. 223–35, 243–5 and passim.
49 Ibid. 238.
50 Idem, 'The labour bill in farming', *Journal of the Royal Agricultural Society of England* 2nd. ser. xi (1875), 120.
51 Ibid. 122.

if asked, would probably assert that his wages were 15s. a week, and inasmuch as that is the standard of wages for ordinary work upon the farm in question, he would be so far justified in his statement. An examination of the books of the master, however, would show that they frequently amounted, even in winter, to as much as 21s. a week, and that (independently of harvest) the average earnings of himself and his family during the summer months were about [30s.] per week.[52]

In fact, Little asserted, 'John Jones' and his family took home a total of almost £100 in a year, adding that labourers enjoyed inexpensive modern cottages and were almost always able to keep a pig.[53] Regretting the 'very aggressive and dictatorial tone' taken by the NALU, Little told his readers that in the pre-union days the 'farmers and labourers were . . . drawn together more by the mutual ties of humanity and esteem for each other, than actuated by the more selfish motives of mercenary contacts' that were associated with labour relations in industry.[54] The veteran James Caird, also writing in the RASE's *Journal*, continued to emphasise the paternalist theme, admitting that although wages before 1872 were low, they had since risen, and the condition of the labourer was better than ever before: 'Compared with the labourer in the towns, his position is one of greater comfort; he lives in a better atmosphere, he is more free from anxiety, and has a closer and more friendly relation with his employers, and with the schoolmaster and clergyman of the parish.'[55] For Caird, these individuals were the very authorities on whose evidence the assessment of rural life should be based; and the members of the Social Science Association agreed. Meeting at Plymouth in 1872, the NAPSS was prompted by the activities of the NALU to initiate a debate on the condition of the agricultural labourer, and Forbes's articles on Warwickshire were discussed.[56] Like the members of the RASE, participants in this congress tended to support the claims of the farming interest. Although the more sympathetic Baldwyn Leighton pointed to the possibility of industrial partnership or co-operation as a solution to the labour difficulty,[57] the farming spokesman, Clare Sewell Read, defended the wages paid to his own labourers, which, although standing at only 12s. a week, had been as low as 9s. twenty years earlier.[58] Mr E. Thorne of Plymouth, emphasising the liberality of systems of payment in kind, reckoned that the English agri-

---

52 Herbert J. Little, 'The agricultural labourer', *Journal of the Royal Agricultural Society of England* 2nd ser. xiv (1878), 775.
53 Ibid. 785–6.
54 Ibid. 771–2.
55 James Caird, 'General view of British agriculture', *Journal of the Royal Agricultural Society of England* 2nd ser. xiv (1878), 302.
56 NAPSS *Transactions* (1872), 415–16.
57 Ibid. 393–401.
58 Ibid. 411–12.

cultural labourers and their wives were 'the most extravagant of the working class in any part of the world', and tended to waste their money on drink.[59] The contributors to this discussion were farmers, landowners or clergymen: as in earlier decades, for the membership of the NAPSS, these men remained the most reliable and authoritative sources of social knowledge in the rural community.

This axis of informants was challenged by the special correspondents of the 1870s, not only by emphasising the importance of the direct consultation of the labouring classes that formed the subject of most of their inquiries, but also through the use of a different set of informants, in particular Nonconformist ministers. Nonconformity upset the traditional paternalist balance of rural communities, and its association with Liberalism appealed to the journalists who aimed to contest the Tory conception of the countryside. A local minister was likely to be socially closer to the labouring classes than was the Church of England parson: many were village artisans and tradesmen, such as Heath's informant William Conduit of Woodford in Wiltshire, a blacksmith who had helped the Woodford labourers to establish a pig insurance society.[60] The association of Methodism, and Primitive Methodism in particular, with the 'Revolt of the Field' politicised the role of the minister in many areas, both as a member of the rural community in which he preached and as an informant in social inquiries. Many agricultural trade union leaders, at both a national and a local level, were active Methodists, and Nigel Scotland has argued persuasively that the culture and structure of Methodism informed, and indeed pervaded, the culture and structure of the unions. He has related the growth of Methodism to the emergence of 'a more literate and articulate agricultural labourer', more able and willing to challenge established rural social structures, and by so doing to challenge the Hodge stereotype.[61] Contemporaries argued that involvement with Nonconformity helped to broaden the horizons of the labourer and in turn to improve his economic and social position. Thus Richard Heath (no relation of Francis), a special correspondent who wrote for various journals in the early 1870s, and a Primitive Methodist preacher himself, remarked on the happiness of labourers he met in Northumberland, which was ascribed to their relatively high level of education and the opportunities they enjoyed for advancement within the hierarchy of the Presbyterian Church. The qualities of these 'noble people' contrasted, for example, with the 'depression and hopelessness' of rural Devonians and the 'superstition, ignorance, immorality, and poverty which prevails in the Weald of Sussex'.[62] For Heath and other NALU sympathisers, parson, landowner and farmer had long conspired to keep the agricultural

[59] Ibid. 415.
[60] Heath, *Peasant life*, pt iv, ch. xi, esp. p. 324.
[61] Nigel Scotland, *Methodism and the revolt of the field: a study of the Methodist contribution to agricultural trade unionism in East Anglia, 1872–1896*, Gloucester 1981.
[62] Heath, *English peasant*, 217, 82, 191–2. The parts quoted were written in the period 1870–4.

labourer in a state of subjection and ignorance, and through Nonconformity the labourer could be drawn into a more active role in the local community. For the social investigator, the minister was, arguably, likely to be able to pass more informed comment on the labourers among whom he lived. The special correspondents, then, did not just move in this period towards a respondent method of inquiry, but also consulted a different range of second-hand informants.

The activities of the special correspondent were met with scepticism from many quarters, especially the Conservative press. Reviewing Francis Heath's *The English peasantry* in the same year, the *Quarterly Review* drew a distinction between the more balanced inquiries in the book and the information collected at first hand by Heath himself: 'although there is something in [the book] of the tendency . . . which, if we might coin a phrase, we should call "Our-own-correspondentism," – there is much valuable information derived from trustworthy sources'.[63] The special correspondent may have carried out fieldwork at first hand, but he was only in the field for a short period, and lacked the experience to comment authoritatively on rural life. Heath seems to have accepted some of this criticism: in his third inquiry into the condition of the south-western labourers in 1880, his own inquiries were supplemented by information from correspondents, for which he had advertised in various newspapers and journals.[64] More notably, Forbes's articles in the Liberal *Daily News* were held up to ridicule by the leader of the opposition, Benjamin Disraeli, in his speech at the Free Trade Hall in Manchester in 1872: the famous 'exhausted volcanoes' speech, in which he set out his version of Conservative principles. Speaking a few days after Forbes reported on his stay with the poor labouring family in Warwickshire, Disraeli claimed that the agricultural labourer had shared in the growth of national prosperity in the form of increased money wages, improved machinery making work easier, and the growth of allotment provision. He directly denounced 'gentlemen of the press going to dine with an agricultural family when he has seven children and only one red-herring for dinner . . . for there seems something so extremely greedy and rapacious in the experiment that it ought to be held up to public condemnation'.[65] Responding to this speech – which was inaccurate, as there were five children in the household, not seven – Forbes immediately travelled to Hughenden, indicting Disraeli with the poor conditions among the labourers there; and Disraeli in turn was defended by his local vicar in a letter to the *Daily News*.[66] This episode illustrates the importance attached to the condition and outlook of the unenfranchised agricultural labourer to the leading political figures of the early 1870s; it also highlights

[63] *Quarterly Review* cxxxvii (1874), 500.
[64] Heath, *Peasant life*, 220.
[65] *Daily News*, 4 Apr. 1872, 3. This section of the speech was not included in T. E. Kebbel (ed.), *Selected speeches of the late right honourable the earl of Beaconsfield*, London 1882, ii. 490–522.
[66] *Daily News*, 4 Apr. 1872, 5; 16 Apr. 1872, 3.

the overtly conflictual character of social inquiry in a politicised rural environment.

Although the special correspondents of the 1870s insisted on the value of the personal contact they had enjoyed with the labouring population, the extent of their penetration into labouring life can clearly be questioned. Heath and Forbes, writing for metropolitan journals, were not averse to the employment of traditional stereotypes in their descriptions of the rural population. Forbes described how, at the first labourers' meeting he attended, he watched as 'heavy-footed, slow-paced men, converged wonderingly' at the Wellesbourne chestnut tree, to have their 'dull intellects' stirred by the oratory of Joseph Arch,[67] while Heath admitted that farm labourers were 'ignorant enough concerning everything outside their own particular sphere'.[68] The success of the mode of inquiry adopted by the special correspondent depended on the co-operation that could be obtained from those he wished to question, and on his personal ability to communicate with the labouring classes at first hand. Heath repeatedly emphasised the helpfulness of his labouring informants,[69] but his explanation that he had gone among them '[p]encil and notebook in hand'[70] suggests a somewhat intimidating character of whom the subjects of inquiry might be rather wary. He paid tribute to the 'simple and earnest kindness' he met with in Devon, and acknowledged the 'respectful salutation' he had invariably received from the rural poor on country roads;[71] but the salutation was deferential, and this deference is reflected in some of the descriptions of his conversations with the south-western rural poor. Indeed, he recorded one housewife as having curtseyed to him before inviting him into her cottage.[72] At Stoke-sub-Hamdon, he found it 'impossible . . . to see such scenes of wretchedness without feeling compelled to tender some relief before quitting the miserable hovels'.[73] He was the patron, they the eager recipients of charity: he was hardly meeting the 'peasantry' on an equal footing.

The political situation in which the special correspondent of the early 1870s found himself made the task of investigation and reporting even more difficult. Some found that an unsympathetic approach could provoke fierce contestation. The NALU had prompted the outburst of investigative energy in the 1870s; it had also given the labourers' spokesmen an outlet for their own views. As one farmer told the readers of Fraser's Magazine, '[t]he newspapers have got hold of the working man . . . [and] the working man has got hold of a newspaper':[74] the Labourers' Union Chronicle. Although not an offi-

67 Ibid. 27 Mar. 1872, 6.
68 Heath, English peasantry, 116.
69 Ibid. 78–9, 107–11.
70 Idem, British rural life and labour, London 1911, 181.
71 Idem, English peasantry, 126.
72 Ibid. 107.
73 Idem, Romance, 43.
74 'A Wykehamist', Agricultural labourer, 9.

cial NALU mouthpiece, the *Chronicle* gave the labourers a chance to hit back at some of their detractors. Thus, when the *Daily Telegraph*'s special correspondent travelled around the south of England in the wake of the strike, mocking the crude political opinions that he heard in the tap-rooms of public houses, and describing with some relish the political ignorance of a class whose representatives were demanding the franchise, the *Chronicle* responded angrily, characterising him as

> 'our own commissioner,' which is another word for 'a reporter' who runs about in search of impressions, which he throws into black and white as quickly as they are made, and sometimes, apparently, before, and which are of the same intrinsic value as thistledown, which is blown hither and thither, bearing everywhere thistle crops of superficial sentiment and opinion, instead of solid corn and wine of earnest thought and heart-feeling. We need hardly say that our 'commissioner' looks down from a pretty considerable elevation upon 'John Whopstraw,' as he pleases to call the agricultural labourer, in weariness of repeating the more hackneyed name of 'Hodge.'[75]

The writer protested that the correspondent was judging the labourers 'by superficial standards, and upon the briefest possible acquaintance': a good example of the possible reactions of a rural population to an apparently intrusive investigator whose representations of them did not accord with their own priorities. Even where a group of labourers had no direct access to the *Chronicle*, they could express themselves in other ways. Archibald Forbes, for example, stumbled across a rhyme recited at a union meeting in Warwickshire, which delivered a rebuke to those supporters of the Union who, it was felt, did not sufficiently acknowledge the labourers' independence of mind:

> We'll tell the Reverend Vicar Leigh
> And Canon Girdlestone
> And Bromley Davenport MP
> We'll call our minds our own.[76]

The agricultural crises of the 1870s, then, prompted a resurgence in rural special correspondent journalism, and initiated a nationwide debate on agricultural conditions from which the political concerns of the period could not easily be disentangled. However, as the initial wave of excitement over agricultural trade unionism died down, and as the 1870s gave way to the 1880s, new concerns about rural labouring life came to the fore. F. E. Green characterised the 1880s as 'The Aftermath of Thistles', the relative calm following the storms of the 1870s;[77] and this relative calm stimulated a more reflective and less conflictual brand of social investigation and commentary. By 1880 it

[75] Quoted in Clayden, *Revolt of the field*, 95.
[76] *Daily News*, 29 Mar. 1872, 3.
[77] F. E. Green, *A history of the English agricultural labourer, 1870–1920*, London 1920, pt iv.

was felt that plenty was known, largely thanks to the efforts of the investigators of the 1870s, about the agricultural labourer and rural social relations. Commenting on the publication of Richard Jefferies's two-volume study of rural life, *Hodge and his masters*, in 1880, one reviewer complained that '[t]he theme is old, the matter is well worn, the subject common to us all, and for a few facts more or less, if they be not romantically conveyed, most of us care nothing'.[78] In the same year – just eight years after Arch's union had awoken the urban world to the plight of the rural worker – Francis Heath wondered whether any reader would be interested in the English agricultural labourer, now that 'the burning lights . . . have been turned away from him and directed to other objects, and he has once more become, so to speak, lost from sight amongst the shadows in which he was before immersed'.[79] Agricultural trade unions went into numerical decline, the membership of the NALU falling from 55,000 in 1877 to 15,000 in 1881;[80] and many of the wage gains secured in the early 1870s were lost as the agricultural depression deepened.[81] Public attention was beginning to focus once more on the urban, and especially the metropolitan, poor. If Manchester had been the 'shock city' of the 1830s and 1840s, London was at the centre of concern about working-class life in the 1880s. In the wake of Andrew Mearns's pamphlet on London's housing, *The bitter cry of outcast London* (1883), an attendant rush of similar publications described the filth and squalor of the capital; and this outpouring of sensationalism, together with outbreaks of urban social discontent such as the Trafalgar Square riots in 1886, established the climate within which Charles Booth initiated his survey of *Life and labour of the people in London*, which itself brought new ideas and techniques to the practice of social investigation.

Other social problems had surpassed rural labour in the public mind; but in addition, a different series of concerns about rural life had replaced the immediate issue of the remuneration of labour which had launched the NALU and provoked the intense debates of the 1870s. The most prominent issues in the rural politics of the 1880s were the franchise, which was conceded to agricultural labourers by the Reform Act of 1884 and first exercised in the general election of 1885; allotments and smallholdings, which gained particular significance with the publication of Joseph Chamberlain's 'unauthorised programme' prior to that election as a response to the altered franchise, and which spawned the slogan 'three acres and a cow'; and county and parish

[78] *Atheneaum*, 10 Apr. 1880, 463.
[79] Heath, *Peasant life*, 219–20.
[80] Ernest Selley, *Village trade unions in two centuries*, London 1919, 77; Groves, *Sharpen the sickle!*, 83; Dunbabin, *Rural discontent*, 80–1.
[81] For recent debates on the effects of agricultural trade unionism on wages see George R. Boyer and Timothy J. Hatton, 'Did Joseph Arch raise agricultural wages?', *Economic History Review* 2nd ser. xlvii (1994), 310–34; J. P. D. Dunbabin, 'Can we tell whether Arch raised wages?', and George R. Boyer and Timothy J. Hatton, 'Did Joseph Arch raise agricultural wages? A reply', ibid. 2nd ser. xlix (1996), 362–9, 370–6.

councils, which were established in 1888 and 1894 respectively. None of these were wholly new concerns: the agitation of the 1870s had raised a number of issues which came to the centre of public discussion of the problems of rural England in the following decade, and to emphasise this the *Labourers' Union Chronicle* was cumbersomely subtitled 'An Independent Advocate of the British Toilers' Rights to Free Land, Freedom from Priestcraft, and from the Tyranny of Capital', demanding, in addition to higher wages, the franchise and the nationalisation of land.[82] Thus the separation between the 1870s and 1880s should not be overstated; the 1880s should rather be seen as a decade in which the labouring classes attempted to consolidate the material gains of the years of union activity with a series of institutional and political advances. In terms of investigative activity, the progressive encroachment of the rural labour force onto mainstream political territory necessitated a different kind of inquiry: the exploratory mode of investigation as employed by the special correspondent was less appropriate to a population about whom much more was known than had been the case fifteen years earlier, and it was also less likely to yield the kinds of political and cultural information that were sought by the investigators of the 1880s. This period saw a developing impetus towards the examination of the political views of the agricultural labourer, a task more difficult than assessing his material condition. As one investigator explained in 1892, '[t]o get at the real political thoughts and aspiration of the agricultural labourer is very difficult ... he is naturally secretive and takes full advantage of the Ballot Act'.[83] Only through sympathetic communication on a personal level with the rural poor could the degree of cultural understanding be obtained which would allow the less tangible aspects of the life of the agricultural labourer to be investigated.

In the rural context the groundswell of social concern in the 1880s cannot be disentangled from aspects of the ruralist ideology that emerged from what Alun Howkins has called the 'discovery of rural England'.[84] Fears of urban deterioration, intensified by revelations of physical and moral degeneration in the London of the 1880s, culminating in *The bitter cry* and *Life and labour*, and overlaid by discourses which interpreted these developments as indicative of the onset of imperial decay, encouraged contemporaries to look to the rural world for the salvation of the nation, the empire and the English race.[85] Rural popular culture was newly privileged as a wholesome alternative to the

---

82 Selley, *Village trade unions*, 51–2. See also Nigel Scotland, 'The National Agricultural Labourers' Union and the demand for a stake in the soil', in Eugenio F. Biagini (ed.), *Citizenship and community: liberals, radicals and collective identities in the British Isles, 1865–1931*, Cambridge 1996, 151–67.
83 P. Anderson Graham, *The rural exodus: the problem of the village and the town*, London 1892, 84.
84 Howkins, 'Discovery'.
85 Gareth Stedman Jones, *Outcast London: a study in the relationship between classes in Victorian society* (1st edn 1971), Harmondsworth 1984, esp. chs vi, xvi.

debased mass culture of the towns, and a revival of pastoral ideology was manifested in the popularity of books and articles on a rural theme. The upsurge of interest in British folklore, which coincided with the revelations of rural poverty in the 1870s and was reflected in the establishment of the Folk-lore Society in 1878, represented one manifestation of the rediscovery of rural culture; and the realisation, intensified by the activities of the NALU, that many of the old certainties about rural life could no longer necessarily be counted upon, gave a new urgency to the project of documenting folkloric 'survivals'.[86] As well as further challenging the Hodge stereotype and, argu-ably, marking the beginning of a process of 'reconstructing' the labourer as the nobler (though still heavily caricatured) 'Lob',[87] these developments encouraged folklore collectors in the practical task of gathering information on the inner beliefs, superstitions and lore of the rural population that would not readily be shared with outsiders. As such, folklore collectors and social investigators shared the need to emphasise their personal credentials as authorities on the rural population, in order to convince their readers of the depth of their understanding, and in this context the resident of a district appeared to have a clear advantage over the visitor. Hence the investigators discussed in the remainder of this chapter could generally claim, like Miss Mitford forty years earlier, 'the merit of . . . that local and personal familiarity, which only a long residence in one neighbourhood could have enabled her to attain'.[88] This local knowledge contrasted with the brief visits of the special correspondent journalist: Thomas Kebbel, for example, claimed that his work was 'founded on actual experience; and on that kind of knowledge which comes from long habits, association, and sympathy, and is not hastily acquired to meet any particular demand'.[89] In conveying information of both sociolog-ical value and folkloric interest, the country parson was a particularly impor-tant figure, but all kinds of literate residents of rural England also found their way into print on the subject of their poorer neighbours.

Perhaps the most notable of all the clerical commentators on rural life in the 1880s was Augustus Jessopp, who became well known to readers of the *Nineteenth Century*. Jessopp (1823–1914), rector of Scarning in Norfolk, former headmaster of the King Edward VI School in Norwich, admirer of Gladstone,[90] antiquarian and social historian, was in his sixties when he wrote his articles, which were subsequently published in book form as *Arcady: for better for worse*, which John Fraser has called 'by far the most sociologically valuable work on the subject [of rural labouring life] before 1901'.[91] The reviewer in the *Spectator* – from a distinctly urban perspective – found it a 'delightful' volume, and 'doubt[ed] if such an account of English village life,

---

86 See Freeman, 'Folklore collection'.
87 Howkins, 'From Hodge to Lob'.
88 Mitford, *Our village*, i, p. v.
89 Kebbel, *English country life*, p. vii.
90 See Jessopp to Gladstone, 28 Oct. 1884, in BL, MS Add. 44487, fos 343–4.
91 Fraser, 'George Sturt', 114.

its bad and good sides, its specialities, its humours, and the odd, gnarled characters it produces, ever has been published'.[92] Perhaps the only investigator to surpass Jessopp's prominence was Richard Jefferies, the popular novelist, nature writer and social commentator, whose *Hodge and his masters* has been called 'an invaluable work for the social historian'.[93] This book consists of a series of more or less fictionalised sketches, describing various aspects of country life, and appeared originally in the *Standard* in 1880. Henry Williamson, of *Tarka the otter* fame, thought the book contained 'the reality of almost the entire world of mid-Victorian country life in England'.[94] Although few copies of the book were sold, it was serialised in the *Standard*, with a daily readership of some 180,000.[95] Jefferies published several other books, and countless articles in such journals as *Fraser's*, *Longman's* and the *New Quarterly*; and Karen Sayer argues that Jefferies, '[u]sing his own experiences as a farmer's son . . . wrote in London for a predominantly urban readership and effectively developed *the* dominant descriptive mode of writing on the countryside'.[96] As Philip Drew has suggested, although often viewed mainly as a quirky literary figure – 'the man who wrote one good book for boys [*Bevis: the story of a boy*] and a lot of bad books about birds' – Jefferies also deserves attention as 'an economist and a realist', who used the medium of the artist to convey information of sociological interest.[97] Although he spent much of his life in London, he based his descriptions of rural life on his residence in rural Wiltshire, and it was from this long residence in one place that his intensive knowledge of the life of the English countryside was obtained.

The travelling reporter, however sympathetic with the labouring people he was investigating, had only a limited opportunity to observe them. Francis Heath, for example, relied on correspondents for his information on labourers' clothing, particularly Sunday clothes;[98] and, to take an example from an annual cycle, he never recorded seeing a hiring fair, an event of particular significance both in the lives of the participants themselves and to investigators such as Thomas Kebbel, who regarded it as a particularly immoral feature of rural life, and devoted much thought to proposals for its removal.[99] The fact of all Heath's tours of inquiry being made in the summer could give him a somewhat misleading impression of the condition and lifestyle of the south-western labourers. Moreover, the acquaintance gained by the roving

---

92 *Spectator*, 7 May 1887, 624.
93 Drew, 'Richard Jefferies', 185.
94 Henry Williamson, 'Introduction', to Richard Jefferies, *A classic of English farming: Hodge and his masters* (1st edn 1880), London 1946, 7. Subsequent references to *Hodge and his masters* will be to the first edition (see p. 11 n. 49 above).
95 Samuel J. Looker and Crichton Porteus, *Richard Jefferies, man of the fields: a biography and letters*, London 1965, 136.
96 Sayer, *Women*, 149. Original emphasis.
97 Drew, 'Richard Jefferies', 181, 186.
98 Heath, *Peasant life*, pt iv, ch. viii, esp. pp. 297–302.
99 Kebbel, *Agricultural labourer*, 118–28, 227–8.

reporter was not only brief but, arguably, superficial, enabling him to bring to light the material difficulties behind the labourers' grievances at a time of social discontent, but not to investigate in depth the social and cultural lives of the rural poor. Heath and his fellow special correspondents were rarely interested in such subjects as superstition and folklore; and in 1880 Heath had to rely on a correspondent – the curate of Heywood in Wiltshire – for his information in this area.[100] Augustus Jessopp laboured under no such disadvantage: he was in his parish all year round, except for brief visits to London to lecture at Toynbee Hall and elsewhere, and was well acquainted with the habits of the labourers. He felt that his long association with the village, six years by the time he wrote his 'Arcady' articles, enabled him to 'give a faithful picture of the habits and ways of thinking, the superstitions, prejudices and grounds for discontent, the grievances and the trials, of the country folk among whom [his] lot was cast'.[101] In particular, on the subject of rural religion, lore and superstition, he noted that 'the people are a great deal too wary to open out to "our own correspondent" if he should come down on a voyage of discovery. Idle curiosity they are quite shrewd enough to detect and to deal with in their own way'.[102] He was able to give an amusing example: 'Old Huggins', a Scarning rustic, who was talkative enough with Jessopp himself, pretended to be deaf when the vicar took a journalist into his cottage.[103] Jessopp explained that the outsider could easily fall foul of the villagers' suspicions of officialdom, whereas the kind of intercourse he enjoyed with his parishioners encouraged the sharing of confidences. Thus some years later he reminded his readers that 'a long chat in the lowly cottages of the aged poor' could result in the hearing of 'most instructive reminiscences of the[ir] daily life and social habits, and ways of thinking and religious sentiment';[104] and it was on this kind of casual intercourse that he based his assessments of the religious and secular life of Scarning. Similarly, another clerical author, J. C. Atkinson of Danby in Cleveland, described how a long and patient association with his moorland parishioners was necessary before they would share any of their folkloric secrets with him: the stranger 'was likely to experience something of the "Heave 'arf a brick at 'im" treatment recorded by George Stephenson as the customary welcome extended by north-country natives to unlucky explorers of the country wilds'.[105]

Jefferies also insisted on the value of the resident's perspective, especially when seeking superstition and folklore, which were 'confined . . . to the inner life of the people, and likely to be overlooked by an outsider'.[106] In *Red deer*,

100 Heath, *Peasant life*, pt iii, ch xii.
101 Augustus Jessopp, *The trials of a country parson*, London 1890, p. v.
102 Idem, *Arcady*, 83.
103 Ibid.
104 Idem, *England's peasantry, and other essays*, London 1914, 135.
105 J. C. Atkinson, *Forty years in a moorland parish: reminiscences and researches in Danby in Cleveland* (1st edn 1891), London 1892, 27–8.
106 Richard Jefferies, *Wild life in a southern county* (1st edn 1879), London 1889, 90.

one of his books in which human life does not feature very much, he expressed an even more pessimistic conclusion:

> Not one word of superstition, or ancient tradition, or curious folk-lore, can a stranger extract. The past seems dead, and they are not to be distinguished from the people of other districts close to the populous centres of industry. But the fact is that this silence is not change: it is a reticence purposely adhered to. By mutual consent they steadfastly refrain from speaking in their own tongue and of their own views to strangers not of the countryside. They speak to strangers in the voice of the nineteenth century, the voice of newspaper, book, and current ideas. They reserve for themselves their own ancient tongue and ancient ideas, their traditions, and belief in the occult.[107]

Not only would the non-resident fail to penetrate the 'inner life of the people', but even the resident could only gain access to it after an extended period of sympathetic and friendly intercourse.[108] Jefferies's counsel to the external investigator did not apply only to folklore collectors: having developed his methods of investigation in the context of social and political conflict in the countryside, he was acutely aware of the resentment and bitterness among the labouring population, which had been intensified in many areas by the development of agricultural trade unionism against which he had railed in 1872. Warning his contemporaries about the depth of the class divide in rural England, he described a 'sullen', 'scornful' and 'desperate' rural poor, which observed middle-class life with a 'savage animosity' that only careful investigation could uncover and understand.[109] Jefferies was convinced that the formal consultation of the labourer would yield little or no useful information for the investigator. To overcome this, he adopted the strategy of the 'Amateur Casual', travelling *incognito* to gather information from west country inns. One of his admirers explained,

> As [Jefferies] had perfect command of the broad Wiltshire dialect, and a close acquaintance with the details of country life, it was easy for him, with a change of dress, to be taken for some kind of superior labourer himself, and so hear and gather the intimate opinions of these men. What seems to have impressed his mind was the gusto with which they would dwell on the coming day when it would fall to their lot to plough up this and the other gentleman's 'bloody park'. . . . The incident shows how futile it is to hope to gain any just idea of the rustic's thoughts by means of formal interrogation. Often the awkward clown who scratches his head, and, before a questioner, seems the picture of stupidity, is glib enough among his own cronies.[110]

107 Idem, *Red deer* (1st edn 1884), London 1900, 242–3.
108 Idem, *Round about a great estate* (1st edn 1880), London 1894, 80–1.
109 Idem, *The life of the fields* (1st edn 1884), London 1899, 19–20.
110 Graham, *Rural exodus*, 84–5.

Hodge and his masters, which was based on these experiences, is full of little incidents which illustrate a seething resentment among the labouring populations of the lifestyles of the better-off.[111] The emphasis on conflict gives Jefferies's work a certain kinship with that of Heath and Forbes in the 1870s, in that all these investigators shaped their inquiries on the understanding that conflict would condition what was revealed to them, and, hence, all emphasised the importance of a sympathetic approach to the labourer which transcended the generalised and largely external information obtainable from other sources.

It was important for these resident investigators to enhance the credibility of their accounts by emphasising the quality of their interaction with the population they described. How far they really enjoyed access to the 'inner life' of their neighbours is another question. As Jefferies's letters to *The Times* in 1872 had shown, his sympathy was not always with the labourers' grievances, and his first (and admiring) biographer admitted that Jefferies 'made his way to the fields through the farmers first and the labourers next'.[112] Others compared his approach to the labourer with his work as a naturalist: he 'minutely noted the habits, dress, food, peculiarities of speech, and action of the labourers', but '[h]is imagination never carried him below the exterior of human life'.[113] These are largely literary assessments, but they are also applicable to Jefferies as a social investigator. In its editorial on Jefferies's letters in 1872, *The Times* recognised the limitations of his perspective on the agricultural labourer, remarking that Jefferies 'describes truly and well what he sees and knows, but then he speaks at large and as if from a survey'.[114] This terminology reflects the 'view from above' from which Jefferies often approached the rural poor; he was from a farming background, and took a farmer's point of view. As for Jessopp, it is not hard to imagine a villager adjusting the contents of a story for the parson's consumption, or lying in order to improve his chances of receiving charitable assistance. Although he was undoubtedly among the group of parsons identified by Brian Heeney as having 'forged links with their people' which included Edward Girdlestone and other campaigning clergymen – standing in contrast to the austerity and unworldliness of the Trollopian 'gentleman-cleric'[115] – Jessopp was forced to admit that while he may have enjoyed 'daily intercourse' with his parishioners 'on the footing of a mere friendly neighbour',[116] a certain 'isolation' in his position was inevitable, even a function of his office.[117] On at least one

111 Jefferies, *Hodge and his masters*, i. 154, 334; ii. 254–5. See also his *The open air* (1st edn 1885), London 1893, 27, and *Life of the fields*, 18.
112 Walter Besant, *The eulogy of Richard Jefferies*, London 1888, 109.
113 Graham, *Rural exodus*, 36–7.
114 *The Times*, 25 Nov. 1872, 9.
115 Heeney, 'On being a mid-Victorian clergyman', 213. See p. 33 above.
116 Jessopp, *Trials*, p. x.
117 Ibid. 38, 52.

occasion Jessopp was not so much isolated as reviled, attracting the hostility of some of his parishioners: when the local labourers revolted against a proposal by the charity commissioners to impose a fee in the Scarning free school, and established their own free school in the Primitive Methodist chapel, one aggrieved group of labourers threw stones through the rectory windows.[118] This incident gives a somewhat different impression from the one of sympathetic harmony which Jessopp presented in his articles, and has wider ramifications for the position of the country parson in the more highly politicised and secularised countryside of the late nineteenth century. As Henrietta Batson, a Berkshire clergyman's wife, admitted in the *Nineteenth Century* in 1892, the labourer 'hates his employer, he hates his squire, but, above all, he hates his parson'.[119] The social and political structure of rural communities set evident limits to the extent of penetration into the world of the agricultural labourers that even the resident investigator could claim.

Both Jefferies and Jessopp described the labourer in terms that owed much to the old Hodge stereotype. Jessopp avoided the word Hodge, but his portrayals of the Scarning labourers incorporated many of the component attributes of the stereotype; and Jefferies was more responsible than any other individual author in the 1880s for the diffusion of a conception of a new kind of Hodge, partially reconstructed for the different circumstances of the 1880s.[120] The beginnings of concern about rural depopulation, which was to become a widespread panic in the 1890s, drew the attention of investigators to the limited social and recreational opportunities in rural England: the overwhelming consensus was that rural life was dull, and had a dulling effect on the population. Thus the material poverty revealed by investigators of the early 1870s was replaced as the focus of concern by a spiritual and cultural poverty, as Jessopp explained:

> The truth is that you have increased the labourer's daily wages, but that is absolutely all that you have done for him. He asks for a decent home, for a chance of *bettering* himself, for the *possibility* of a future which may raise him to the rank of a small proprietor; for *some* prospect of trying his luck with a cow or a horse and cart; for *some* innocent recreation and amusement when his day's work is done; for *some* tiny playground for his children in the summer evenings; for *some* object of ambition. . . . The very beer is so bad that it has ceased to tempt him to debauch.[121]

Again, these themes were not wholly new to the rural social commentary of the 1880s – Francis Heath, for example, had touched on the scant 'amusements' of the south-western labourers[122] – but they marked a reappraisal of the social and political position of the labourer and a reinforcement of the

[118] L. Marion Springall, *Labouring life in Norfolk villages, 1834–1914*, London 1936, 114.
[119] Henrietta M. Batson, 'Hodge at home', *Nineteenth Century* xxxi (1892), 178.
[120] This reconstruction is explored in Freeman, 'Agricultural labourer', 177–82.
[121] Jessopp, *Arcady*, 27. Original emphases.
[122] Heath, *Peasant life*, pt iv, ch. xiii.

importance of a series of reforms – the franchise, the provision of allotments and smallholdings and the democratisation of village life – that were perceived as essential to halt a longer-term decline in the quality of rural life. These proposals for reform rested on the assumption of the emptiness of rural life and the demoralisation of the labourer. There are traces of relish in some of the descriptions of labourers that appear in books like Jessopp's *Arcady*. In one passage he described the young men of Scarning, who, at an age when they may have enjoyed a small margin of disposable income to spend on wholesome recreational activities, lounged around displaying (as far as Jessopp could see) no interest or ambition:

> In Arcady one never hears people laugh. . . . You may see half-a-dozen hulking young men literally sprawling in the ditch smoking their pipes, and sunning themselves on their stomachs in the summer evenings, doing the only thing they have any power of doing – nothing. Do you wonder if these young fellows get tired of it, and vaguely find it dull?[123]

Jessopp's labourers retained some of the animalistic qualities of earlier descriptions: their eating habits, for example, were compared to 'chewing the cud', a phrase also used by Jefferies.[124] Language like this recurs in many other descriptions of the agricultural labourer that appeared during this period. An observer from Hertfordshire thought the labourer 'prefer[red] slouching to any other condition';[125] the west country labourers 'appeared to have lost even the desire to better themselves';[126] a Leicestershire commentator summed up much of the problem when he pointed to the labourers' '[i]ncessant work . . . the same dully [sic], dreary mode of life, without a chance of bettering their condition';[127] in Wiltshire the 'slow, plodding' labourer lacked 'push and enterprise' and even a 'mental object';[128] and as for the Scarning labourers, '[l]ogic can they no more understand than they can understand the Differential Calculus'.[129]

These descriptions are very similar to those that might have been found in the mid-nineteenth century, but it is important to note that in the 1880s the Hodge stereotype was invested with new features. The new Hodge was partly an urban creation, and was explained in terms of the pernicious encroachment of urban cultural patterns into rural communities. Although the identification in the 1880s of physical and moral degeneration in metropolitan centres of casual employment encouraged urban elites to look to the land for

123 Jessopp, *Arcady*, 112–13. Original emphases. See also pp. xviii, 27, 74–5.
124 Ibid. 74; Richard Jefferies, *The toilers of the field* (1st edn 1892), London 1907, 180.
125 Scrivener C. Scrivener [sic], *Our fields and cities, or misdirected industry*, London 1891, 80.
126 Heath, *English peasantry*, 45.
127 Quoted in Liz Bellamy and Tom Williamson (eds), *Life in the Victorian village: the* Daily News *survey of 1891*, London 1999, i. 106.
128 Richard Jefferies, 'After the county franchise', *Longman's Magazine* iii (1884), 372.
129 Jessopp, *Arcady*, 124.

solutions to the problems of urban England, rural England was itself being fatally corrupted by urbanism. It had affected rural speech. The Scarning labourers spoke with the 'townsman's gabble': 'it is as if their sentences are made by machinery'.[130] Jefferies noted that many of the songs sung in rural communities were the products of music halls, and could as easily be heard sung by London street-arabs.[131] Jefferies, a naturalist himself, was especially concerned at the lack of interest shown by the bulk of the rural population in the wildlife of the countryside, and incorporated this into his indictment of Hodge (in this case using the name Roger, from which Hodge was derived):

> Roger did not interest himself in these things, in the wasps that left the gate as he approached . . . in the bright poppies brushing against his drab unpolished boots, in the hue of the wheat or the white convulvulus; they were nothing to him. . . . His life was work without skill or thought, the work of the horse, of the crane that lifts stones and timber. His food was rough, his drink rougher, his lodging dry planks. . . . Of thought he thought nothing; of hope his idea was a shilling more wages; of any future for himself of comfort such as even a good cottage can give – of any future whatever – he had no more conception than the horse in the shafts of the wagon . . . why should he note the colour of the butterfly, the bright light of the sun, the hue of the wheat? This loveliness gave him no cheese for breakfast; of beauty in itself, he had no idea.[132]

The apparent demise of the traditional lore of the countryside, its inhabitants' knowledge and understanding of the natural world surrounding them, was in part the product of the substitution by the younger generation of urban cultural forms for the more 'real' and timeless culture of the 'folk'. Some resident investigators admitted complicity in this demise: Jessopp, for example, thought it a mistake on the part of the rural clergy to have acquiesced in the abandonement of fairs, wakes, maypoles and other pagan indulgences.[133] (Even the barbaric practice of cock-fighting, he argued, had at least given the agricultural labourer something in which to take an interest.) Others tried to recreate the former sense of community that they believed had existed in earlier times: J. C. Atkinson, for example, reintroduced the old 'harvest home' to Danby, partly in an attempt to bring the church closer to the community, but also as a means of revitalising the communal and social life of the parish.[134] Jefferies contrasted the English labourer with the continental peasantry, who enjoyed fete days and retained a sense of their own history:[135]

130 Ibid. 36, 50.
131 Jefferies, *Hodge and his masters*, ii. 204–5.
132 Idem, *Open air*, 100–1.
133 Jessopp, *Arcady*, 230–2.
134 William Sheils, 'Church, community and culture in rural England, 1850–1900: J. C. Atkinson and the parish of Danby in Cleveland', in Simon Ditchfield (ed.), *Christianity and community in the west: essays for John Bossy*, Aldershot 2001, 272–3; Atkinson, *Forty years*, 239–45.
135 Jefferies, *Toilers*, 97.

as for the English rural population, they 'have no myths; no heroes. They look back on no Heroic Age, no Achilles, no Agamemnon, and no Homer. The past is vacant. They have not even a "Wacht am Rhein" or "Marseillaise" to chant in chorus with quickened step and flashing eye'.[136] In this context the collection of folkloric 'survivals', often the pastime of eccentric amateur collectors such as Atkinson of Danby, took on a greater social and political importance, and the activities of the 'county collectors' had a close methodological affinity with the social investigators of the period.[137] The collection of survivals was essential as a matter of historical record, but also reflected the hope for a more distant future when the rural population, or the much-discussed 'folk', might be encouraged to reclaim its cultural heritage.[138]

The occupation of land was viewed by many observers as an essential prerequisite for the reinvestiture of the English labourer with his old qualities of independence. The roots of the demise of rural popular culture were located historically in the enclosure movement, and as such were closely related to the debates on smallholdings and allotments that characterised the 1880s. Charles William Stubbs, a Christian socialist influenced by Charles Kingsley and Frederick Denison Maurice and the incumbent of a number of country parishes across this period,[139] saw the occupation of land as serving to 'fire the imagination of the agricultural labourer',[140] giving him a stake in the soil, and through the soil a stake in his community as well. Stubbs, later bishop of Truro, encouraged the development of thrift among the labourers through local philanthropic effort – such as the establishment of penny savings banks and sick clubs – but viewed cultivation as the best incentive to self-sufficiency. The smallholding inculcated virtues of 'growth, parental love, filial obedience, household thrift, cleanliness, modesty, chastity, self-respect, piety and simplicity of heart';[141] and Stubbs gave practical effect to these ideas by devising allotment schemes on his glebe land. Behind these initiatives lay a continued subscription to the idea of Hodge, an idea which also underpinned many arguments for the concession of the franchise. Stubbs, speaking in 1877, told an audience that the franchise would perform a similar service to the spread of landholding, being 'the first step in raising [the labourer] from the condition of an eating, drinking, and toiling *animal* to the true dignity of a working *man*'.[142] The franchise was only the first step: Jessopp admitted that it would be some time before 'the vote of the agricul-

---

[136] Idem, *Hodge and his masters*, ii. 204.
[137] Freeman, 'Folklore collection'.
[138] See Boyes, *Imagined village*.
[139] Stubbs, *Charles Kingsley*.
[140] Idem, *The mythe of life: four sermons, with an introduction on the social mission of the Church*, London 1880, 19, and *The land and the labourers: facts and experiments in cottage farming and co-operative agriculture* (1st edn 1884), London 1893, 29.
[141] Idem, *Land and the labourers*, 27–8.
[142] Idem, *Village politics: addresses and sermons on the labour question*, London 1878, 191. Original emphases.

tural labourers can represent anything better than the views of those who happen to dominate over them',[143] and recognised that, whatever was done for them, there would remain a substantial 'residuum' for whom there was no future on the land.[144] Similarly, in his essay on 'One of the new voters', Jefferies described a young labourer whose very fitness to exercise his democratic right was called into question by the monotony and emptiness of his existence.[145] Elsewhere, Jefferies contrasted agricultural labourers with workers at the Great Western Railway works in Swindon, whom he found to be generally intelligent, well-travelled, well-read and disinclined to drunkenness and immorality. Even amongst this huge workforce, there was a perceptible *esprit de corps*, and the cream of them, intellectually speaking, were 'full of social life, or, rather, of an interest in the problems of social existence'.[146] For Jefferies, the way to raise the agricultural labourer to this level of political and social awareness was the establishment of parish councils, through which Hodge would once again be empowered to participate in the kind of village life that had, supposedly, characterised the pre-enclosure countryside.

If part of this empowerment was to be achieved through the establishment of political institutions within which the labourers could exercise a degree of self-government – and parish councils were eventually established in 1894 – another impetus towards it was provided by locally initiated philanthropic action. Stubbs, a perhaps unusually active country parson, not only provided labourers with the opportunity to occupy small parcels of land, but also organised winter lectures and night schools in his parishes, recognising that the elevation of the labourer necessitated the social involvement of village elites. Stubbs argued that the country parson served a function analogous to that of the university settlements in the large towns:[147] the Church of England placed a member of the educated middle classes in each rural parish, thereby facilitating the class dialogue that Canon Barnett, the founder of Toynbee Hall, envisaged as the first step towards the social regeneration of urban communities. Toynbee Hall, the earliest and most influential of the university settlements, was established in Whitechapel in 1884, the same year as the concession of the wider rural franchise, and, as Standish Meacham has shown,[148] those who took up residence there were acutely conscious of the obstacles that stood in the way of effective communication with the metropolitan poor. There were no rural imitators of Toynbee Hall in this period, although in 1894 a proposal for rural settlements was considered at a confer-

143 Jessopp, *Arcady*, p. xviii.
144 Ibid. 210.
145 Jefferies, *Open air*, 94–111.
146 Idem, *The hills and the vale*, London 1909, 129.
147 Charles William Stubbs, *The church in the villages, principles and ideal: an address to the church council and wardens of the united parishes of Stokenham, Chivelstone, and Sherford*, Dartmouth 1887, 39, and *Village politics*, 174.
148 Standish Meacham, *Toynbee Hall and social reform, 1880–1914: the search for community*, New Haven, Conn. 1987, esp. ch. ii.

ence on 'Land, Co-Operation and the Unemployed' at Holborn Town Hall.[149] T. Locke Worthington, the proposer, hoped such settlements would make rural life more interesting and thereby help to prevent the exodus of the most intelligent labourers to the towns, and particularly wanted them to 'organise and improve the educational advantages of the town in the country districts, not forgetting, above all things, the recreative needs'.[150] These proposals came to nothing in the short term, and the nearest rural manifestation of the impulses that drove the activities of the settlement pioneers was the social mission of the Church, as articulated by groups such as the Christian Social Union, and diffused to many other country parsons in this period. If the settlement served as a centre of both social work and social investigation in the large town, the parson fulfilled a similar function in rural communities. If members of the metropolitan middle classes were experiencing a 'consciousness of sin' in the 1880s, as identified retrospectively by Beatrice Webb,[151] which lay behind the outpourings of social concern of which the settlements were one institutional manifestation, a similar consciousness of sin was affecting members of rural elites in the same period. Men like Stubbs were becoming aware of the class isolation that had kept the labourer in ignorance and dependence, and that had also helped to maintain the Hodge stereotype. Thus Stubbs agreed that his fellow clerics were partly responsible for the creation of '[a] class of men, the stolid helplessness of whose ignorance has become proverbial'.[152]

Insofar as the representations of the labourer engendered by these interpretations of rural life were the result of social interaction of a fundamentally unequal kind, they continued to reflect the perceptions of observers who, for all their professed sympathy with the poor in their midst, enjoyed only an external perspective on the lives of the poor. They operated, as investigators and as reformers, within a middle-class agenda packed with the conventional middle-class cultural preoccupations of the 1880s. Men like Jefferies and Jessopp were not discouraged by their unflattering representations of their labouring neighbours from taking information from them at first hand – indeed, there would have been no other way to obtain the information they sought – but their approach entailed a 'survey'-type attitude that resulted in often condemnatory accounts of the rural poor. Unsurprisingly, therefore, their findings were open to contestation, especially on the grounds of their frequent reinforcement of the Hodge stereotype. Although Jessopp avoided the label Hodge, his sometimes condescending attitude to the labourer drew

[149] T. Locke Worthington, 'Proposal for rural university settlements', in J. A. Hobson (ed.), *Co-operative labour upon the land, and other papers: the report of a conference upon 'Land Co-operation and the Unemployed' held at Holborn Town Hall in October 1894*, London 1895, 111–16.

[150] Ibid. 115.

[151] Beatrice Webb, *My apprenticeship* (1st edn 1926), Harmondsworth 1971, 191–3.

[152] Stubbs, *Village politics*, 191.

criticism, even from other clerics. When, in a throwaway remark in his essay on *The trials of a country parson*, he referred to his parishioners as 'a handful of bumpkins',[153] one anonymous clergyman was infuriated:

> It must be remembered too that those whom the author speaks of as 'a handful of bumpkins' have souls, they have their trials and sorrows. The term 'bumpkin' is a familiar one; it may be a 'racy' one, it certainly is not a 'clever' one. On the contrary, when applied to CHRIST'S poor by a clergyman it is little less than contemptible, and not the language which a Pastor ought to use. . . . We have no right to take liberties with the poor. If we look upon them merely in the light of 'a handful of bumpkins,' no wonder they resent it.[154]

More vitriolic condemnation of the stereotype came from the labourers themselves. The establishment of the NALU in the 1870s had given the agricultural labourer access to a newspaper, and labourers and their spokesmen continued to publish their own accounts of English rural society in the 1880s. For example, an anonymous 'agricultural labourer', writing in 1885, admitted that features of the Hodge stereotype reflected the reality of the labourer's condition, but turned this into an indictment of the rural elites:

> What do these rich men tell you my fellowmen, they tell you that you are ignorant, and I am sorry to say that to some extent it is true. But who is it that has kept you ignorant? Why these rich lords and squires and capitalists, they have ever tried to keep you ignorant to serve their own ends, and yet these people will taunt you with being ignorant . . . and it is they who are to blame for it, they have ever tried to keep you back in your ignorance, and why? because they know that when you had more knowledge, you would not be contented with your miserable condition.[155]

Much of the criticism aimed at derogatory accounts of the agricultural labourer focused on methodological issues, the portrayal of an ignorant and dependent labourer being associated with a failure among investigators to penetrate effectively the life they sought to describe. For Thomas Hardy, for example, Hodge was the creation of external observers. Hardy had himself attracted criticism for crediting the agricultural labourer with too much intelligence. The *Athenaeum*, reviewing his novel *The hand of Ethelberta* in 1875, had remarked that Hardy 'does not seem to appreciate the exceeding scantiness of ideas in the brain, and words in the mouth, of a modern rustic', and suggested that the labourer's vocabulary was confined to fewer than 200 words.[156] Hardy's suggestion to those who believed in Hodge, however, was

---

153 Jessopp, *Trials*, 93.
154 Anon., *Other views on the trials of a country parson*, London 1891, 19–20, 31. Original capitalisation.
155 'An agricultural labourer', *The position of the agricultural labourer in the past and in the future*, London [1885], 50.
156 Quoted in Edmund Blunden, *Thomas Hardy* (1st edn 1942), London 1967, 40.

this: they should go to Dorset ('where Hodge in his most unmitigated form is supposed to reside'),[157] and take up residence in a cottage. He suggested that, after some time living among the labourers, the resident 'would find that, without any objective change whatever, variety had taken the place of monotony . . . Hodge, the dull, unvarying, joyless one' would cease to exist.[158] Such an investigator would obtain an intimate knowledge which would be at variance with his prior external perspective. He would find, like the country parson and publisher Charles Kegan Paul, remembering his Oxfordshire cura-cies, that the rural poor 'are not stolid and stupid, as is so often assumed. What they lack is book-learning, but for one who can talk their language and understand their thoughts, there is much to repay the attempt to know them better'.[159] Remembering her childhood of the 1890s in the same county, Flora Thompson remarked of her own village that '[i]f a stranger had gone there looking for the conventional Hodge, he would not have found him'.[160] Accounts of rural labouring life that came to some degree 'from the inside' would modify significantly the assumptions made by investigators who enjoyed only an external perspective.

The methodological challenges to which the work of men like Jefferies and Jessopp were subjected in the 1880s are indicative of a developing tradi-tion of cultural anthropology in the English countryside, a mode of social investigation that provoked contestation no less significant than the output of the special correspondent journalists of the 1870s. Both the 'journalistic method'[161] of Forbes and Heath and the intensive methods employed by Jessopp and Jefferies, although marginalised in the historiography of social investigation, were viewed as important channels of information about rural life during a period in which the condition and outlook of the agricultural labourer had come to be viewed as a matter of fundamental national impor-tance. Impressionistic and essentially unverifiable explorations like these were one means through which the lives of the rural – and indeed the urban – poor were communicated and represented, and they provided important if contestable information about a population that remained essentially hidden from urban middle-class view. Naturally, the findings of these social inquiries were presented according to various literary conventions, and their wide circulation and influence can be attributed to the popular appeal of the countryside. Jefferies's *Gamekeeper at home* and *Amateur poacher* presented a pleasing image of a countryside populated by quaint rustic characters who were repositories of naturalists' folklore and harmless superstitions. Many other authors found their way into print and circulation as a result of the success achieved by Jefferies, and contributed to the diffusion of this fantasy

157 Thomas Hardy, 'The Dorsetshire labourer', *Longman's Magazine* ii (1883), 252.
158 Ibid. 253–4.
159 C. Kegan Paul, *Memories* (1st edn 1899), London 1971, 187–8.
160 Flora Thompson, *Lark Rise to Candleford* (1st edn 1945), Harmondsworth 1973, 50.
161 Wells, *Local social survey*, 14 n. 1.

of the countryside. As William Sheils has pointed out, one of these books, J. C. Atkinson's *Forty years in a moorland parish*, first published in 1891, owed its fame 'to the timely way in which it provided, through its descriptive vigour, a homespun view of rural society to a readership on whose walls hung romantic rural scenes but who remained largely ignorant of the reality behind'.[162] The role of the social investigator was frequently that of describing this reality of rural life, and awakening the conscience of urban and rural elites to the condition of the bulk of the rural population. That the revelations of Heath and Forbes in the 1870s were contested vigorously in the newspaper and periodical press, and among groups such as the NAPSS, was hardly surprising given the greater access to these means of dissemination enjoyed by rural social elites. However, the NALU press and the union meeting gave the labourer a chance to hit back at his detractors; and as the special correspondent gave way to the resident investigator in the 1880s, the resultant representations of the labourer continued to provoke dissent. The controversial adoption of the respondent method of inquiry, and its more intensive adoption by resident investigators, was the issue around which methodological debate coalesced; and, as the next chapter will show, this debate continued into the 1890s, when rural depopulation was the main concern among social investigators in the English countryside.

[162] Sheils, 'Church, community and culture', 276.

3

The 'Passion for Inquiry': Rural Depopulation and the Social Investigator

If the burning lights had been turned away from the English agricultural labourer in the 1880s, they shone with redoubled brightness in the following decade. So strong did the investigative impetus become that Russell Garnier, a conservative historian of the British 'peasantry', wondered in 1895 'whether this passion for inquiry . . . may not become extravagant'.[1] The passion grew from the dominance of two themes – depression and, especially, depopulation – in the late 1880s and the 1890s. As early as 1879 a royal commission was established to investigate the 'depressed condition of the agricultural inter-est'; and it was a measure of how far the labourer had come since the 1860s that Joseph Arch and other agricultural trade union officials were invited to give evidence to this inquiry,[2] which was followed by another commission on 'the agricultural depression' in the 1890s.[3] More important, perhaps, the steady (though unspectacular) revival of agricultural fortunes during the 1890s contrasted with a deepening dissatisfaction among the labouring classes with life on the land. The reports of the census of 1891 provided stark evidence of the numerical decrease of the rural population, and prompted another wave of investigative activity which sought reasons and remedies for the disturbing state of rural affairs. The most impressive venture was the Royal Commission on Labour, which included a separate rural inquiry carried out using the by now traditional device of the itinerant assistant commis-sioner, and which added to the mass of evidence for the 'rural exodus'; and there was also a revival of rural special correspondent journalism in the national newspapers, culminating in Rider Haggard's inquiry for the *Daily Express* in 1901. This chapter examines these and other manifestations of the 'passion for inquiry' spawned by rural depopulation, showing how their

1 Russell M. Garnier, *Annals of the British peasantry*, London 1895, 407.
2 *Minutes of evidence taken before Her Majesty's Commissioners on Agriculture, volume III*, PP 1882, C. 3309–I, 1–10, 36–47, 67–94, 111–22. The commissioners also interviewed John Cockbill, an allotment-holder at Minster Lovell in Oxfordshire (257–8). See also Horn, *Joseph Arch*, 158–9. Arch also served as a member of the RC on the Aged Poor in 1893–4, and was offered, but declined, a place on the RC on the Agricultural Depression in 1893: ibid. 203–4. Alfred Simmons's evidence is noted in Armstrong, *Farmworkers*, 119, and Mick Reed and Roger Wells, 'An agenda for modern English rural history?', in Reed and Wells, *Class, conflict and protest*, 221.
3 *RC on the Agricultural Depression: first report, minutes of evidence*, PP 1894, C. 7400; *Minutes of evidence*, PP 1896, C. 8021.

methods and findings were challenged, and in some ways refined, through the processes of dialogue that they engendered. The respondent method was widely used in this period, and although its adoption was by no means an uncontested activity, a growing body of opinion believed that the outlook of a class could best be estimated through the kind of close association that had been enjoyed by many of the resident investigators active in the 1880s. Where sufficient account was not taken of the evidence and opinions of the agricultural labouring classes, the inquiries concerned provoked an often highly critical response.

Depopulation seemed to threaten both urban and rural communities. As Gareth Stedman Jones has shown, in the metropolitan social turmoil of the 1880s fears were continually expressed that the ongoing migration of coun-trymen to London and other large cities resulted in progressive racial deterio-ration.[4] The physical strength of the agricultural worker was attenuated by two or three generations of casual labour – accompanied by inefficiency, malnutrition and vice – in an urban industrial environment. Rural poverty and the agricultural depression played their part in this process, in driving the labourers from the land to seek higher wages in the towns. The dockers' union, whose strike in London in 1889 was further evidence of the growing strength of organised labour in the ranks of the unskilled, therefore attempted (with at best moderate success) to mobilise agricultural labourers' unions, hoping to keep on the land those whose competition would otherwise further depress wages in the over-stocked metropolitan labour market.[5] Charles Booth, whose survey of *Life and labour of the people in London*, begun in 1887, was perhaps the most spectacular result of the 'passion for inquiry', drew attention to the influx of migrants and its effects on both the immigrant and native populations. On of his assistants, Hubert Llewellyn Smith, using published and unpublished census data, showed that, on top of its large natural increase, London's population was increased to the extent of over 10,000 a year (not to mention the rapid expansion of extra-metropolitan districts such as West Ham) through immigration from the country districts.[6] He drew the conclusion that the metropolis was

> to a great extent nourished by the literal consumption of bone and sinew from the country; by the absorption every year of large numbers of persons of stron-ger physique, who leaven the whole mass, largely direct the industries, raise the standard of health and comfort, and keep up the rate of growth of the great city only to give place in their turn to a fresh set of recruits, after London life for one or two generations has reduced them to the level of those among whom they live.[7]

4 Jones, *Outcast London*, chs vi, xvi.
5 Ibid. 146–7.
6 H. Llewellyn Smith, 'Influx of population (East London)', in Charles Booth (ed.), *Life and labour of the people in London* (1st edn 1889; 2nd edn 1892–7), London 1902–3, iii. 62.
7 Ibid. iii. 65–6.

Although this theory of urban degeneration was flawed,[8] and although Booth himself never explicitly assented to a model of generational deterioration, his employment of the language of the 'residuum' contributed to developing discourses around the term.[9] Later, when reports of the widespread unfitness of military recruits during the second Boer war added a new urgency to the situation in the early 1900s, drawing attention to the savage conditions in towns, and prompting a whole series of concerns about 'national efficiency',[10] the Balfour government was driven to appoint an Interdepartmental Committee on Physical Deterioration to examine the whole question, and its report focused largely on the problems associated with urban life.[11]

For several decades, various political groupings had looked to the land for their solutions to the problems of England's towns – and they were joined in the 1880s by Booth, who proposed a scheme of rural labour colonies to house London's large class of casual workers[12] – but this vision was compromised by the discovery that deterioration also occurred in the countryside. Indeed, this was a logical extension of the theory of urban degeneration. Drained of its youngest, healthiest and most intelligent inhabitants, the land was left with a 'residuum' of the less efficient, which in turn threatened the future of the rural population. This development, no less than the degeneration associated with the urban environment, entailed a serious threat to the future progress and economic competitiveness of the nation, to say nothing of the strategic importance of an efficiently cultivated countryside. The rediscovery of rural poverty in the 1870s and the effects of the agricultural depression worsened the gloom that was coming to surround the problems of the countryside. Thus as early as 1883 Richard Jefferies could tell the readers of *Longman's Magazine* that

A race for ever trembling on the verge of the workhouse cannot progress and lay up for itself any saving against old age. Such a race is feeble and lacks cohesion, and does not afford that backbone an agricultural population should afford to the country at large. . . . They are the last line of defence – the reserve, the rampart of the nation. Our last line at present is all unsettled and broken up, and has lost its firm and solid front.[13]

8   Jones, *Outcast London*, 130–44.
9   José Harris, 'Between civic virtue and social Darwinism: the concept of the residuum', in Englander and O'Day, *Retrieved riches*, 67–87.
10   See, for example, G. R. Searle, *The quest for national efficiency: a study in British politics and political thought, 1899–1914* (1st edn 1971), London 1990; Bernard Semmel, *Imperialism and social reform: English social-imperial thought, 1895–1914*, London 1960; *Report of the Interdepartmental Committee on Physical Deterioration*, PP 1904, Cd. 2186.
11   But see pp. 103–4 below.
12   John Brown, 'Charles Booth and labour colonies, 1889–1905', *Economic History Review* 2nd ser. xxi (1968), 349–60.
13   Richard Jefferies, 'The Wiltshire labourer', *Longman's Magazine* iii (1883), 60.

Thus the legislative programmes of the period paid more attention to the problems of rural life than they had previously done; and the various proposals were framed in the light of both urban and rural needs. In the 1890s, for example, the radicals' 'Newcastle Programme' 'bristl[ed] with such Collectivist measures as . . . Compulsory Powers to Local Authorities to acquire and hold Land for Allotments, Small Holdings, Village Halls, Places of Worship, Labourers' Dwellings, and other public purposes',[14] while many Conservatives, such as Henry Chaplin (president of the Board of Agriculture in the early 1890s) and Rider Haggard, saw in the provision of smallholdings a means of recreating a lost class of yeoman farmers.[15] Such measures as the various Small Holdings and Allotments Acts of 1882, 1887, 1892, 1894 and 1908, it was hoped, would both reverse the deterioration of the urban population and revitalise English rural life.[16] Similarly, in terms of social inquiry, the 'passion for inquiry' in rural England paralleled the attention given to urban conditions in the 1880s, and cannot be viewed in isolation from it: as Arthur Acland commented in 1892, '[p]ublic opinion has been awakened [both] by the sad and impressive pictures of the life of the poor, presented in such works as [Life and labour of the people in London], and by the spread of knowledge concerning the grievous hardships of village life in many parts of the country'.[17]

Rural issues were thus central to national political concerns in the 1890s, in part because of the role of organised labour, and especially the participation of agricultural labourers in the political process. In the 1870s agricultural trade unionism had been in its infancy and disputes were usually localised and arguably took the place of an institutionalised political framework for the airing of grievances. The concession of the widened rural franchise in 1884 marked an important turning-point; and the creation of county councils in 1888 and rural district and parish councils in 1894 represented a further institutionalisation of the previously somewhat informal (and undoubtedly archaic) rural political and administrative machinery. Agricultural trade unions increasingly looked to these new institutions, attempting to organise the election of sympathisers to them.[18] Furthermore, in this period there were three general elections in eight years – in 1892, 1895 and 1900 – in all of which agricultural labourers participated, and in all of which, especially the first two, land reform was a central plank of the Liberal campaign. Marion

14 Fabian Society, 'To your tents, oh Israel!', Fortnightly Review lx (1893), 571.
15 Roy Douglas, Land, people and politics: a history of the land question in the United Kingdom, 1878–1952, London 1976, 105–6; Avner Offer, Property and politics, 1870–1914: landownership, law, ideology and urban development in England, Cambridge 1981, ch. xxi; E. H. H. Green, The crisis of conservatism: the politics, economics and ideology of the British Conservative party, 1880–1914, London 1995, 121–2, 128.
16 Douglas, Land, people and politics, 103–6; Hasbach, History, 235–41, 303–21.
17 A. H. D. Acland, 'Introduction', in J. A. Spender, The state and pensions in old age, London 1892, p. xvii.
18 Groves, Sharpen the sickle!, 88–9.

Springall, a Norfolk historian writing in the 1930s, explained that '[a]s the agricultural depression deepened, the economic rather than the social side of the problem came uppermost in men's minds. Village politics grew more concerned with the land and less with the Church'.[19] The publication and wide dissemination of Henry George's *Progress and poverty* (which first appeared in 1880); the campaiging activity of groups such as the Land Nationalisation Society and the English Land Restoration League, whose vans travelled round rural England serving both an investigative and a propagandist purpose; and above all the evident and frequently emphasised link between the land question and rural depopulation, all ensured that the ideological conflicts associated with the most fundamental of economic resources would impose themselves onto the structure and methodology of social inquiry in the English countryside. The result was a more conflictual period of social investigation, and one which saw the maturing of some of the debates that had ensued in fledgling form from the agricultural upheavals of the 1870s.

Depopulation dominated the rural investigations of the Royal Commission on Labour, one of the largest investigative endeavours of the period and one whose ramifications extended far beyond its envisaged role. It was appointed in 1891, 'to inquire into the questions affecting the relations between employer and employed, the combination of employers and employed, and the conditions of labour, which have been raised during the recent trade disputes'.[20] This remit was somewhat out of date as far as agriculture was concerned: the upsurge of trade unionism in the countryside had come two decades earlier, and although the National Union and some other bodies enjoyed a modest revival in the late 1880s and early 1890s, it could not realistically be argued that labour combination *per se* was a threat to the social stability of agricultural communities.[21] Nevertheless, it was felt that 'the condition of agriculture, the diminution of employment on the land, the migration of labourers from rural districts, and their competition with other classes of labour, had exercised an important influence on the labour question generally',[22] and the special case of agriculture seemed to necessitate a method of inquiry that went beyond the simple cross-examination of witnesses that the commissioners considered sufficient for the investigation of every other industry. Therefore, as in the inquiries of 1843 and 1867, assistant commissioners were sent out to explore rural Britain. Under the guid-

19 Springall, *Labouring life*, 115.
20 *Fifth and final report of the RC on Labour, part I: the report*, PP 1894, C. 7421, 3.
21 Selley, *Village trade unions*, 77–9; Groves, *Sharpen the sickle!*, 85–8; Dunbabin, *Rural discontent*, 80–1. The NALU expanded from a low of 4,254 members in 1889 to a peak of around 15,000 in 1891–2, but dwindled rapidly to just 1,100 in 1894, and was dissolved in 1896. The figure of 4,254 is mistakenly given as 2,454 in Selley, *Village trade unions*, 77. The Eastern Counties Labour Federation grew from 2,183 members in 1890 to a peak of 16,881 in 1892; it too was dissolved in 1896.
22 *Fifth and final report of the RC on Labour, part I*, 10.

ance of senior assistant commissioner W. C. Little, who was responsible for the final report of the agricultural section of the commission, six men were sent out to different regions of England. (Assistant commissioners were also sent to Ireland, Wales and Scotland, but the discussion here will focus on the English inquiry.) They were instructed to report under nine headings: the labour supply; conditions of engagement; wages and earnings; cottage accommodation; gardens and allotments; benefit societies; trade union activity (if any); the 'General Relations between Employers and Employed'; and 'The General Condition of the Agricultural Labourer'.[23] In addition, Cecil Chapman, who reported on Shropshire and seven southern counties, used an additional category, the 'Character of Labourers'.

The assistant commissioners, like those of 1867, were mostly barristers, enjoying a reputation for impartiality and rigour. All had experience of social investigation or knowledge of rural life, or both: Arthur Wilson Fox, for example, was an active member of the Royal Statistical Society and later carried out investigations into the wages and earnings of agricultural labourers for the Board of Trade, where he was comptroller-general of the Commercial, Labour and Statistical Departments from 1906 until his death in 1909;[24] William E. Bear and Roger C. Richards contributed articles on agriculture to a number of periodicals;[25] Aubrey Spencer was an expert on agricultural and land law; and Cecil Chapman was a former assistant commissioner for the Markets and Fairs Commission (1887–8). The structure of their inquiries was very similar. Each was allocated a number of counties; and in each county a representative and as far as possible 'distinctly agricultural' poor law union was selected: in England, agriculture predominated in thirty-three of the thirty-eight unions investigated.[26] The concentration on one union in each county, Little asserted, allowed 'greater exactness than would be possible in any general survey'.[27] In each union, one or two notable officials, often including the chairman of the board of guardians, were contacted in each district, and these would put the commissioner in touch with other authorities – usually clergymen, farmers and landowners – who would be interviewed or invited to supply written evidence. In addition, the commissioners were instructed to hold public meetings of labourers in order

---

[23] Ibid. 199.
[24] A. Wilson Fox, 'Agricultural wages in England and Wales during the last fifty years', *Journal of the Royal Statistical Society* lxiv (1903), 273–359; see pp. 164–8 below.
[25] See, for example, William E. Bear, 'The principle of tenant right', *Contemporary Review* xli (1882), 645–55; 'The agricultural problem', *Economic Journal* iii (1893), 391–407, 569–83; 'Our agricultural population', *Economic Journal* iv (1894), 317–31; and 'The land and the cultivator', in James Samuelson (ed.), *The civilisation of our day: a series of original essays on some of its more important phases at the close of the nineteenth century by expert writers*, London 1896, 1–25; Roger Charnock Richards, 'The landlord's preferential position', *Fortnightly Review* liii (1890), 881–95.
[26] *Fifth and final report of the RC on Labour, part I*, 203.
[27] Ibid. 199.

to hear their side of the question. Thus, for example, when Wilson Fox carried out a fairly typical inquiry at Thingoe in Suffolk, he began by sending a copy of the 'Notes of Inquiry' to the union's forty-three guardians, fifteen of whom replied; then through these contacts he visited farmers in the union, staying at the homes of four large farmers, one of whom was also the chairman of the board of guardians, and one the deputy chairman of Suffolk County Council. He staged nine public meetings, entry to which he attempted to restrict to labourers, and held a 'public inquiry' in the guildhall at Bury St Edmunds. He visited labourers' cottages in the company of the local sanitary inspector, and took additional evidence from 'landowners, land agents, clergymen, school-masters, relieving officers, doctors, workhouse officials, labourers, and members of the Eastern Counties [Labour] Federation'.[28]

On the face of it, this was a fairly broad profile of informants, but to what extent the assistant commissioners drew on evidence from different sources in compiling their reports is difficult to tell. Only for Wilson Fox's inquiry at Swaffham in Norfolk is it possible to assess the balance: in an appendix he quoted and attributed all the evidence cited in the report.[29] As a rough guide, this can be broken down into evidence obtained from employers, from labourers and from miscellaneous sources. In this report Wilson Fox cited employers' evidence 101 times, labourers' evidence thirty-six times and other evidence three times (see table 1): one informant was a medical officer of health, one a clergyman and one a solicitor. Much of the labourers' evidence was obtained at public meetings, although some individuals were also quoted. This breakdown compares unfavourably with the witness profile of the commission as a whole when taking evidence in the normal way: as the secretary, Geoffrey Drage, pointed out, of the 583 witnesses examined, 350 were representatives of the employed, 163 representatives of employers and 70 'miscellaneous'.[30] When Wilson Fox's evidence is broken down by subject, the results are even more striking. It is perhaps unsurprising that for information on the subjects of the numbers employed and the effects of the depression Wilson Fox relied almost wholly on interviews with employers; but on earnings, trade unions, labour relations and the general condition of the labourer, there is a marked bias towards evidence from the employing classes. The inherent contestability of the real value of the agricultural wage, therefore, was barely acknowledged, while the condition of the labourer and the role of trade unionism were represented almost wholly from the standpoints of the elites with whom the direction of the investigation rested.

By contrast, some of Wilson Fox's colleagues on the commission more

---

[28] RC on Labour: assistant commissioners' reports on the agricultural labourer, volume I: England, PP 1893–4, C. 6894, iii. 33.
[29] Ibid. iii. 85–95. On the subject of piece-work and allotments, some of the evidence used was unattributed, and this is excluded from the table.
[30] Fifth and final report of the RC on Labour, part II: secretary's report on the work of the office: summaries of evidence (with index); and appendices, PP 1894, C. 7421 (i), 10.

Table 1
Evidence used by Arthur Wilson Fox in his report on Swaffham, Norfolk, for the Royal Commission on Labour

Subject	Evidence from employers	Evidence from labourers	Evidence from miscellaneous sources
Numbers employed	17	2	–
Efficiency of labour	16	–	–
Piece-work	4	5	–
Women and gangs	5	10	1
Earnings	13	–	–
Cottage supply	–	5	–
Cottage building	4	–	–
Allotments	2	5	–
Trade unions	8	1	–
Labour relations	17	5	1
General condition of labourer	9	–	1
Depression	4	–	–
Length of service	2	–	–
Labourers' budgets	–	3	–
Total	**101**	**36**	**3**

Source: *RC on Labour*, iii. 85–95.

Note: As many informants were quoted several times in Wilson Fox's report, the figures given above should not be taken as indicating that 101 different employers and thirty-six different employees were cited. The section 'Numbers employed' embraces the separate section on 'Numbers employed per 100 acres'. The three pieces of evidence quoted under the heading 'Labourers' budgets' are inferred to have been obtained from labourers because of their content, although they may have been supplied by poor law guardians or some other authority.

frequently acknowledged the discrepancies between the evidence of employers and employees. Cecil Chapman noted the conflicting opinions on the subject of piece-work: the 'masters' told him that it had '[v]ery much gone off. Men are not up to it, as the young men have gone away'. The 'men' retorted: 'Price so bad, and soil so heavy, that men can hardly earn day pay at it.'[31] In the Wantage union, '[i]n the opinion of the labourers their condition is worse than it used to be, but in the opinion of a majority of the masters it is better'.[32] On the subject of labour relations in Truro, farmers and labourers agreed that cordiality had diminished, but attributed this to different causes, the labourers to the pride and haughtiness of the farmers, who were 'all for

[31] *RC on Labour: assistant commissioners' reports*, ii. 26.
[32] Ibid. ii. 69.

hunting and meets', and the farmers to the labourers' lack of interest in their work. The employers here were 'unanimous in their opinion that great improvements have taken place . . . they speak in exaggerated language of the comforts and luxury of the men's existence, which the men themselves resented with a good deal of feeling'.[33]

Because of such discrepancies, the assistant commissioners often preferred the evidence of medical officers of health, clergymen, relieving officers and sanitary inspectors. Generally not direct participants in the economic relationships that the commissioners were sent to investigate (although relieving officers might also be employers of agricultural labour), such men could be presented, by William Bear for example, as 'disinterested' and 'impartial'.[34] However, they were often used to supply information about the condition or the moral character of the labouring classes, whom they knew in a particular professional or other capacity, and hence viewed from a distinctive standpoint. The commissioners' inquiries, therefore, were operational on the labourers in that their political and moral agenda was set within a clear social hierarchy within each poor law union. Thus Cecil Chapman's moral analysis of the 'Character of Labourers' was based largely on the evidence of clerical informants, and some farmers,[35] while at Wigton in Cumberland, Wilson Fox examined four informants on the subject of the labourer's 'standard of morality': Mr Moore and Mr Beeton, relieving officers, Mr Holliday, a farmer, and the board of guardians as a group.[36] At Woburn in Bedfordshire and Thakeham in Sussex, William Bear asked clergymen and similar authorities about the 'moral condition of the people'.[37] The relative unwillingness of these investigators to consult the subjects of inquiry on their own terms reflected a cultural distance that located the inquiry within elite discourses in which representations of labouring life were likely to conform to established and enduring stereotypes.

Even where labourers were involved directly at public meetings they were consulted according to an agenda shaped within this structure of investigation. They were, explicitly, the objects of inquiry – although the remit of the commission as a whole was to investigate the labour question in all its aspects, the rural reports were about 'the agricultural labourer' – and their condition was objectivised within an agenda that prioritised the supply and efficiency of labour, while the 'general condition' of the labourer was viewed through the prisms of established moral authorities. The evidence taken at public meetings was frequently represented as untrustworthy: Aubrey Spencer remarked that the evidence taken at the meetings in Pershore

---

[33] Ibid. ii. 114.
[34] Ibid. i. 18, 55, 63.
[35] Ibid. ii. 126, 150–1.
[36] Ibid. iii. 158.
[37] Ibid. i. 25, 64.

(Worcestershire) was 'of a rather one-sided nature, and not wholly reliable',[38] while at Woburn, William Bear heard from a group of labourers that the land was 'labour-starved', but reported that he had found no evidence to support their claim.[39] Spencer remembered that at public meetings labourers' spokesmen often criticised employers, arguing that they should employ more labour at higher wages, but he did not 'think that too much weight should be attached to this demonstration of feelings, as the discontented men who exist in every class and occupation of life naturally come to the front at a public meeting, while the more contented ones remain silent'.[40] Even the establishment of the public meeting was usually in the hands of local elites. At Nantwich in Cheshire Roger Richards drew up his plan of inquiry in consultation with the mayor of Crewe and the clerk to the local board of guardians, and put it to a public meeting of farmers and landowners for approval before the investigation began.[41] When a public meeting of Nantwich labourers challenged the farmers' assertion that labour was less efficient than formerly, it was found that 'upon being tested, they substantially confirmed the accuracy' of the farmers' complaints, being unable to carry out traditional rural tasks such as hedging and roofing.[42] At Thame in Oxfordshire Cecil Chapman tried to encourage the labourers to organise public meetings themselves, but found that this 'usually resulted in the attendance of small numbers and all of the same way of thinking',[43] and thereafter relied on the clerks to the boards of guardians and other officials. Moreover, although where the labourers organised meetings, as at Thame, they were sometimes held in the local club-room or even public house, the meetings generally took place in the village schoolroom, on the territory of local elites and in an environment shaped by them.

The predominance of evidence obtained from employers and local elites gave the commissioners ammunition to mount the defences of rural life traditionally advanced by farmers' spokesmen. The depiction of the system of payment in kind is a good example: although most despaired of obtaining an accurate assessment of the real value of the labourer's earnings, in view of the importance of perquisites in the wage structure, W. C. Little, in his final report, argued that to an extent the variety in the payment of 'extras' across the country cancelled out the variations in cash wages. Thus in the highest-wage districts earnings were 11.4 per cent in excess of wages, whereas in the lowest-wage unions they exceeded cash wages by 33.4 per cent, and in one union, Pewsey in Wiltshire, by 47.6 per cent.[44] On one Shropshire farm Cecil

---

[38] Ibid. v. 91.
[39] Ibid. i. 18.
[40] Ibid. v. 19.
[41] Ibid. iv. 95.
[42] Ibid. iv. 96.
[43] Ibid. ii. 7, 51.
[44] Fifth and final report of the RC on Labour, part I, 207.

Chapman found that ordinary labourers received four different 'allowances', waggoners seven and horsemen and shepherds nine, not including potato ground or free beer.[45] Assistant commissioner Edward Wilkinson called such payments 'little helps';[46] and Roger Richards thought the labourer's aggrieved comparison of his own lot with that of his urban counterpart did not take into account these extra benefits: 'he is most impressed by what is obvious, and the most obvious thing to his mind is the hard cash difference'.[47] Wilson Fox added that the decline of the system of payment in kind meant that the labourers were worse fed than formerly.[48] Ideologically the perquisite system was central to the commissioners' defence of the old paternalist order. Chapman thought these payments 'bind [the labourers] more closely still to their employers', and regretted that labourers were becoming increasingly disaffected with this dependence,[49] while Little thought it unfortunate that in many cases '[t]he bond . . . has become a commercial one, or . . . "merely a cash *nexus*" '.[50] However, the country-dweller still enjoyed many advantages over the townsman: William Bear pointed out that in villages poor people 'find kind helpers among the well-to-do people who know them',[51] and Wilson Fox remarked that rural life 'has some advantages over a town one, and among these may be mentioned lower rents, gardens, allotments, fresher air, purer food and the friendships that exist in a village community'.[52]

This approach, and these findings, were challenged by other groups of social investigators and representatives of the labouring classes of the countryside. In 1894 a conference of Labourers' Union delegates protested against what they saw as the too favourable portraits of rural life drawn by the commission;[53] and other bodies carried out their own inquiries that issued direct challenges to aspects of the assistant commissioners' reports. For example, each year between 1891 and 1897 the English Land Restoration League (founded as the Land Reform Union in 1883) sent out red vans into the countryside to hold political meetings in support of Henry George and the single-taxers, and to gather information about rural life.[54] The vans thus served both an investigative and a propagandist purpose, intending to spread the gospels of land reform and agricultural trade unionism. As the League

[45] RC on Labour: assistant commissioners' reports, ii. 130.
[46] Ibid. vi. 19.
[47] Ibid. iv. 50.
[48] Ibid. iii. 16.
[49] Ibid. ii. 21.
[50] Fifth and final report of the RC on Labour, part I, 215–16, quoting Canon William Bury; see also RC on Labour: assistant commissioners' reports, iv. 20. Original emphasis.
[51] RC on Labour: assistant commissioners' reports, i. 12–13.
[52] Ibid. iii. 71.
[53] ELRL, Special report, 1893: among the agricultural labourers with the 'red vans', London 1894, 7; Special report, 1894: among the agricultural labourers with the 'red vans', London 1895, 18.
[54] The Land Nationalisation Society embarked on a similar, though smaller-scale, campaign using yellow vans: Douglas, Land, people and politics, 106–8.

explained, '[i]t was felt from the first that a large part of the usefulness of the campaign would consist in the collection of information at first hand about the social condition of the agricultural villages, and in the diffusion of the information so gained among the town workers':[55] this emphasised the importance of the depopulation question to both country and town. A daily report form was prepared, on which information was recorded about the access to land, local landowning patterns and labourers' wages and rents (*see* appendix). The regular revelations of poor conditions in villages were reported by Frederick Verinder (the League's general secretary) and others in the *Church Reformer*, a Christian socialist journal, in which the investigators complained of the condition of '*slavery*' in which the labourers lived;[56] and blamed depopulation – the fact of which was undeniable – on the '*Survival of Serfdom*'.[57] The League's meetings were held on village greens: public spaces, used famously and well within living memory for meetings of the National Agricultural Labourers' Union and its branches, in contrast to the village schoolrooms into which labourers were drawn by the assistant commissioners to supply information within a structure dictated to them by an outside inquirer. The greens were also symbolic of the common land whose demise the land reformers regretted.[58] The meetings themselves became theatres of conflict: the League's right to use village greens was contested;[59] and at Aylesbury in May 1896 a red van was physically attacked.[60] In 1892 Lord Bateman, as lord lieutenant of Herefordshire, prevented the League from holding a meeting on a public highway, and as landlord at Shobdon denied them access to a local public house.[61] For their part, the League and the *Church Reformer* reported the victimisation of union members and other instances of the tyranny of landlord and farmer and the evils of land monopoly.[62]

The League's reports directly contested the findings of the labour commission. In 1894 a red van visited Alderminster in Warwickshire, where a public meeting had been held two years earlier by assistant commissioner Roger Richards. Richards claimed that his meeting 'was entirely composed of labourers, who were invited by the schoolmaster . . . [and were] evidently on excellent terms with Mr [James] Stokes, [the landlord's] agent, who came in during the evening'.[63] Richards valued the Alderminster labourers' average weekly earnings, including 14s. cash, a cheap cottage and piece work, at 19s. 7d. When the red van visited, the lecturer explained:

---

55 ELRL, *Special report, 1891: among the Suffolk labourers with the 'red vans'*, London 1891, 9.
56 *Church Reformer* xi (1892), 41. Original emphasis.
57 ELRL, *Special report, 1891*, 13. Original emphasis.
58 *Church Reformer* xi (1892), 15.
59 ELRL, *Special report, 1893*, 10.
60 ELRL, *Special report, 1896: with the 'red vans' in 1896*, London 1897, 5–6.
61 *Church Reformer* xi (1892), 161.
62 Ibid. xii (1893), 63–4, 212–13.
63 *RC on Labour: assistant commissioners' reports*, iv. 31, quoted in ELRL, *Special report, 1894*, 18.

At our meeting last night I read out this description to the audience, and the men, as well as the vicar, who was present, and with whom I had a long conversation afterwards, characterised the report as misleading and inaccurate. I ascertained that the meeting, which the Commissioner says was 'composed entirely of labourers,' consisted of about 30 working men, the schoolmaster, the landlord's agent, and the vicar. I was also informed that none of the labourers present answered any of the questions put by the Commissioner. A small employer of labour told me that he and a gardener were the only two men who answered. As for himself, the Commissioner asked him what were the average weekly wages of labourers, and he replied 'from 10s. to 12s.,' whereupon the agent at once interposed and said: 'That is not fair; there is So-and-so receiving 14s., a week.' It would appear from the Commissioner's Report that, in spite of the fact that the meeting was 'composed entirely of labourers,' he was much more ready to take the word of the agent than the testimony of the working man.[64]

The League claimed that wages had since been further reduced; and in October 1894 the red van returned to Alderminster to help establish a branch of the Warwickshire Labourers' Union. Naturally, it suited Verinder and his colleagues to give as pessimistic an account as possible of the condition of the agricultural labourer; but the episode highlights the contestability of the findings of even the most apparently detached inquiry. By relying more heavily on the information supplied by labourers and trade unionists, the League's investigators were challenging the tradition of the informant method of inquiry within a political context of land reform, and challenging the established bodies that engaged in social investigation to adopt a respondent method of inquiry and to trust the findings that resulted.

Similar debates were taking place among the special correspondent journalists whose newspapers responded to the panic over depopulation by sending them out into the field to report on social conditions in much the same way as they had done in the 1870s. These correspondents had fewer resources at their disposal than the assistant commissioners, although they were arguably more independent in that they had no official duties to fulfil. Like their predecessors such as Francis Heath, they were operating within an exploratory tradition; and like the assistant commissioners, their reports exhibit many of the tensions underpinning the processes of social investigation. Their output had a large readership, spanning the strata of literate society, and as such played an important role in framing urban middle-class perceptions of rural life. The character of their reports was shaped by the districts they chose to visit, the questions they chose to ask and the informant structure they selected. There remained an abundance of misleading information about labouring life in circulation; and correspondents stressed the importance of thorough fieldwork. Peter Anderson Graham, a Northumbrian journalist and later editor of *Country Life*, who undertook tours of inquiry for

---

64 ELRL, *Special report, 1894*, 18.

the *St James's Gazette*, Edinburgh's *National Observer* and the *Morning Post*, told his readers that 'heart-rending but utterly unfounded descriptions of rural wretchedness' could be avoided only if the investigator realised that 'the only reliable authorities in regard to rent or wages are those who pay and those who receive them'.[65] Moreover, as we have seen and as Graham recognised, the reliability of these authorities was itself compromised by ideological and epistemological issues that stood between the investigator and what he liked to think of as objective truth. In his influential book on *The rural exodus* (1892), Graham acknowledged that landowners, farmers and parsons were all 'inclined to take an exaggerated view of Hodge's income' by ascribing too high a value to payments in kind and perquisites – and in the case of farmers overstating their own benevolence towards their employees – while the labourer, on the other hand, 'exaggerates his toil, and minimises the reward of it'.[66] The correspondent, as an explorer, had to choose who was to be his guide; and this decision, as the major parties concentrated their attention on the land question and the position of the agricultural labourer, was becoming increasingly political. Thus Graham went on to explain how the radical investigator was likely to rely on the evidence of Dissenting ministers, village tradesmen and, above all, the agricultural labourers themselves, whereas the Conservative would consider landowners, farmers and Church of England parsons as the most reliable sources of information.[67]

As an archetype of the radical special correspondent, Graham cited George Millin, who undertook a two-month tour of East Anglia and the home counties for the *Daily News*, beginning in August 1891. Millin's articles, reprinted in book form as *Life in our villages*, which went through a number of editions, were widely circulated, and, like Archibald Forbes's contributions to the same newspaper, attracted a substantial volume of correspondence. As Liz Bellamy and Tom Williamson have pointed out, '[t]he letters from farmers, parsons and labourers published in the *Daily News* soon outweighed the offerings of the commissioner, while in other papers the debate itself became an item of news'.[68] The *Daily News* became a forum in which any reader could express his views on the progress of the inquiry, and confirm or take issue with any of the points made – subject, of course, to editorial constraint. Millin took the bulk of his information from the labourers he met at work or in the street. For example, one group of labourers in a field in Essex told him that although their wages were nominally 11s. a week, they lost money when the weather conditions prevented them from working, and one man often took home only 5s. or 6s. in a week; Millin did

---

[65] *St James's Gazette*, 5 Jan. 1892, 5.
[66] Graham, *Rural exodus*, 108.
[67] Ibid. 41–2, 106–8.
[68] Bellamy and Williamson, *Life in the Victorian village*, i. 1.

not verify this story from other sources.[69] In a village in Oxfordshire he took the word of the labourers who told him that they earned only 9s. a week, rather than accepting the higher estimate given to him by the local parson, who unsympathetically suggested that if labourers did not like their rates of pay they could always go and work somewhere else.[70] Millin preferred the evidence of Nonconformist ministers to that given by parsons. Some correspondents wrote to the *Daily News* criticising this approach, but Millin retorted that the Dissenters he met on his travels tended to show more sympathy for the labouring classes than did village clergymen.[71] At Steventon in Oxfordshire, for example, he fell in with a Wesleyan preacher, who 'had been fighting the poor man's battle . . . he thoroughly understands the people, and is in active sympathy with them, and the consequence is that they trust him and talk over their troubles with him. I found that everybody knew him, and he knew everybody, and all their circumstances'.[72] Millin accepted that drunkenness and immorality might be features of labouring life, but remained imbued with a belief in the labourers' reformability and an acceptance of environmental reasons for many of their less endearing behavioural traits that others were quick to castigate, asking '[w]hat can be expected of people who know little but penury and privation and hardship, and almost entire exclusion from the many influences that have placed these superior croakers themselves so high above all human frailties?'[73] His investigations relied on a genial interaction with the labouring population. He advised the investigator to 'stroll down the village and gossip with the people . . . you can get some valuable side-lights on village life, and most of the folks have something valuable to say'.[74]

This interaction with village 'gossip', indicative of a basic faith in the respondent method of inquiry, was challenged by Millin's most direct antagonist, Arthur Cooper, who scorned such uninformed sources of information, preferring the more trustworthy evidence of the traditional paternalist axis of farmer, parson and landowner. Cooper, a Tory paternalist whose tour of inquiry was initiated in direct response to the *Daily News* survey,[75] concentrated on the higher-wage districts of the north of England and presented a much more optimistic assessment of the labourer's position. Where Millin, like many land reformers, had blamed much of the labourer's economic and social backwardness on the 'tyranny' of the closed village, where squire and parson exercised a firm benevolent despotism that stultified the social life of

---

[69] [G. F. Millin], *Life in our villages, by the special commissioner of the* Daily News, *being a series of letters written to that paper in the autumn of 1891*, London 1891, 36.
[70] Ibid. 119–23.
[71] Ibid. 116–24.
[72] Ibid. 118.
[73] Ibid. 161.
[74] Ibid. 73.
[75] A. N. Cooper, *Our villages: another view: a reply to the special commissioner of the* Daily News, London 1891, 5.

the community and gave the labourers no say in local governance,[76] Cooper advanced a strong defence of the role of the traditional rural hierarchy in relieving the dullness of country life. He looked to the 'awakened responsibility' of village elites as a means to solve many of the admitted problems that remained.[77] Where Millin had dedicated his book to William Gladstone, Cooper's pamphlet was dedicated to Lady Legard of Ganton in Yorkshire, 'the model lady of a model village'. Cooper tried to place himself in a tradition of social investigation that transcended the political role of the special correspondent, and understood rural life on its own terms rather than in terms of metropolitan misunderstandings and prejudices. This construction of the role of the investigator deliberately privileged the evidence of rural social elites:

> The *Daily News* Commissioner does not pretend to be deep in his subject. He is the rough-and-ready writer, journeying from village to village, using his eyes, looking into accounts, picking up gossip from farmers, labourers, and old women, all of which he duly chronicles in a pleasant, chatty style. When Arthur Young wrote his famous travels, he was a farmer and employer of labour, looking with an experienced eye on other farmers and their labourers. The *Daily News* writer never pretended to be anything but the Londoner on the jaunt. This may go far to account for the false impression the commissioner has received.[78]

Drawing on a tradition of social and agricultural inquiry that could be traced back over a century, Cooper presented what he saw as a more trustworthy account of rural social conditions, claiming to 'differ from the assertion that the labourers are always in the right and the gentry always in the wrong'.[79] By contrast, Millin was sceptical of the claims of the 'gentry' to really know what was happening in their midst. Describing the outwardly pleasant impression of the nevertheless poverty-stricken village of Ixworth in Suffolk, he claimed that Ixworth 'strikes the stranger as a pleasant and prosperous village ... Tory guardians and Tory parsons, being of a caste altogether separate from the cottagers, would never have found out that anything was wrong in it'.[80]

Anderson Graham, whom the *Spectator* called '[a] most unusually able and temperate contributor',[81] and whose findings were published in book form in Swan Sonnenschein's *Social Science* series, adopted a method that lay somewhere between the two paradigms he identified among his fellow special correspondents. However, he also argued the necessity of attempting more rigorously to understand the outlook of the labouring classes rather than simply the material conditions in which they lived; and as such he was influenced by the methodological developments of the 1880s. Although sceptical

76 Millin, *Life in our villages*, 106–13.
77 Cooper, *Our villages*, 21.
78 Ibid. 5–6.
79 Ibid. 6.
80 Millin, *Life in our villages*, 44.
81 Quoted in *St James's Gazette*, 2 Dec. 1891, 12.

of the labourers' estimates of their earnings, he insisted that to discover the causes of rural depopulation, it was necessary to consult the labourers themselves.[82] He was also, like Millin, attracted to Nonconformist opinion, arguing that the clergyman, usually a product of Oxbridge who mixed socially among the gentry and large farmers, moved in a very different sphere from the bulk of his parishioners. By contrast, Graham thought, labourers saw the minister as 'just like one of ourselves',[83] making him a more reliable source of information. This claim is likely to have overstated the wider social knowledge of the minister, who was more likely to be able to comment with authority on members of his own denomination than on village life as a whole, but it does reflect the importance to investigators in this period of ascertaining something about the labourer's opinions rather than simply unveiling the conditions in which he lived. As Graham explained, '[m]any influences are at work that cannot be expressed in figures . . . [t]he talk [the labourer] hears at the public house is, in determining his conduct, as important a factor as the condition of his cottage or the rent of his allotment'.[84] To understand depopulation, it was essential to understand why the labourers wanted to leave the land; depopulation therefore represented a considerable spur to a more widespread (though clearly not universal) adoption of a respondent method of inquiry. Local knowledge was important to the investigator: thus when Graham undertook an intensive investigation into the circumstances of a semi-depopulated Northumberland village, he claimed that such an inquiry would have been impossible had he not enjoyed a prior personal familiarity with its inhabitants.[85] The kind of information sought transcended the simple details of the labourers' remuneration and cottage accommodation, and suggested that the fleeting visits of the special correspondent might not be sufficient in revealing the conditions of rural labouring life.

Graham's attraction to the respondent method of inquiry was paralleled in other, perhaps more surprising quarters. Thomas Kebbel, the patrician Tory whose book on *The agricultural labourer*, published in 1870, was essentially a distillation of the findings of the Royal Commission on the Employment of Children, Young Persons and Women in Agriculture,[86] brought out a second edition in 1887, heavily reliant on his own inquiries among farmers, and found himself criticised for a failure to empathise with the labouring population. Kebbel, who insisted rather unconvincingly on the broadness of his informant base,[87] remained obsessed with such issues as the immoral implications of the statute fair as a method of hiring labour (a central concern of the

82 P. Anderson Graham, *The revival of English agriculture*, London 1899, 15.
83 Idem, *Rural exodus*, 52.
84 Ibid. p. vi.
85 *St James's Gazette*, 11 Nov. 1891, 4.
86 See pp. 39–41 above.
87 T. E. Kebbel, *The agricultural labourer: a short summary of his position: a new edition brought down to date*, London 1887, 19.

investigators of an earlier generation), the injurious effects of the public house and the possibility of inculcating thrift through the promotion of benefit societies and co-operation. Such preoccupations were denounced in a review in the *Spectator* as 'variously important as incidental to the labourer's well-being; [but] . . . not of the essence of his daily life'.[88] For example, Kebbel seemed unaware of the labourers' hatred of the compulsory school fee; and more generally he paid little attention to the aspects of labouring life that lay behind the drift of the population to the towns. When in 1891 he turned his attention to depopulation, he acknowledged the comments of this reviewer,[89] and strove accordingly to 'get behind mere appearances, and to penetrate to their inner motives'.[90] The apparent inconsistency between an undoubtedly improving material position and a continuing exodus to the towns necessitated a deeper knowledge of 'what is passing in the minds of . . . the peasantry . . . [and] what would keep the better ones at home, or stimulate the worse to greater exertions and to a more lively interest in the work they are called upon to perform'.[91] Kebbel, echoing the reports of Jessopp, Jefferies and Stubbs, thought the broadening horizons of the labourer, the dullness of village life (in particular the demise of old communal festivals) and the apparent opportunities of economic and social betterment in urban centres all played their part in the exodus.[92] Nevertheless, Kebbel's approach was at bottom one which viewed the labourers as a resource, described in terms of 'better' and 'worse' and occupying a set station in life ('the work they are called upon to perform'). The son of a Leicestershire parson, and an admirer of Disraeli, Kebbel, admitting that '[i]t is difficult to say exactly what thoughts are passing through [the labourers'] brains at this moment',[93] remained broadly aligned with the informant method of investigation and with the traditional interpretation of rural England as a benevolently hierarchical society. Yet he was not immune to the challenges laid down by a more confident and mobile labouring class and a more 'democratic' approach to social inquiry.

If many investigators were beginning to take account of the potentialities of the respondent method of inquiry, the same cannot be said for Rider Haggard, whose inquiry of 1901 was the largest, and arguably the most impressive, unofficial inquiry into rural depopulation during this period. Haggard, a popular novelist, Norfolk landowner and practical agriculturalist,[94] together with Arthur Cochrane, a friend acting in a secretarial capacity, travelled around the country, visiting twenty-seven counties and two Channel

88 *Spectator*, 15 Oct. 1887, 1393.
89 Kebbel, *English country life*, 165 n. 1.
90 Ibid. 165.
91 Ibid. 176.
92 Ibid. 180–93.
93 Ibid. 196.
94 Victoria Manthorpe, *Children of the empire: the Victorian Haggards*, London 1996.

Islands, interviewing different authorities on rural life, with the intention of enquiring into the state of English agriculture and the problem of rural depopulation. For Haggard, an unsuccessful Conservative candidate at the general election of 1895, depopulation threatened the future of the English race. The exodus of the best and fittest countrymen to the towns – 'there, in obedience to the laws of nature, to wither and deteriorate'[95] – left behind on the land the oldest, feeblest and least efficient, who in turn fathered and mothered the next generation of country-dwellers. Haggard attributed British setbacks in the second Boer war to 'the pitting of town-bred bodies and intelligences . . . against country-bred bodies and intelligences'.[96] Thus he saw his task as one of national and imperial importance, whose ramifications extended beyond the confines of the rural areas he investigated. The *Express* agreed, declaring at the outset of the inquiry that Haggard was 'undertaking a task as truly patriotic as that of any soldier who goes out to fight for the flag'.[97] Haggard and Cochrane carried out a total of 484 interviews,[98] sent out hundreds of printed questionnaires and received in addition many unsolicited written communications. The reports of the interviews were published in a series of articles entitled 'Back to the land', which appeared twice weekly in the *Daily Express* between April and October 1901, in the *Yorkshire Post* under the title 'State and outlook of the English countryside', and in whole or in part in a variety of local newspapers. The fortunes of the *Express* were intimately bound up with the inquiry: for most of its run it appeared on page 4, opposite the 'Matters of moment' editorial column, and the articles were accompanied by considerable editorial comment. As a new newspaper, just under a year old when Haggard's articles began, the *Express* was trying to set out its stall as a newspaper that presented serious views on rural life.[99] On the envelope in which the newspaper sent out circulars advertising Haggard's tour was emblazoned the slogan 'Of supreme importance to all interested in agriculture':[100] as agriculture and rural life in general were in a period of confusion, change and perhaps crisis, the *Express* was articulating an essential contemporary concern. In 1902 the articles, together with accompanying evidence gathered from correspondents, were published as a two-volume book, *Rural England*, which has become a standard source for historians of rural life.[101]

95 *Daily Express*, 12 Apr. 1901, 4.
96 H. Rider Haggard, *Rural England, being an account of agricultural and social researches carried out in 1901 and 1902*, London 1902, ii. 568.
97 *Daily Express*, 17 Apr. 1901, 4.
98 The figure of 484 interviews is derived from Arthur Cochrane's interview notebooks, Rider Haggard papers, NRO, MS 4692/22–3, and does not reflect the number reported in the published report of the inquiry. Some interviews were conducted by Haggard without Cochrane's assistance and were recorded separately: ibid. MS 4692/24B.
99 See Stephen Koss, *The rise and fall of the political press in Britain*, London 1981, ii. 420.
100 Rider Haggard papers, MS 4692/25 (counties unvisited).
101 See also Mark Freeman, 'Rider Haggard and *Rural England*: methods of social enquiry in the English countryside', *Social History* xxvi (2001), 209–16.

Haggard saw himself as operating within the tradition of inquiry epitomised by the royal commission. The *Express* announced his tour as 'the work of a Royal Commission undertaken by a single man',[102] and if this overlooked Cochrane's important contribution, it did at least indicate the intended scale and scope of the investigation. It also unconsciously betrays the attitude with which Haggard approached his task: his was to be a more accessible equivalent of the official inquiry, and was to involve the consultation of a similar range of informants. The larger readership that Haggard, writing in an organ of the popular press, could attract was seen as giving his survey a potential influence wider than that of an official inquiry. A letter to the editor of the *Express* from George Lambert, a member of the 'Eversley' commission on agriculture in the 1890s, explained:

> A series of descriptions & conclusions arrived at by personal inquiry, and illuminated by Mr Rider Haggard's graphic pen, on the agricultural conditions of our country cannot but do good. If nothing else they will attract attention to a subject that is received with too much apathy by the country at large. The last Royal Commission on Agriculture offered many valuable suggestions, but as one of its members I am downhearted at the scant efforts made to carry them into effect.[103]

Elsewhere, Haggard remarked on the inaccessibility of the reports of offical inquiries to the general reader:

> Blue-books never have been and probably never will be a popular branch of literature. However difficult it may be, indeed, to collect the material and to write a treatise of this nature, it is undoubtedly far more difficult to persuade any one to study the same when written. Whether it is the colour that repels, or the size, or the big, closely printed page, the fact remains that no one reads a blue-book unless he is absolutely compelled so to do, and then not infrequently he contents himself with the Synopsis of Documents at the beginning and, perhaps, the concluding paragraphs.[104]

The serial publication of Haggard's survey, and other reports by special correspondent journalists, made them more digestible; and he identified himself with the long tradition of agricultural inquiry that he traced back to Arthur Young. His tour was modelled on Young's – he even claimed later that the idea of emulating Young came to him, in classical fashion, while having a bath[105] – and, like Young, Haggard's background was agricultural and he was interested in agricultural techniques and experiments. Like Millin, Cooper

---

102 *Daily Express*, 1 Oct. 1901, 1.
103 Lambert to *Daily Express*, 15 Apr. 1901, Rider Haggard papers, MS 4692/25 (Devon).
104 H. Rider Haggard, *The poor and the land, being a report on the Salvation Army colonies in the United States and at Hadleigh, England, with scheme of national land settlement and an introduction*, London 1905, p. v.
105 Idem, *The days of my life: an autobiography*, London 1926, ii. 134–5.

and Graham, Haggard was a special correspondent journalist, but he did not identify with this mode of investigation, preferring, like Cooper, to locate himself within a longer genealogy of agricultural investigators that began with Young and included William Marshall, Frederick Eden, William Cobbett and, chronologically the latest of those whom Haggard acknowledged, James Caird.[106] *Rural England* was subtitled 'Agricultural and social researches carried out in 1901 and 1902': the 'social' was subordinated to the 'agricultural'.

However, in a largely favourable review of *Rural England* in the *Economic Journal*, the economist L. L. Price saw Haggard's survey as having much in common with Charles Booth's *Life and labour* and Seebohm Rowntree's 1901 survey of York, which was itself adduced in *Rural England* as evidence of unenviable urban social conditions.[107] As Price pointed out, Haggard's approach, based on the qualitative interview and a questionnaire not designed to facilitate a quantitative presentation of its results, could not hope to achieve the mathematical exactness of Booth's and Rowntree's conclusions, but Haggard aimed rather 'to draw a picture which is broadly true; and, if it be proverbially questionable whether in the multitude of counsellors real wisdom can be found, we may at any rate allow that from a host of interviews a general notion of men's feelings may be drawn'.[108] Haggard's adoption of a more formally structured interview method may have owed something to Booth: he explained that the methods used by Caird, Cobbett and Young were all 'open to the objection that they are too liable to be coloured to the tint of the author's own mind', whereas his own method, involving diligent note-taking (usually by Arthur Cochrane), enabled him 'to preserve, together with something of their personalities, the individual experiences of many witnesses' which may otherwise have been coloured in their presentation by Haggard's own views.[109] How far Haggard succeeded in this aim is questionable: as Rosemary O'Day has shown in her study of Booth's interviews, the interviewer's neutrality was compromised by the selection for preservation in note form of those subjects which interested him most, raising 'the whole issue of bias and of the nature of the interaction of interviewer and interviewed'.[110] Haggard's correspondence suggests that the method produced inaccuracies;[111] and the interview method may have been used to steer his informants into telling him what he wanted to hear. The tour was advertised as an investigation of depopulation; therefore, the most enthusi-

---

[106] Idem, *Rural England*, i, pp. viii–xi. For an acknowledgement of Eden see Haggard's personal notebook, Rider Haggard papers, MS 4692/24A, p. 46.

[107] *Economic Journal* xiii (1903), 204–15; Haggard, *Rural England*, ii. 566.

[108] *Economic Journal* xiii (1903), 207.

[109] Haggard, *Rural England*, i, p. xi.

[110] Rosemary O'Day, 'Interviews and investigations: Charles Booth and the making of the religious influences survey', in Englander and O'Day, *Retrieved riches*, 157.

[111] Freeman, 'Rider Haggard', 212–13, and 'Social investigation in rural England, 1870–1914', unpubl. PhD diss. Glasgow 1999, 154–6.

astic respondents to his call for information would be those who had definite views on the subject; and in the interviews themselves Haggard would attempt to draw out the opinions of his interviewees on what he saw as the most pressing of matters, and to reinforce his conclusions – already expressed forcefully two years earlier in his book *A farmer's year*[112] – about the labourer and depopulation.

Haggard's informants were mainly landowners, farmers, land agents and auctioneers. Across the country, he and Cochrane would stay with a local landowner, visiting farmers, often tenants of the landowner in question, in his company. For example, in Cambridgeshire they stayed with Charles Allix of Swaffham Prior House, a landowner and practical farmer of 500 acres, interviewing seven others in his presence; and later at Wilburton Manor, home of the landowner and Conservative MP Albert Pell. In Northamptonshire, they stayed at three centres: Fawsley, the home of Sir Charles Knightley, who owned 9,000 acres; Courteenhall, with the family of Sir Hereward Wake, another large local landowner; and Northampton, where they interviewed a land agent and the secretary of the chamber of agriculture.[113] Haggard moved within the networks with which he was familiar – it was not uncommon for friends and family to introduce him to potential informants[114] – and sought trustworthy authorities on rural life. He was assisted, for example, by Clare Sewell Read, a Norfolk neighbour, 'whose opinions, at least where East Anglia is concerned, are entitled to as much weight as those of any agricultural expert in England'.[115] Read's long experience as a farmers' spokesman in parliament and elsewhere (including the Social Science Association) gave him as great an authority as anyone's to represent the views of the farming interest;[116] and, as his exchanges with Canon Girdlestone thirty years earlier had shown, he was tenacious in arguing that pictures of labourers' distress were frequently over-painted.[117] Arthur Wilson Fox, who 'knows as much about British agriculture at large as any man in the country', assisted with the itinerary in Hertfordshire and Lincolnshire.[118] It was men like this who shaped the framework within which Haggard's inquiries were conducted.

112 H. Rider Haggard, *A farmer's year, being his commonplace book for 1898*, London 1899.
113 For a more detailed examination of the Cambridgeshire and Northamptonshire inquiries see Freeman, 'Social investigation', 158–60.
114 Silas J. Weaver to Mrs Maddison Green, 18 May 1901, and Jessie Hartcup to Cochrane, 4 Mar. 1901, Rider Haggard papers, MS 4692/25 (Worcs.); Bevan to Haggard, n.d., MS 4692/25 (Cambs.); various letters in MS 4692/25 (Norfolk).
115 Haggard, *Rural England*, ii. 528.
116 J. R. Fisher, *Clare Sewell Read, 1826–1905: a farmers' spokesman of the late nineteenth century*, Hull 1975.
117 See pp. 41–2 above, and Read's remarks on the condition of the labourer in response to Arthur Wilson Fox's paper to the Statistical Society: Wilson Fox, 'Agricultural wages', 351–3.
118 *Daily Express*, 26 July 1901, 4; letters in Rider Haggard papers, MS 4692/25 (Herts.) and (Lincs.).

Some correspondents questioned the reliance at certain points on the evidence of landowners and their agents: a writer from Hertfordshire, on reading Haggard's account of his interview with Lord Salisbury's agent, remarked that such an informant 'understands matters from a very different standpoint to that of the actual farmer who has to make ends meet'.[119] Indeed, Haggard was aware that the farmers might take a less optimistic view of the local labour supply than their landowner.[120] However, the most significant feature of the informant structure was that it did not reach down to the labourers themselves. It was, of course, much more difficult to meet labourers in an inquiry of this kind: they worked long hours, often in remote corners of farms, and could not be contacted in advance to arrange an interview. The labour commission's investigators who were at work during the harvest period of 1892 pointed out that it was difficult to consult labourers, who were often at work in the fields from dawn to dusk.[121] Moreover, the associational lives of the agricultural population were more limited than those of their urban counterparts: William Bear had attempted to use the working men's clubs at St Neots (Cambridgeshire) and Basingstoke (Hampshire) for gathering information, but found that very few agricultural workers were members.[122] By contrast, the farming interest had the advantage of organised groups, such as agricultural clubs and chambers of agriculture, which often invited Haggard to meet groups of representative agriculturists, and although Haggard disliked this form of information-gathering,[123] he regularly interviewed representatives of such groups who were able to give him opinions based on a range of their members' experiences.[124] By contrast, there were no meetings with representatives of agricultural trade unions; and only on a few occasions were labourers interviewed.[125]

This exclusion resulted in a largely uncritical acceptance of the opinions of employers about the character and quality of their workforces. *Rural England* is full of complaints of the relative inefficiency of labourers compared with their ancestors. In Leicestershire, the men 'either could not or would not work', and only 'the old men, the cripples, and the dullards' remained on the land;[126] in Herefordshire the 'young men who are worth anything went away, only the dregs remaining on the land';[127] and in Sussex 'no one who was fit for

[119] Gardiner Wilson to Haggard, 12 Aug. 1901, Rider Haggard papers, MS 4692/25 (Herts.). See Haggard, *Rural England*, i. 578–80, for Haggard's response to Wilson's criticisms.
[120] *Daily Express*, 2 July 1901, 4; Haggard, *Rural England*, i. 426–7.
[121] *RC on Labour: assistant commissioners' reports*, i. 55.
[122] Ibid. i. 35, 75.
[123] Haggard, *Rural England*, ii. 320.
[124] Bannister to Haggard, 13 Apr. 1901, Rider Haggard papers, MS 4692/25 (Yorks.); Hunt to Haggard, 15 Apr. 1901, MS 4692/25 (Gloucs.); *Daily Express*, 17 Apr. 1901, 4; Haggard, *Rural England*, ii. 141.
[125] Haggard, *Rural England*, i. 247, 300, 444, 458–60; ii. 369–70.
[126] Ibid. ii. 249.
[127] Ibid. i. 304.

anything else stopped on [the land] now-a-days'.[128] Haggard did not acknowledge the contestability of these assessments; and his characterisation of the
labouring classes as a feeble and inefficient residuum both derived from and
reinforced their exclusion from the mechanisms of the investigation. Such a
residuum was unlikely to be considered as a potential base of reliable informants. The very concentration in the survey on the quality of work done,
rather than on the social and economic condition of the labourers themselves, reflected the location of the inquiry within a framework dictated by
the concerns of landowners and employers. Labour was commodified:
Haggard often quoted the labour cost per acre rather than the wages paid, and
in his questionnaire wages were relegated to a subsidiary question, after the
more pressing concern of labour supply (*see* appendix). As one correspondent
remarked at an early stage of the tour, '[s]o far your articles have smacked too
much of the Royal Agricultural Society. . . . You have told us much about the
landlords' losses . . . but not much about the common labourer'.[129] Indeed,
when Haggard wished to give 'the labourer's point of view', he turned to Dr
Killick of Williton in Somerset, 'a Medical Officer who had [*sic*] Studied the
Views of the Workers'.[130] Haggard also spoke to medical officers of health at
Gainsborough in Lincolnshire and Yeovil in Somerset;[131] sometimes interviewed parsons, including Augustus Jessopp, 'who is so well known through
his able and delightful writings on antiquarian and country matters';[132] and
elsewhere recognised the value of the testimony of village schoolmasters to
an investigation of depopulation, given their intimate acquaintance with
rural youth.[133] Even where Haggard did interview labourers directly, on at
least one occasion the interview was recorded in his personal notebook,[134]
rather than in Cochrane's interview notes, suggesting that the labourer was
regarded as a curiosity rather than as a full participant within the formal
structure of the investigation.

Like any other large-scale inquiry, Haggard's survey became a source of
contention among contemporaries. It was widely discussed in the agricultural
community at large and in the national press. For example, the Tunbridge
Wells Farmers' Club held an adjourned debate on the articles, which Haggard
was invited to attend; and H. E. Palmer, editor of the *Yorkshire Post*, saw the
survey 'referred to constantly at agricultural shows'.[135] It was not always
praised, even by those in whose interests it was written: a group of farmers at
the Hertfordshire Agricultural Show expressed strong disagreement with

---

128 Ibid. i. 113.
129 Sweetman to Haggard, 25 Apr. 1901, Rider Haggard papers, MS 4692/25 (Essex).
130 *Daily Express*, 30 May 1901, 4.
131 Haggard, *Rural England*, i. 254; ii. 234–8.
132 Ibid. ii. 505.
133 *Daily Express*, 20 June 1901, 4.
134 Rider Haggard papers, MS 4692/24A, pp. 37–8.
135 Durrant to Haggard 17 June 1901, ibid. MS 4692/25 (Kent); Palmer to Haggard, 28 July
1901, MS 4692/25 (Yorks.).

Haggard's articles on their county.[136] Many communications criticised his methodology, and much of this criticism had an overtly political dimension. J. Martin White, a former Gladstonian Liberal MP, a prominent member of the Sociological Society and a substantial financial backer of Patrick Geddes and the London School of Economics, wrote, initially in response to the articles on Wiltshire, recommending the taking of some labourers' evidence; and he later suggested contacting the Liberal agent in each area visited, 'because the farmers and landlords are mostly Unionists, whereas I understand you want to get the two sides of the question'.[137] A number of letters recommended that Haggard consult some labourers, some mentioning particular individuals by name;[138] and one from a labourer pointed out that '[t]his subject is not one that has been often – if at all – written upon from the labourers [sic] point of view . . . [and] I trust that I may be able to give some information from the labourers [sic] standpoint'.[139] This labourer was, arguably, unusually articulate – he had contributed articles on rural life to the *Standard* and to his local newspaper – but he illustrates the availability of rural working-class opinion to the investigator who sought it.

There is evidence that a more 'democratic' informant structure would have resulted in different findings in some key areas, because the reasons given for the exodus of the rural population by labourers or those intimately acquainted with them – and those of a Liberal political complexion – often differed from those typically advanced by farmers and Conservatives. In particular, insecurity of cottage tenure was mentioned much more often by Liberal investigators; and as many farmers had a vested interest in the perpetuation of the tied cottage system, they were unlikely to give it the same prominence. A letter from 'a grateful reader' explicitly linked the non-identification of this cause of depopulation with the methodology adopted in Haggard's survey. Haggard published part of this letter in *Rural England*; the unpublished section is italicised below:

> *May I venture, very respectfully, to suggest the desirability of other sources of information. With only one or two exceptions landlords, farmers, land agents, auctioneers and others of the owning and employing fraternity have been your informants. Let me suggest to you Clergymen, Non-Conformist Ministers, Village Blacksmiths & men of his [sic] type, Leaders of village Chapels, and above all the Labourers themselves. Until now* . . . *your articles are obviously one-sided.* My idea is, when you extend the scope of your enquiries, you will discover that after all Farmers are not in such a bad way. . . . You, when you consult another class will learn the true explanation of the labour difficulty. The slavish system of Tied Cot-

136 Haggard, *Rural England*, i. 512.
137 White to Haggard, 25 Apr. 1901, Rider Haggard papers, MS 4692/25 (counties unvisited); 3 (quoted), 9, 11, 13 May 1901, MS 4692/25 (Wilts.).
138 Gastling to Haggard, 13 Apr. 1901, ibid. MS 4692/25 (Suffolk); Muscott to Haggard, 7 May 1901, MS 4692/25 (Oxon.); Harper to Haggard, 19 May 1901, MS 4692/25 (Gloucs.).
139 [Triveby?] to Haggard, 17 Apr. 1901, ibid. MS 4692/25 (Hunts.).

tages is the great factor. The farmers use this as a whip, and drive away the best of the labourers. . . . Security of tenure would mean, as any one can see, security of labour.[140]

The suggestions of the 'grateful reader' were clearly not to Haggard's liking, and elsewhere in the same chapter he advanced a strong defence of the tied cottage system, based on his personal experience.[141] By contrast, White mentioned it first in his list of causes of depopulation;[142] Millin had given it a central place in his analysis;[143] and it featured regularly in investigations of rural housing at the turn of the century.[144] Indeed, the English Land Restoration League showed in 1894 that more than half of all cottages in forty-five parishes in Wiltshire and Norfolk were tied, and remarked that '[t]he labourers contend that under circumstances like these, the Parish Councils Bill will but mock them with an empty pretence of self-government, for a vote not approved of by the masters of the village will render the voter workless and homeless within a fortnight'.[145] As we will see in chapter 6, such circumstances also influenced the methods adopted by investigators of rural working-class housing.

The preponderance of farmers and landowners in the informant base of Haggard's inquiry ensured that in his findings the interests of the labouring classes were subsumed beneath those of their employers and landlords. Unsurprisingly, Haggard concluded that, within rural communities, the small landowners had suffered the most from the crisis in agriculture, the farmers now did 'no more than make a hard living', but that the labourers were 'more prosperous to-day than ever before'.[146] Unlike Millin's survey, Anderson Graham's inquiries of the 1890s, and even some of the reports of the labour commission, *Rural England* gave the reader little insight into the world of the agricultural labourer. Lacking access to the mechanisms of the inquiry, labourers had to react to Haggard's articles in other ways. At St Neots in Huntingdonshire, Haggard interviewed Tom Stone, once a labourer himself but by 1901 a publican, who clearly enjoyed a somewhat higher social standing. Reporting Stone's remarks in detail, Haggard wrote in the *Express* of 20 August that the St Neots labourers were lazy, ignorant and unintelligent.[147] Somehow these remarks made their way back to the labourers of the district and, unsurprisingly, 'upset the tempers of the working men', a group of whom gathered outside Stone's house, hooting and jeering him until after

---

140 'A grateful reader' to Haggard, [?] June 1901, ibid. MS 4692/25 (Wilts.), repr. (with corrections) in Haggard. *Rural England*, i. 48–9.
141 Haggard, *Rural England*, i. 38–9.
142 White to Haggard, 3 May 1901, Rider Haggard papers, MS 4692/25 (Wilts.).
143 Bellamy and Williamson, *Life in the Victorian village*, i. 68–9, 171–2 and passim.
144 See pp. 161–2 below.
145 ELRL, *Special report, 1893*, 17–18.
146 Haggard, *Rural England*, ii. 543–5.
147 *Daily Express*, 20 Aug. 1901, 7.

midnight, and threatened him with physical harm if he strayed from the premises.[148] It may be that examples like this could be multiplied; at least it suggests a far from passive response by the investigated populations to what were often highly critical and certainly judgemental articles written almost entirely from the standpoint of rural elites, over the shaping of which the bulk of the agricultural population had little influence. Haggard's articles, then, were contestable pieces of social research, whose methods and findings could spark debate and disagreement among a wide readership.

It is easy to contrast Haggard's remoteness from the labouring classes with the more 'democratic' methodologies of other investigators. For example, when Anderson Graham, during his tour for the *Morning Post* in 1899, talked to a group of harvesters about the rural exodus, having gained access to their society by helping them with their work, he put Haggard's views (as expressed, presumably, in A *farmer's year* or in periodical publications) to them, and found that they disagreed with his assessment that low wages were the main reason for depopulation.[149] However, the self-proclaimed intimacy of the special correspondent with the agricultural labourer can be challenged: like their predecessors in the 1870s, these men sometimes had difficulties interacting with the labourers on their own territory. Millin found himself in an awkward position in a village inn, where he insisted on drinking tea instead of beer while he 'studied village life in the tap-room'.[150] Denham Jordan, a Kentish marshland nature-writer and son of a skilled artisan, who published under the *nom-de-plume* of 'a son of the marshes', found that in roadside inns across the south of England he was eyed suspiciously by local inhabitants, who referred to him as the 'furrin feller', and reassured themselves that he was not there 'tu mek inquirations'.[151] When Jordan moved to the woodlands of Surrey, one of the more easily accessible counties for the London-based investigator of rural life, he found himself on the wrong end of the 'passion for inquiry', and explained in 1893 that he had little sympathy for the fleeting investigator:

> Those who come into the country for a few weeks or months, as the case may be, to write on rural matters, go away little wiser than they came. If there is one thing these people dislike more than another, it is being questioned; and if the course is persisted in, strangers get told a good deal, but little that is useful. To one rash individual who tried to interview me I gave valuable information, which if published would outdo Baron Munchausen. Brain-suckers are out in force just now, and our villages and rural population get too much written about.[152]

---

[148] Stone to Haggard, n.d., Rider Haggard papers, MS 4692/25 (Hunts.). See also Freeman, 'Social investigation', 291–2.
[149] Graham, *Revival*, 14–17.
[150] Millin, *Life in our villages*, 75.
[151] 'A son of the marshes', *Drift from longshore*, ed. J. A. Owen, London 1898, 183.
[152] 'A son of the marshes', *With the woodlanders and by the tide*, ed. J. A. Owen, London 1893, 30.

Jordan, in the tradition of the resident investigators such as Augustus Jessopp and Richard Jefferies, emphasised the long process of social and cultural assimilation that was required before the outsider, even a working-class outsider like himself, could speak with authority on behalf of another class. As Anderson Graham admitted, 'it is an exceptional man of any class who can see from the point of view of another'.[153]

Moreover, the findings of these inquiries, even those superficially sympathetic to the labouring population and its grievances, resulted in the suggestion of imposed solutions to the problem of depopulation which did not necessarily accord with the priorities of those who were leaving the land. For example, investigators of depopulation – including Haggard[154] – often recommended that rural education should be more clearly directed towards specifically rural objectives, which would encourage village youth to appreciate the joys of the country life in which they participated; but this proposal entailed an educational agenda that was at variance with rural working-class notions of personal advancement. They did not want to acquire skills for agricultural employment, nor did they wish their children to be condemned to it. E. N. Bennett pointed out in 1913 that the adoption of a rural curriculum designed to foster a taste for agricultural labour (as Jesse Collings had proposed) entailed an assumption that rural children were predestined to a future as agricultural workers, and this would be a retrogressive step.[155] Many investigators realised that reversing depopulation artificially by settling townsmen on the land was not viable. Haggard himself, addressing an audience of Charity Organisation Society activists soon after completing his survey, read a letter from a London stevedore who had been set up on the land in Somerset by a charitable body, but who found himself ill-equipped for the work and the environment unpleasant:

> if I stop here I know I shall be dead . . . even the villagers tell us what a dreadful place we are in they say it is a shame to bring people from their comfortable london homes to bury their lives in a place like this . . . their is 9 months of winter here and when I told the villagers the farmer said he thought if we all come together I would get on better with my family round me they all laught they can see we was led in a trap. . . . I got to work harder than I did in london for 12 Shillings a week and my wife work twice as hard for five a sixpence a week and their is no rest at all . . . my wife says that if there was a shop she would sell her home off and go strait into the workhouse in london rather than stay here.[156]

153 Graham, *Rural exodus*, 15.
154 H. Rider Haggard, 'Agriculture and the unemployed question: an address', in Loch, *Methods of social advance*, 68.
155 E. N. Bennett, *Problems of village life*, London 1914, 99–101.
156 Quoted in Haggard, 'Agriculture and the unemployed question', 72n. (spelling exactly as in original).

Haggard adduced this as evidence that 'useless and unfit persons' should not be sent into the countryside;[157] but it also suggests that the descriptions by Haggard and others of the unenviability of the position of the casual labourer in towns compared with that of the agricultural worker did not necessarily match the experience of those about whom they wrote. If 'even the villagers' thought their Somerset home 'a dreadful place', it suggests that any attempt to make rural life seem attractive to more than a small minority was doomed to failure. Similarly, C. Deane of Horncastle wrote to Haggard in 1901, having read his account of depopulation in Lincolnshire in the *Stamford Mercury*, presenting 'another side of the question' of smallholdings: his father, aged sixty-nine, had been unable to pay the rent on the small farm that had been in the family for thirty-nine years, and now had 'nothing but the Work House before him', while Deane himself, together with his wife and seven children, was homeless.[158]

Most of these inquiries were reactions to depopulation, and few made any significant policy recommendations. The findings of the special correspondent journalists could be reduced either to the argument that labourers left the land because of the tyranny of parson and squire (of which low wages, poor housing and limited social opportunities were a by-product), or to the assertion that parson, landowner and farmer were doing their best in trying circumstances for an ungrateful body of labourers who rarely appreciated the advantages of country life until they had experienced, and been disappointed by, life in a large town. Neither approach really advanced the prospects of reform; indeed, realistically, reform seemed hardly possible. Haggard, although he suggested some minor changes which he hoped would improve the position of agriculture as an industry, despaired of a solution, deciding that English agriculture was 'fighting against the Mills of God'.[159] He was unwilling to campaign explicitly for tariff reform – which was to force its way onto the Conservative agenda within two years of his tour – although he recorded privately his maxim 'protect or perish!'[160] Beyond protection, which he rejected as a 'chimera', he could propose little: beyond a general endorsement of improved access to allotments and smallholdings, his most significant suggestion was the establishment of an agricultural post under a strengthened ministry of agriculture to improve supply to domestic markets and help to counter the effects of foreign competition.[161] (Even these limited proposals attracted hostility from some sections of the Conservative press, notably the *Quarterly Review*, which regretted the level of government intervention that they entailed.)[162] Returning to the depopulation theme in 1905,

---

157 Ibid. 72.
158 Deane to Haggard, 6 Sept. 1901, Rider Haggard papers, MS 4692/25 (Lincs.)
159 Ibid. MS 4692/24A, p. 63; Haggard, *Rural England*, ii. 536.
160 Rider Haggard papers, MS 4692/24A, p. 29.
161 Haggard, *Rural England*, ii. 566–8.
162 Peter Berresford Ellis, H. *Rider Haggard: a voice from the infinite*, London 1978, 162–3.

Haggard carried out an inquiry under the auspices of the Colonial Office, during which he visited labour colonies in the USA and the Salvation Army's colony at Hadleigh in Essex. Having interviewed 'General' Booth for the 1901 investigation, and finding himself attracted to the Salvation Army's plans 'to get this [urban] riff-raff, and take them back to the land',[163] he was impressed with the work of these schemes, but still held out little hope for 'the scum and dregs of our city race', who were beyond any sort of redemption save that offered by charity and the workhouse.[164] There was more hope for their children, who might be resettled on the depopulated land of England or in the virgin lands of the colonies. Yet in 1912 Haggard lamented the failure of successive governments to take account of either his specific proposals or his more general plea for greater consideration to be given to the countryside: 'I suppose it will go on – the devouring cities growing more and more bloated, and the starved land becoming more and more empty.'[165]

The principal result of the 'national efficiency' panic with which depopulation was associated was the appointment of the Interdepartmental Committee on Physical Deterioration, whose report in 1904 was primarily concerned with 'deterioration' in its urban context, but gives some indications of the rural side of the problem. The committee did not endorse the more hysterical fears of progressive deterioration that the second Boer war had brought to the forefront of political debate, but it recognised that there was much to deplore in the condition of the urban masses. As far as rural areas were concerned, it reported that not only was depopulation taking place, but that in the opinion of some observers there was a parallel exodus of the 'debilitated' urban population back into the villages.[166] The dangers posed by this unwanted repopulation suggested that the enforced removal of the urban 'residuum' to a rural environment was not a viable option. Already, the committee heard from the trustworthy professional men who formed the bulk of its informants, those who remained on the land were the worst specimens of the race: G. H. Fosbroke, medical officer of health to Worcestershire County Council, believed that the worst class of labourers remained on the land and bred an even worse class of children,[167] and H. J. Wilson, HM Inspector of Factories in Newcastle-upon-Tyne told its members that 'cripples and imbeciles, and that sort of people, are left about country villages'.[168] As

---

[163] Haggard, *Rural England*, i. 498.
[164] Idem, *Poor and the land*, p. xxv.
[165] Idem, *Days*, ii. 203. The book was written in 1912, but not published until after Haggard's death.
[166] *Report of the Interdepartmental Committee on Physical Deterioration*, 34.
[167] *Interdepartmental Committee on Physical Deterioration: minutes of evidence*, PP 1904, Cd. 2210, 263.
[168] Ibid. 84.

Wilson and other authorities consulted by the committee recognised, however, the evidence to support these claims was only impressionistic, and was not supported by any anthropometric data or scientific evidence.[169] Fosbroke also had to admit that his evidence was based only on impressions and on the complaints of farmers;[170] and more systematic inquiry was required to ascertain whether the complaints had any factual basis.

Nevertheless, the view gained wide currency, and persisted through the Edwardian period. For example, the self-educated countryman Alfred Williams, the 'hammerman-poet', who travelled each day from his Wiltshire village to work at his skilled trade in the Great Western Railway works at Swindon, noticed that only the 'feeble and decrepit' still worked in agriculture in the vicinity, as higher wages and better opportunities were available through industrial employment.[171] Others related these economic (and arguably racial) developments to cultural decline: in *The condition of England* (1909) C. F. G. Masterman lamented the 'vanishing life' of the countryside, the end of 'a life which had once stood for the bedrock life of England', and 'the silence that broods over a doomed and departing race'.[172] The late Victorian realisation that '[t]he countryside which many sought to offer as a refuge from the problems of the city was itself in manifest difficulties',[173] and the reassessment of English ruralism that this provoked, resulted in a great diversity of schemes of reform designed to reinvigorate a rural life whose problems could no longer be ignored. In the Edwardian years groups across the political spectrum formulated their land reform plans, including the Independent Labour Party, Keir Hardie pleading in 1904 for 'one harmonious combined attempt to re-people the deserted idle land of England with an industrious peasant class'.[174] Behind this spirit of reform lay a conception of the English countryside, rooted in a selective historical diagnosis of its problems, that emphasised the permanence of the countryman and his environment in contrast to the transience of urban culture, a diagnosis rooted in the 'discovery' of rural England that had been proceeding apace since the 1880s. The fullest political consequences of the diverse schemes of reform, however, were not to be seen in the 1890s; and even in the 1900s little was done legislatively, beyond minor adjustments to smallholding and housing legislation, to attempt to reverse the tide of internal migration. Indeed, the absolute numbers resident in rural districts in England and Wales rose slightly in the first decade of the twentieth century (although as a proportion of the total

---

169 Ibid. 84–5, 439.
170 Ibid. 263.
171 Alfred Williams, *Life in a railway factory*, London 1915, 296.
172 C. F. G. Masterman, *The condition of England*, London 1909, 195, 199, 201.
173 Simon Dentith, *Society and cultural forms in nineteenth-century England*, Basingstoke 1998, 98.
174 J. Keir Hardie, *The unemployed problem, with some suggestions for solving it*, London 1904, 10.

population they fell from 28 per cent in 1891 to 21.9 per cent in 1911), as did the numbers employed in agriculture; and by this time social investigators, although still concerned with depopulation, had begun to focus on a variety of other matters.

The information transmitted by the social investigators examined in this chapter was all open to contestation. The agendas of the different investigators shaped the way they carried out their inquiries, but even where these agendas were specifically acknowledged and the methodology unashamedly adopted accordingly, the basis of the approach taken could be challenged. If Haggard relied primarily on the testimony of farmers, a correspondent could retort that 'the farmer is a confirmed grumbler [and] I never believe a word he says';[175] if Millin based his inquiry on what the labourers told him, he could be accused of unjustly assuming that 'the labourers are always in the right and the gentry always in the wrong'.[176] The investigator whose approach lay somewhere in between these two extremes and who reflected more than most on his methodology, like Anderson Graham, could find himself perplexed by the difficulties of lifting the often politically constructed veil of misinformation that seemed to hide what should have been simple truths about rural labouring life. Naturally, these truths were not so simple as was suggested, and indeed any attempt to make meaningful generalisations about rural life was frustrated by the great regional disparities in both the material condition and the cultural and aspirational lives of agricultural labourers. Certainly the mere creation of an apparently detached machinery for investigation, as attempted by the labour commissioners and by Rider Haggard, did not prevent fierce contestation from other quarters. Perhaps the best that could be said for the project of investigating depopulation, as manifested in the various methods of inquiry that were brought to bear on it, was to express the hope, as Arthur Cooper did, that 'truth is struck out from the clash of conflicting opinions'.[177] It is difficult, however, to draw from most of these inquiries any sense of a middle way, and the clearest conclusion that emerges from reading them is that agreement even on the character and extent of the problem, let alone the possible remedies, was found almost impossible. Only the very localised study could not be directly challenged with contradictory evidence, and, as both Roger Richards and Tom Stone found, even the reporting of localised information was potentially contestable and could reverberate back onto the community from which it was obtained. If nothing could be agreed, little could be done; and in this period not much was done to arrest or reverse the steady depopulation of England's rural areas. To frame an investigation which could yield uncontestable results and provide the basis

[175] Murray to Haggard, 17 Apr. 1901, Rider Haggard papers, MS 4692/25 (counties unvisited).
[176] Cooper, *Our villages*, 6.
[177] Ibid. 5.

for a legislative reappraisal of the situation, a different approach was required, one which brought 'scientific' inquiry to bear on rural communities and sought to arrive at incontrovertible conclusions. Such inquiries are the subject of the next chapter.

4

Poverty Surveys and the English Countryside

The desire for accurate knowledge about rural life upon which reforms could be based paralleled the need in urban areas which the social surveys of Charles Booth and later Seebohm Rowntree and Arthur Bowley appeared to meet.[1] Booth and Rowntree in particular are usually credited, to a greater or lesser extent, with defining poverty as an economic concept and bringing new methods of inquiry to bear upon it. This chapter examines the activities of Booth and Rowntree in rural areas, which are usually overshadowed by their better known urban surveys; and also analyses the poverty surveys that were carried out in rural areas in the 1900s under the influence of Rowntree's survey of York, which essentially involved the application of concepts and methods derived from urban social surveys to the investigation of rural social problems. Although the rural community was a different theatre of inquiry from the town or city, most of the methods used in urban surveys could be applied with some modifications; however, the cultural constraints that operated on social investigators of rural life could not wholly be removed simply through the adoption of a 'scientific' methodology. Poverty, defined for the purposes of the social survey in economic terms, was not understood in a value-free context, and in its rural manifestations it was overlaid by constructions of rural England that drew on a long tradition of pastoralism, built upon by the complex discourses that had emerged since 1872. The methodological issues that investigators had become more aware of in the 1870s, and contested sometimes very bitterly in their inquiries into depopulation in the 1890s, did not vanish with the arrival of the social survey. Indeed, even within the distributional social survey as carried out by Booth and Rowntree, the differences between the informant and respondent methods bore a significance that arguably compromised the detachment that sociological objectivity was supposed to entail. Thus while Catherine Marsh has seen Booth's London survey as an epitome of the informant method of inquiry and Rowntree's *Poverty: a study of town life* (1901) as an important milestone in the transition to respondent investigation,[2] the social survey as carried out in rural England presents a more complex picture of the interplay between the

---

1   Booth, *Life and labour*; B. Seebohm Rowntree, *Poverty: a study of town life* (1st edn 1901), London 1902; A. L. Bowley and A. R. Burnett-Hurst, *Livelihood and poverty: a study in the economic conditions of working-class households in Northampton, Warrington, Stanley and Reading*, London 1915; A. L. Bowley and M. H. Hogg, *Has poverty diminished? A sequel to Livelihood and poverty*, London 1925.
2   Marsh, 'Informants', 215–17.

two methods. This complexity in turn translated into contested definitions and interpretations of rural poverty.

Furthermore, the surveys described in this chapter were clearly and at times explicitly associated with the 'very distinctive moral assumptions' that lay behind Edwardian social legislation.[3] Historians have very effectively questioned Charles Booth's claims to empirical rigour in his London survey, showing how his careful inquiries were methodologically and conceptually underpinned by conventional Victorian assumptions about personal morality; and how at the same time he exhibited an arguably naïve obsession with the collection of 'social facts', without applying (or even acquiring) the statistical techniques that might facilitate a more sophisticated analysis of such material.[4] Although large-scale aggregative social investigation, for Booth, was a means of gathering information to inform social action, the policies he advocated were often based on the 'individualistic' principles of the poor law and the Charity Organisation Society, and the maintenance of rigid distinctions between the 'deserving' and 'undeserving' poor. Thus while he supported the provision of old-age pensions, at the same time he proposed that a substantial proportion of the population of London should be removed to rural labour colonies, where they were not in danger of competing economically with, and morally corrupting, the 'respectable' poor.[5] John Brown, who has described Booth's attitudes to the labour colony, has to some extent exonerated Rowntree from being tarred with the same brush, arguing that the latter 'consciously tried to avoid any unfavourable judgement of those living in poverty';[6] but Rowntree's claims to objectivity have also been effectively challenged by a number of historians. Arguably, by separating poverty into two – poverty caused by insufficient income, and poverty caused by uneconomical application of income – Rowntree perpetuated Victorian moral distinctions between different sections of the poor.[7] In fact, an examination of two of Rowntree's inquiries to which Brown does not refer demonstrates at least a flirtation with the idea of the labour colony;[8] and Rowntree and his rural imitators can also be shown to have entered upon their

3   Brown, 'Charles Booth and labour colonies', 350.
4   Ibid; E. P. Hennock, 'Poverty and social theory in England: the experience of the eighteen-eighties', Social History i (1976), 67–91; Jane Lewis, 'Social facts, social theory and social change: the ideas of Booth in relation to those of Beatrice Webb, Octavia Hill and Helen Bosanquet', in Englander and O'Day, Retrieved riches, 49–66; Harris, 'Between civic virtue and social Darwinism'; Hanan C. Selvin, 'Durkheim, Booth and Yule: the non-diffusion of an intellectual innovation', Archives européennes de sociologie xvii (1976), 39–51.
5   Brown, 'Charles Booth and labour colonies'; Lewis, 'Social facts', 50, 61 and passim.
6   Brown, 'Charles Booth and labour colonies', 352.
7   For example, Karel Williams, From pauperism to poverty, London 1981, 345–68; cf. J. H. Veit-Wilson, 'Paradigms of poverty: a rehabilitation of B. S. Rowntree', Journal of Social Policy xv (1986), 69–99 (repr. in Englander and O'Day, Retrieved riches, 201–37).
8   Rowntree, Land and labour, 490–2, 510; B. Seebohm Rowntree and Bruno Lasker, Unemployment: a social study, London 1911, 199.

researches with a set of moral and cultural assumptions that, to the historian, clearly compromise their claims to 'scientific' objectivity. Some of these assumptions were specifically associated with the rural locations of the inquiries, and will be examined in particular detail in this chapter.

The publication, from 1887 onwards, of Charles Booth's seventeen-volume survey of *Life and labour of the people in London* was an undoubted milestone in the history of social investigation. It in fact consisted of three separate surveys – of 'poverty', 'industry' and 'religious influences' – each of which was further subdivided into several parts. The importance of Booth's study, especially the poverty survey, has been reiterated by historians and sociologists,[9] and Booth undoubtedly made some significant advances in methods of social research. In particular, his poverty survey was presented as a scientific response to the proliferation of haphazard and impressionistic accounts of metropolitan distress, and appeared to contemporaries to set new standards for the quantitative investigation of social problems. Nevertheless, Booth's strategy, which involved interviewing school attendance officers about the condition of the families over whom they were employed to watch, and classifying the population accordingly into groups defined either by lifestyle or by income bracket, still relied ultimately on impressionistic evidence gathered at second hand. David Englander, in an examination of Booth's notebooks, has shown that Booth's metropolitan informant base, especially in the industry series of *Life and labour*, was socially more eclectic than historians who are acquainted only with the printed volumes of the survey have tended to acknowledge;[10] however, the bulk of the informants for the poverty inquiry were school attendance officers, and as such brought to the inquiry the preconceptions of a group whose dealings with the urban working classes were official and, in some respects, resented.[11] In any case, when he turned his attention to rural theatres of inquiry, Booth insisted on the adoption of an informant method of inquiry. Thus in 1891 he advised Herbert Samuel (who was himself considering carrying out a rural survey) to 'consult existing local authorities such as schoolmasters, rate collectors, postmasters, relieving officers, the clergy (Church and Dissent), and the doctors, and only to supplement and enliven the information from such sources with what the inquirer himself sees and hears from the people themselves'.[12]

When Booth investigated rural life himself he relied on an even more restricted set of informants. In the early 1890s he carried out a study of

9   See, for example, Simey and Simey, *Charles Booth*; O'Day and Englander, *Mr Charles Booth's inquiry*; Englander and O'Day, *Retrieved riches*.

10 Englander, 'Comparisons and contrasts', 126–7, 132–3.

11 For a discussion of the role of school attendance officers (or 'School Board Visitors') see Kevin Bales, 'Charles Booth's survey of *Life and labour of the people in London* 1889–1903', in Bulmer and others, *The social survey*, 66–110, esp. pp. 83–9.

12 Booth to Samuel, 10 Nov. 1891, Herbert Samuel papers, House of Lords Record Office, A/155 I/10, also quoted in Gertrude Himmelfarb, *Poverty and compassion: the moral imagination of the late Victorians*, New York 1991, 98n.

old-age pauperism and poverty, which had a special focus on the rural dimension. Like his London survey, it was a team effort: he installed a small staff in an office at the headquarters of the Royal Statistical Society.[13] Collaboration was unavoidable: Booth had many other commitments, and for much of the period was out of the country recovering from illness. His attention was never fully given over to this investigation, and he was glad when its completion gave him time to return to his work on the industry series of *Life and labour*.[14] Booth's role in the rural inquiry was two-fold: to write up the results – which he published as *The aged poor in England and Wales* in 1894, while he was serving on the Royal Commission on the Aged Poor – and to supply the funds.[15] He also appears to have been able to use his influence to gain access to certain important sources of evidence. The study grew out of a controversial paper presented by Booth to the Royal Statistical Society in 1891, in which he advocated the provision of old-age pensions.[16] It was overseen by Arthur Acland, whom Booth credited with its suggestion and inception;[17] and Booth was assisted by the Liberal journalist J. A. Spender, twice a resident of Toynbee Hall, whose book on *The state and pensions in old age*, published in Swan Sonnenschein's *Social Science* series in 1892, was a progress report on the investigation.[18]

The inquiry was divided into two parts: a general survey of the condition of the aged poor in urban and rural districts, and a special study of the rural aspects of the problem. The general survey used information 'supplied chiefly, though not exclusively' by the clergy.[19] The informants were asked to fill in a questionnaire, in order that the information received might be standardised and tabulated. Replies were received from 360 of the 648 poor law unions in England and Wales. The coverage was weakest in large towns, where the clergy had a less intimate knowledge of the circumstances of their aged parishioners, and this shortfall was partly made up by information supplied by members of the Charity Organisation Society.[20] The second study was carried out by Booth and Spender with the assistance of Miss Mary C. Tabor of Boston in Lincolnshire (who had worked on the poverty series of *Life and*

[13] [Mary Booth], *Charles Booth: a memoir*, London 1918, 141–54.

[14] Booth to Alfred Marshall, 25 May 1894, Charles Booth papers, University of London Library, MS 797 I/1352.

[15] J. A. Spender remembered that Booth 'subscribed handsomely to the expenses': *Men and things*, London 1937, 63.

[16] Charles Booth, 'Enumeration and classification of paupers, and state pensions for the aged', *Journal of the Royal Statistical Society* liv (1891), 600–43.

[17] Idem, *Aged poor*, 335.

[18] The book also described pension provision in Germany, France, Denmark and Italy.

[19] Booth, *Aged poor*, 106.

[20] Booth also specifically thanked Henry Marton of Birmingham and Frederick Scott of Manchester, who was an active member of the Manchester Statistical Society and carried out a poverty survey (prompted by Booth's work on London) in Manchester in 1889: ibid.

labour)[21] and Miss H. G. Pearce. They consulted the bishop in each Church of England diocese, through whom the incumbents of various rural parishes were contacted. The clergy who assisted with this survey had more detailed work to do than did those who helped with the first; and their role was comparable to that of the school attendance officers who provided the essential information on individual households for the poverty series of *Life and labour*. The clergy were asked to provide, as far as possible, answers to a series of questions about each person over the age of sixty-five in their parish (*see* appendix). Altogether returns were received from 262 parishes representing 231 different unions, and data obtained for 9,125 people. Of particular interest, as the questions make clear, and unsurprisingly given that the object of the study was to investigate the case for old-age pensions, was the old people's means of financial support. Booth dealt with the information statistically, as had been clearly envisaged in the framing of the questionnaire, but the statistical summary of the returns was supplemented by the presentation of more detailed information about ten parishes from across the country.

The involvement of the clergy is illustrative of an important difference between the investigation of town and country as Booth envisaged it. In studying the metropolitan aged poor, Booth's investigators had access to the records kept by the Tower Hamlets Pension Committee, which provided weekly pensions to the 'deserving' poor of Whitechapel and Stepney. These cases, which had themselves been investigated by members of the COS, were supplemented by others derived from COS records. Such information was not readily available for rural districts, where COS informants could not be drawn upon: Spender's interim report contained only brief descriptions of rural cases, communicated by unidentified correspondents. This reinforced the importance of the country parson, in the absence of the alternative, supposedly unbiased sources of information that were available in urban districts. Moreover, there was an ideological dimension to the use of parsons as informants in rural areas: whereas the COS could deal with only a limited number of cases of urban destitution and poverty, the country parson (in theory) could know all the cases of old-age poverty and pauperism in his parish in some depth, and supply a reliable picture of the social conditions in his district. With this intensive knowledge, he was also in a position to bestow charity more efficiently. Booth repeatedly emphasised the neighbourliness of rural life, which obviated the need for large-scale organised charity;[22] and argued that it was easier to obtain the sort of detailed information that he required in the countryside:

> There is a natural and very broad distinction between urban and rural districts in regard to the conditions of life in old age, and in seeking to understand the

21 Kevin Bales, 'Lives and labours in the emergence of organised social research, 1886–1907', *Journal of Historical Sociology* ix (1996), 116, 134.
22 Booth, *Aged poor*, 47, 329, 357.

facts, different methods of inquiry come into play. In small country parishes everyone is known by reputation as well as by sight, and the old especially are familiar figures, whose lives, as seen by those who dwell among them, involve comparatively few unknown quantities.[23]

This conception of social relations in the countryside probably overstated the sense of community that existed in all but the most Arcadian villages, but it does stress the more manageable scale of the rural community for the social investigator. Other investigators had noted this: Charles William Stubbs had commented on the difference in size between his Sheffield parish of 20,000 or more inhabitants and his rural Buckinghamshire parish of 350;[24] and Arthur Cooper remarked that after twenty years living in London he had never received a pastoral visit from his local clergyman, and contrasted this with the social involvement of the country parson.[25] These examples emphasise at least the potential for the country parson to know his flock. Nevertheless, it is questionable how far Booth's informants were likely to be given access to such information as the aged poor's sources of income. The poor had a clear interest in presenting as low a figure as realistically possible in order to maximise their chances of securing charity, in the administration of which the parson was usually in some way involved. Indeed, some of Booth's correspondents recognised this: one noted that '[c]hildren, &c., contribute more than is supposed – but amount will be concealed as long as Guardians help destitute only',[26] while another despaired that '[t]hose who have saved money are reticent about it, lest charity should be affected'.[27]

The parson, however, was seen as a reliable witness, and one able to make moral judgements on the poor in his midst as well as to detail their financial circumstances. Like the school attendance officer in London, he supposedly knew working-class families well enough to enable an informant method of inquiry to be used. Booth, despite his metropolitan eclecticism, preferred the use of elite informants to gain access to information about rural working-class conditions. Thus the methods adopted in the rural survey were akin to the 'wholesale' methods of the *Life and labour* survey as characterised by Beatrice Webb. She argued that, while each individual came to the interview with his own biases and prejudices, the consultation of a large group would enable these biases to be cancelled out.[28] However, whereas in the London survey the groups consulted formed a relatively wide cross-section of middle-class opinion, the rural sample was almost wholly confined to the clergy. Thus, while Booth was justified in pointing to the consistency of opinion among his

[23] Ibid. 335.
[24] Stubbs, *Mythe of life*, 5.
[25] Cooper, *Our villages*, 19.
[26] Booth, *Aged poor*, 167.
[27] Ibid. 161.
[28] Webb, *My apprenticeship*, 236–40; Beatrice Webb and Sidney Webb, *Methods of social study*, London 1932, 207–8.

informants once the inevitable biases were discounted,[29] the informants themselves were drawn from a narrow social group, and necessarily reflected the general outlook of that group. Booth's surveys, urban and rural, were representative of a desire for exact quantitative information about social conditions: as Spender remembered of his generation as they lived through the 1890s, 'we grovelled in the concrete . . . we wanted to know the facts'.[30] Yet however carefully gathered, these facts were representative of the stand-point of a limited sector of rural society, and in their presentation were over-laid by a conception of country life that even the most ostensibly scientific investigator was unable wholly to abandon.

While Booth was conducting his inquiry, Joseph Ashby and Bolton King were carrying out a survey of sixty-nine parishes in South Warwickshire, which entailed a partial reconciliation of informant and respondent methods of inquiry. The two main articles resulting from this inquiry, which appeared in the *Economic Journal* in 1893,[31] were, according to Wilhelm Hasbach, a historian of the English rural labourer, 'more trustworthy as regards their facts and [went] deeper as regards their science than the majority of contemporary publications on the agricultural labour problem'.[32] King, a product of Balliol and Toynbee Hall, was secretary of the Mansion House Committee on the Unemployed and a member of the committee of the Agricultural Banks Asso-ciation (founded in 1893), and conducted experiments in cooperative farming in the Midlands. He was a member of the developing community of social investigators schooled under the 'consciousness of sin' of the 1880s which saw in dispassionate inquiry a basis for effective social reform.[33] Ashby, by contrast, was from a labouring background, and was by this time a surveyor and a freelance journalist. The different backgrounds from which the two men came gave them access to different, but complementary, sources of infor-mation: King used his contacts among the clergy and magistracy, while Ashby visited labourers' households and gathered information on domestic budgeting at first hand. In one respect, at least, Ashby was probably unique among social investigators of the period: he had his own allotment, the balance sheets from which were presented in the articles.[34] Carried out during the depopulation panic of the 1890s, the focus of the survey was on allotments, the main conclusion being that they made an important contri-bution to the family economy and were therefore 'the most effective check on migration'.[35] Ashby and King were conscious of a need for impartial investi-gation of social conditions and the procurement of facts in order to 'make

---

29 Booth, *Aged poor*, 107.
30 Spender, *Men and things*, 61.
31 Joseph Ashby and Bolton King, 'Statistics of some midland villages: I', and 'Statistics of some midland villages: II', *Economic Journal* iii (1893), 1–22, 193–204.
32 Hasbach, *History*, 322.
33 Webb, *My apprenticeship*, 191–3.
34 Ashby and King, 'Statistics: I', 14.
35 Ashby and King, 'Statistics: II', 198.

ill-informed talk an anachronism'.[36] They presented what they called 'careful inquiries',[37] and Ashby's more impressionistic gleanings from the research were relegated to a series of articles in the Warwickshire press.[38] The articles presented detailed quantitative information in the form of balance sheets and tables of statistics, claiming a scientific authority that was denied to other social investigators. Nevertheless, they still found space for reflection on moral issues. For Ashby and King, the allotment, as well as being a valuable material resource, was a source of 'stability and self-respect', had 'stimulated the labourer's observation and inventiveness' and helped to keep villagers away from the public house.[39] Partly as a result of the spread of allotment provision, the extent of drunkenness had declined significantly; at the same time village wakes were 'no longer the orgies they used to be, though the statute fairs still have a bad repute'.[40] Despite their desire to distance themselves from unsystematically acquired preconceptions about rural social conditions, rooting social diagnosis in objective and unbiased facts was not the unproblematic activity they assumed it to be.

Nevertheless, the coming of the poverty survey, characterised by strictly defined 'poverty lines' based on systematic research and resting on accurate information about household incomes, appeared to herald the possibility of an objective approach to investigating the conditions of the working classes of both town and country. Seebohm Rowntree's York study in particular had supplied much information that was at that time unavailable for rural districts. Rowntree, employing various methods of fact-gathering, ascertained the economic circumstances of every working-class household in York. He sent to each house an investigator, who obtained occupational and other information, and who decided, on the basis of the appearance of the household and the opinions of neighbours, whether that household was in poverty. By this method 27.84 per cent of the population was shown to be living in a condition of poverty. In addition, Rowntree drew a distinction between 'primary' and 'secondary' poverty. Primary poverty was defined as a condition in which household income was not sufficient for the maintenance of physical efficiency, and was measured by establishing a poverty line and including in the category all those whose incomes fell below it, having obtained information on earnings from local employers. Secondary poverty was a condition in which household income would have been sufficient for the maintenance of physical efficiency but for some non-essential expenditure. The extent of secondary poverty was calculated by subtracting the numbers in primary poverty from those living in poverty. Using these methods Rowntree demon-

---

[36] M. K. Ashby, *Joseph Ashby of Tysoe, 1859–1919: a study of English village life*, Cambridge 1961, 145.
[37] Ashby and King, 'Statistics: I', 1.
[38] Ashby, *Joseph Ashby*, 149–51.
[39] Ashby and King, 'Statistics: I', 18.
[40] Ibid. 20.

strated that 9.91 per cent of the population of York lived in primary poverty and 17.93 per cent in secondary poverty (*see* table 2). Rowntree also divided the population into classes, following Booth's attempts to classify the London population by income and lifestyle; and supplemented his survey with information on the physique of the population, an analysis of a selection of York family budgets and information on public houses, schools, churches, friendly societies and poor relief. He also attempted to enumerate the immediate causes of poverty in York, finding, significantly, that over half of all the city's primary poverty was caused by low wages. The largest single cause of secondary poverty, he thought, was expenditure on drink, but no specific inquiry was made on this point. Although information on the earnings of the chief wage-earner in each household was obtained from employers (or, if unobtainable, then estimated), Rowntree's use of the house-to-house survey and his reliance at many points on information supplied at first hand by the subjects of inquiry represented a shift in the dominant methodology of the social survey. Or, to put it another way, although the information supplied by householders was supplemented by additional evidence from 'voluntary workers, "district visitors", clergymen, and others',[41] the household inquiry appeared to mark a move away from the 'wholesale' interviewing of Booth's survey and towards 'retail' interviewing.[42] Although the reliability and originality of Rowntree's methods, the validity of his conclusions and the impact of his findings have been continually debated by historians, sociologists and social policy-makers,[43] it is clear that his survey was one of the most significant pieces of social research carried out in the period, one which spawned many imitators and generated much contemporaneous debate.

Although interested in rural problems in Britain and abroad, Rowntree never attempted to replicate his York study on a rural community. This was partly because of an awareness that no rural community could necessarily be taken as typical of conditions across England (let alone Britain) as a whole; by contrast, Rowntree had been able to argue (albeit somewhat unconvincingly) that York was a typical provincial town and that his findings there might be expected to apply elsewhere.[44] Thus when Rowntree and May Kendall turned their attention to the problems of rural England, they presented forty-two domestic budgets from various parts of the country,[45] including both high- and low-wage districts, accompanying each with a

---

41 Rowntree, *Poverty*, 14.
42 Bulmer and others, *The social survey*, 22.
43 For recent examples see Jonathan Bradshaw and Roy Sainsbury (eds), *Getting the measure of poverty: the early legacy of Seebohm Rowntree*, Aldershot 2000; Veit-Wilson, 'Paradigms'; Alan Gillie, 'The origin of the poverty line', *Economic History Review* 2nd ser. xlix (1996), 715–30; Hennock, 'Concepts'.
44 Hennock, 'Measurement', 213–14.
45 10 were from Oxfordshire, 8 from Essex, 4 from Berkshire, 1 from Bedfordshire, 4 from Leicestershire and 15 from Yorkshire, of which 9 were from the North Riding, 4 from the East Riding and 2 from the West Riding.

detailed description of the household and its circumstances. Rowntree had used the analysis of budgets to supplement the broad picture supplied by his York survey, but the budgets themselves formed the bulk of the text of *How the labourer lives*, published in 1913. They were accompanied by a commentary, derived from 'some hundreds of visits to labourers' homes in many parts of the country',[46] on 'The labourer's outlook', which was necessarily impressionistic and based only on very thin statistical generalisations. They did include, for what it was worth, a statistical summary of the forty-two budgets, but this clearly could not be employed in making any meaningful generalisations. This is not to say that the study was not scientific in aim: each budget was analysed in terms of the deficiency of calories and proteins consumed by the household, and very precise figures were arrived at, which showed that every investigated household bar one fell below what Rowntree considered the 'standard requirement' of either proteins, calories or (usually) both.[47] But it appeared that conditions in rural communities were inappropriate to the kind of income-based poverty survey that Rowntree had carried out in York. As Charles Booth told the Interdepartmental Committee on Physical Deterioration in 1904, '[c]ountry conditions are very different, both as to the way in which they try to live and as to the extra chances they have in garden produce, and so on. I am not able to give you a comparison'.[48]

Two other investigators, however, did attempt to carry out a Rowntree-type survey of rural communities in the Edwardian period. Harold Mann surveyed the village of Ridgmount in Bedfordshire in 1903, publishing his results in the *Sociological Papers* for 1905; and Maud F. Davies investigated her home parish of Corsley in Wiltshire in 1905–6, the findings appearing as *Life in an English village* in 1909.[49] Mann, whom F. E. Green called the 'first independent investigator to present us with a carefully drawn picture of village life in the early years of the twentieth century',[50] was a Yorkshireman, born in 1872, who enjoyed a long career in agriculture, much of it spent in India. His background, like Rowntree's, was scientific:[51] his connection with Ridgmount was derived from a period working at the Woburn Experimental Station, and the survey was carried out during a period of leave from an appointment as Scientific Officer of the Indian Tea Association in Calcutta. He described himself as a 'man of science', and applied this to his social study:

---

46 Rowntree and Kendall, *How the labourer lives*, 6.
47 Ibid. table between pp. 36 and 37.
48 *Interdepartmental Committee on Physical Deterioration: minutes of evidence*, 54.
49 H. H. Mann, 'Life in an agricultural village in England', *Sociological Papers* i (1905), 163–93; Maude [sic] F. Davies, *Life in an English village: an economic and historical survey of the parish of Corsley in Wiltshire*, London 1909. The wording of this sentence is very deliberate: Mann's survey was of the *village*, Davies's of the whole *parish*. Davies's first name is spelt here as on the spine of the book, but elsewhere is spelt 'Maud', and that spelling has been followed in the text above.
50 Green, *History*, 153.
51 Briggs, *Seebohm Rowntree*, 9–10, 12.

Table 2
Proportion of households and proportion of the population in poverty, in York (1899), Ridgmount (1903) and Corsley (1905–6)

	Households		Persons	
	Number	Percentage	Number	Percentage
Primary Poverty				
York	1,465	[–]	7,230	9.91
Ridgmount	40	31.5	160	34.3
Corsley	28	(12.73)	144	[17.48]
Secondary Poverty				
York	[not given]	[–]	13,072	17.83
Ridgmount	10	(7.9)	33	7.1
Corsley	37	(16.82)	128	[15.53]
Total in Poverty				
York	[not given]	[–]	20,302	27.84
Ridgmount	50	(39.4)	193	41.4
Corsley	65	(29.55)	272	[33.01]

Sources: Rowntree, *Poverty*; Mann, 'Agricultural village'; Davies, *English village*.

Note: The figures in round brackets are not given in the texts, but have been calculated from information contained within them. The figures for Corsley in square brackets represent the proportion of the population in poverty assuming a population of 824, as recorded in the 1901 census. Mann gave his percentages to one decimal place only, which has been followed here. The number of households in poverty and secondary poverty are not given in Rowntree's York survey, and no attempt has been made here to estimate the proportion of households in primary poverty. In the first edition of *Poverty* (of which the 2000 edition edited by Jonathan Bradshaw is a facsimile), the table on p. 120 gives the figure of 1,463 households, an evident miscalculation, the correct figure of 1,465 being given on p. 111. Freeman, 'Investigating rural poverty', fig. 12.1, misleadingly gives only the percentage of households in poverty in Corsley, suggesting that the distribution of primary and secondary poverty was similar to that in York; the above calculations show this not to be the case.

reviewing Rowntree's *Land and labour: lessons from Belgium*, he argued that '[w]e shall never . . . get beyond vague generalizations with regard to the social and economic conditions of the people unless we face the problem and go and get the facts at first hand for ourselves'.[52] Having applied these principles to English village life, Mann went on to undertake surveys of social problems in India, most notably the housing and employment of the 'untouchable' classes.[53] Nevertheless, as Daniel Thorner has pointed out, his 'fame in

[52] H. H. Mann, *The social framework of agriculture: India, Middle East, England*, ed. Daniel Thorner, London 1967, 18.
[53] Idem, 'The untouchable classes of an Indian city', *Sociological Review* v (1912), 42–55.

agriculture and the natural sciences always overshadowed his remarkable achievements in the field of social study',[54] despite the eager endorsement of Patrick Geddes, Sidney Webb and other leading figures in the development of Edwardian social inquiry. Ridgmount, the site of his inquiry, was a 'closed' village, part of the duke of Bedford's estate, and an almost wholly agricultural community. The old industries of straw-plaiting and lacemaking had all but disappeared;[55] and as Peter Laslett has emphasised, '[n]ot so much as a loaf of bread was baked in the village; it all came in horse vans from the towns'.[56] Mann revealed levels of poverty even higher than those uncovered by Rowntree in York: 41.4 per cent of the population was living in poverty, of which 34.3 per cent was in primary and 7.1 per cent in secondary poverty (*see* table 2).

Maud Davies was a native of Corsley, her father being the local landowner, Bryan Martin Davies of Corsley House. She was a member of the London County Council's school care committee – she wrote a short book on the work of such committees[57] – and of the Fabian Women's Group.[58] She was also a registered Fabian lecturer, her specialities being 'Care of School-children. Rural Revival. Women in Local Government. Sweated Industries in the Rural Districts. Woman's [sic] Suffrage.'[59] Davies aligned herself clearly within the social-scientific mode of operation. Her survey was, according to a reviewer in the *Economic Journal*, 'a new departure in sociological investigation' but still 'typical of the aims of modern sociology, which endeavours above all things to get knowledge, and seeks to know before it attempts to reform'.[60] The inquiry was carried out under the auspices of the London School of Economics; and Sidney and Beatrice Webb advised her 'on how to investigate and where to look for possible sources of information'.[61] Their influence was reflected in the presentation of the study, which began with a long section on the history of the parish, concerned in particular with institutions such as the poor law. She gave detailed consideration to the enclosure movement and the proletarianisation of the agricultural workforce, a historical theme from which Davies was unable wholly to extricate herself in the name of detached scientific inquiry. Davies was also responsible for a brief study of married women's work in rural districts for the Women's Industrial

54 Daniel Thorner, 'Introduction', to Mann, *Social framework*, p. xix.
55 Mann, 'Agricultural village', 165, 173. See also *RC on Labour: assistant commissioners' reports*, i. 24.
56 Laslett, *World we have lost*, 217.
57 M. F. Davies, *School care committees: a guide to their work*, London 1909.
58 Cohen, 'Life and works of M. Loane', 22.
59 'Lecturer list of the Fabian Society' (1912), British Library of Political and Economic Science, Fabian Society archive, C62/1, fo. 177.
60 *Economic Journal* xx (1910), 610.
61 Davies, *English village*, p. vii.

Council,[62] published posthumously in 1915: she had committed suicide two years earlier.[63] Unlike Ridgmount, Corsley, as Dennis Mills has pointed out, exhibited a relatively broad occupational structure, and Davies pointed to the importance of secondary and supplementary incomes in her study.[64] Nevertheless, she showed that 29.55 per cent of the households of Corsley lived in poverty, of which 12.73 per cent were in primary and 16.82 per cent in secondary poverty (see table 2). She also showed that the number of individuals in primary poverty, 144, was higher than the number in secondary poverty, 128, and that the main causes of primary poverty were low wages and large families, between them even more predominant as a cause of poverty than in York and Ridgmount. As she did not give the exact population of Corsley, it is impossible to express these figures as percentages, but table 2 makes the closest possible comparison (based on the population of Corsley recorded at the census in 1901) between the figures obtained by Rowntree, Mann and Davies.

Neither Mann nor Davies followed Booth and Rowntree in dividing the population into classes based on lifestyle or income;[65] and neither was as explicit as Rowntree in their explanations of their methods of calculating primary, secondary and total poverty. Both based their primary poverty lines on Rowntree's, making small adjustments in the light of the rural locations of their surveys and the changes in prices that had occurred since Rowntree had carried out his survey in 1899. Davies, like Rowntree, arrived at a total poverty figure using impressionistic methods, ascertained the proportion of Corsley households in primary poverty using the poverty line and as accurate an assessment as possible of each household's earnings, and then subtracted this figure from the total in poverty to arrive at a figure for secondary poverty. She has one claim to conceptual and methodological innovation (although it did not diffuse to other inquiries): she included in her secondary poverty category those households with a margin of less than 1s. above the primary poverty line. Davies justified this on the grounds that the primary poverty line did not include such items as old-age and health insurance (of which the investigator could not in all fairness morally disapprove); but it can also be viewed as a tacit recognition of the impossibility of managing the household economy with the stringency implied by the primary poverty line.[66] Mann was vaguer than Davies about his methods, but he appears to have proceeded somewhat differently, by examining the circumstances of each household and deciding whether it was in primary poverty, secondary poverty or not in

---

62 M. F. Davies, 'Rural districts', in Clementina Black (ed.), Married women's work, being the report of an enquiry undertaken by the Women's Industrial Council, London 1915, 230–51.
63 The Times, 6 Feb. 1913, 8; 14 Feb. 1913, 3.
64 Dennis Mills, Lord and peasant in nineteenth-century Britain, London 1980, 54–60; Davies, English village, 124–30.
65 The reasons for this are explored in Freeman, 'Social investigation', 190–3.
66 Davies, English village, 145.

poverty at all, and then adding the first two figures together to obtain his total of those in poverty. Although Mann had little space in which to elaborate on the results of his investigation, Davies extended her inquiries into the history, the social life (including, like Rowntree, a survey of activity in public houses), and the moral character of the Corsley population; and both she and Mann employed Rowntree's concept of the poverty cycle to show how the majority of the people of Corsley and Ridgmount were likely to pass through a condition of primary poverty at some point during their lives.[67] Like Rowntree, Davies supplemented her survey with a more detailed analysis of a number of domestic budgets from families in varying circumstances in the parish.[68]

In all these surveys, the primary poverty figures rested on the reliability of the information obtained on household incomes. Rowntree's information on wages was obtained, as far as possible, from employers in York, but as he recognised, the adult male cash wage was not necessarily the only source of income in an urban household. Supplementary incomes, charitable gifts, poor relief and money sent home by absent children could all make an important contribution to household income, and Rowntree had enumerated these additional resources in York with as much precision as possible. In rural communities, however, there were additional practical problems associated with conducting an economic survey of this sort. Many rural households had irregular incomes; indeed, the widespread custom of harvest payments made irregularity of income general even for those regularly employed. Where the amount received at harvest was not known, Davies estimated it at £2 12s., equal to 1s. a week, while Mann estimated (or as he put it, 'calculated') such earnings at a maximum of 1s. 6d. a week.[69] Neither gave a good reason for these estimates. Both also found that a large range of additional earnings and resources, many of which were not generally available in towns, had to be taken into consideration in the calculation of household income; indeed Davies despaired that '[a]ny accurate analysis is rendered wellnigh impossible by the fact that in Corsley it the exception rather than the rule for each man to depend on one source of income alone'.[70] In Ridgmount, Mann considered ten different sources of non-wage income: money sent home by children; allotments; harvest money (or additional piece work); parochial charities; home industries; pigs and fowls; odd jobs; seasonal work at the Woburn experimental fruit farm; pensions; and poor relief.[71] Although Mann found no payments in kind surviving in Ridgmount (or, if he did, he ignored them), the practice lingered in Corsley, although Davies noted that those with a low

[67] Ibid. 149, 287; Mann, 'Agricultural village', 192.
[68] On these budgets see D. J. Oddy, 'Working-class diets in late nineteenth-century Britain', *Economic History Review* 2nd ser. xxiii (1970), 314–23.
[69] Mann, 'Agricultural village', 172.
[70] Davies, *English village*, 105.
[71] Mann, 'Agricultural village', 169–76.

cash wage also tended to receive little in kind.[72] As had been made clear by earlier investigators, the evaluation of perquisites, along with the assessment of the economic value of allotment and garden produce, were particularly challenging and contestable tasks.

Of the forty-two households whose budgets were analysed by Rowntree and Kendall in 1913, twenty-five received perquisites of one kind or another, and the families obtained an average of 4.3 per cent of their total protein consumption from perquisites and charitable gifts, the highest proportion being 17.7 per cent.[73] Non-cash resources, then, could be important elements in the working-class domestic economy; and their value had to be estimated. This was usually done by deciding on the value of a particular perquisite and adding this to the cash income of each household that received it. Davies, for example, estimated the free house and garden enjoyed by many labourers as worth 1s. 6d. a week, and free beer where given at 1s. a week.[74] These were, of course, necessarily arbitrary measures, and could not represent the real value of non-pecuniary income to the family. Beer, for example, quite apart from the moral questionability of supplying it at all, was consumed only by those working in the fields and could not really be considered a household resource. Free milk, received by a number of families in Corsley, was allotted its market value, 3d. per quart.[75] This was a fair measure, but an inaccurate reflection of family circumstances: if a free quart of milk were replaced by an extra 3d. on the wage, the money would probably not have been spent on a quart of milk. If nothing else, the milk supply in rural areas was often irregular at best: as the Royal Commission on Labour's senior assistant commissioner W. C. Little, commenting on Scotland, had asserted, '[w]ith regard to milk, which is a very usual allowance in kind, the substitution of money for that article would probably result in depriving the labourer's family of any opportunity of obtaining it'.[76] Valuing any of these perquisites necessarily involved processes of cultural judgement; and the techniques used were contestable. The self-consciously economic investigations in urban areas reduced poverty to a question of the adequacy of pecuniary income, and if this was a limited definition in an urban context, it was perhaps even more limited in a rural area.

The produce of gardens and allotments was also an important feature of the domestic economy of many rural labouring families. Rowntree had been able to dismiss the importance of allotments in his calculations of poverty in York, as there were only about 120 in the city, mostly kept by 'well-to-do working men', and had found the number keeping pigs and hens 'insignifi-

---

[72] Davies, *English village*, 118.
[73] Rowntree and Kendall, *How the labourer lives*, table between pp. 36 and 37. One household obtained 19.3 percent of its protein from charitable gifts, but this was a special case, as it was a family whose breadwinner boarded with his employer.
[74] Davies, *English village*, 115.
[75] Ibid. 116.
[76] *Fifth and final report of the RC on Labour*, 229–30.

cant',[77] but such considerations were far more important in the rural context. Rowntree and Kendall pointed out in 1913 that 'many labourers have gardens or allotments on which they can raise an important proportion of their total food requirements',[78] implying that such produce might raise a family above the poverty line. Eleven of the forty-two households in their sample had allotments, and two had a share of common land. A majority obtained some of their food from gardens or allotments, and in one case 23 per cent of the total protein consumed came from home produce.[79] The average figure for the forty-two households was 7.5 per cent of protein consumed. Yet it was difficult, if not impossible, to translate information of this sort into an assessment of economic value. As F. E. Green explained (in a book aimed at allotment-holders and gardeners themselves rather than at social investigators),

> It is very difficult to get accurate information on the total value of a year's produce from an allotment or a private garden. Those who work them, naturally enough pick the crops as they mature for their own table, perhaps only a few pounds at a time, and this kind of thing is not conducive to good book-keeping.[80]

Like Rowntree, Davies found that the allotment or garden was a 'valuable asset' to the labourer, but found it difficult to ascribe a value to the food produced except where it had been sold for money rather than consumed by the family itself.[81] She circumvented this difficulty in her income calculations by assuming that the value of garden produce in all cases equalled the rent paid for the cottage.[82] Mann estimated the available profit from an average allotment and added this to the income of all households that had one.[83] Beyond the arbitrariness of these calculations lay the cultural dimensions of the allotment: it was not only a material resource, but a value-laden commodity, a reflection of the moral superiority of rural life. For Thomas Kebbel, while working on an allotment, 'the labourer is merged into the husbandman, and begins to understand, for the first time, what is meant by the dignity of industry ... [the allotment] is the source of a common interest to the whole family, and the pride they take in it sheds a humanising influence on the otherwise cheerless tenor of their lives'.[84] Allotments and gardens, and, even more so, smallholdings, held a great moral authority, and even for the town-dweller represented a potential avenue for personal economic and social advancement. Thus in his survey of social conditions on the

---

[77] Rowntree, *Poverty*, 113.
[78] Rowntree and Kendall, *How the labourer lives*, 31.
[79] Ibid. 51, table between pp. 36 and 37.
[80] F. E. Green, *Everyman's land and allotment book*, London 1915, 83.
[81] Davies, *English village*, 136–7.
[82] Ibid. 141.
[83] Mann, 'Agricultural village', 170–2.
[84] Kebbel, *Agricultural labourer*, 71.

land in Belgium Rowntree looked to the Belgian model of living in the countryside but working in the town – earning industrial wages but enjoying the health and dignity of an independent country lifestyle – as a means of reinvigorating the moral and physical condition of the British worker.[85] On the other hand, Rowntree and Kendall were careful to point out the disadvantages attached to allotment-holding in rural communities: work on an allotment was the same as the work the labourer did for wages, and did not constitute a valuable and invigorating change.[86] The assessment of material conditions, then, was inextricably bound up with the moral and cultural dimensions of life on the land.

This is even more clearly illustrated by these investigators' attitudes to secondary poverty. Rowntree defined secondary poverty as a condition in which physical efficiency could theoretically be maintained were the household income not inefficiently spent: this expenditure, as he pointed out, could be 'useful or wasteful'.[87] He also pointed out that 'the point at which "primary" passes into "secondary" poverty is largely a matter of opinion, depending on the standard of well-being which is considered necessary'.[88] These remarks have been interpreted by some historians as evidence of an approach to poverty which encompassed both material and cultural dimensions, and as indicative of Rowntree's subscription to a relativist conception of deprivation.[89] Nevertheless, following his father Joseph Rowntree's work on temperance, Rowntree still blamed a substantial proportion of secondary poverty on drink and gambling.[90] Likewise, Davies ascribed a proportion of secondary poverty in Corsley to 'drink or other wasteful expenditure, or bad management'.[91] Mann, similarly, defining secondary poverty as poverty 'due to an uneconomical application of earnings',[92] believed that half the families in secondary poverty in Ridgmount were in that condition because of drink 'and its associated vices'.[93] The most noticeable feature of Mann's findings, however, is the limited extent of secondary poverty that he uncovered: only 7.1 per cent of the population. Mann's explanation for this was related to land tenure in the village: 'In a village lying in the heart of the agricultural districts of England, and of which the bulk of the place belongs to landlords who are particular as to the character of their cottage-tenants, the amount of

---

85 Rowntree, *Land and labour*, 288–94. See also his comments on the Garden City movement: *Interdepartmental Committee on Physical Deterioration: minutes of evidence*, 205, 207.
86 Rowntree and Kendall, *How the labourer lives*, 31–2, 332.
87 Rowntree, *Poverty*, 87.
88 Ibid. 141, quoted in Veit-Wilson, 'Paradigms', 212.
89 Veit-Wilson, 'Paradigms', 203, 212, 214; Briggs, *Seebohm Rowntree*, 34; Hennock, 'Concepts', 199.
90 Rowntree, *Poverty*, 140–5.
91 Davies, *English village*, 146.
92 Mann, 'Agricultural Village', 169.
93 Ibid. 185.

secondary poverty is necessarily limited.'[94] The concept of rural poverty was thus located firmly within wider discourses on the social structure of rural communities and the land question. This was explicitly recognised by Rowntree and Kendall, whose book was prefaced with the caveat that 'such important questions as the system of land tenure, rural education, small holdings, [and] the relative advantages to agriculturists of Free Trade and Protection' were not considered.[95] Elsewhere, Rowntree told public audiences during the years after the publication of his York survey that 'the most important factor in determining social conditions was the tenure of land'.[96] Rural poverty in particular, then, was located in a wider cultural and political context which helped to determine the agenda of the social investigator.

Whatever their cultural preoccupations and however questionable some of their calculations, the investigations of Mann and Davies appeared to show that poverty was as widespread in rural districts as in York and London. In one sense at least Mann's findings were even more striking than Rowntree's in York, as nearly five-sixths of Ridgmount poverty, covering 34.3 per cent of the population, was primary. One reviewer of Mann's survey remarked that it showed that 'the condition of agricultural England, at any rate in the Midlands and the South, is definitely worse than town life, so far as measurable poverty is concerned'.[97] Measurable poverty aside, some commentators adduced other evidence to argue that the poor wages in the countryside were overridden by compensating factors, but paradoxically, these very features of rural life could contribute to worsening the problem of poverty. Thomas Kebbel had pointed to the longevity of agricultural labourers as evidence of their better conditions:[98] they may have been healthier, but their longer old age meant that they spent more time in poverty. Infant mortality was also lower in rural areas:[99] this could be seen as a reflection of the healthier conditions of rural life, but it meant that families were often larger, and the poverty cycle was therefore intensified. Thus Davies found that of twenty-eight cases of families in primary poverty in Corsley, seventeen were due to low wages or largeness of family.[100] Furthermore, seventy-six of the 121 children of labourers in the parish were in primary poverty, and Davies remarked that the remaining forty-five probably had been or could expect to be at some time in

94   Ibid.
95   Rowntree and Kendall, *How the labourer lives*, 9–10.
96   'Mr Seebohm Rowntree at Cambridge', press cutting, B. Seebohm Rowntree papers, Borthwick Institute of Historical Research, York, LEC/21.
97   Press cutting, ibid. LEC/19/1.
98   Kebbel, *Agricultural labourer*, 223.
99   See Dr J. F. W. Tatham's report to the Interdepartmental Committee on Physical Deterioration, in which he showed that infant mortality in rural counties was 138.8 and 111.0 per 1,000 for males and females respectively, compared with 180.0 and 149.2 in urban counties: *Report of the Interdepartmental Committee on Physical Deterioration*, appendix Va.
100 Davies, *English village*, 142–3.

their lives.[101] To take another example, the figures from J. A. Spender's report on pensions suggest that it was possible that later middle-age poverty might be alleviated by a longer active working life in agriculture than was usual in other sectors,[102] but at this age it was likely that the family with many children would in any case be in a state of comparative material well-being because of supplementary incomes which would lift it out of poverty. Social and cultural defences of rural life could still be advanced: although charitable provision in Ridgmount appears to have been limited to a small parochial Christmas dole and some pensions paid by the duke of Bedford,[103] and although Davies did not deal with charity in Corsley at all, it was still possible (as Charles Booth's attitude to rural investigation demonstrates) to make the argument that charity was more liberally and efficiently bestowed in the countryside. Edwardian country writers often presented an image of country life that incorporated none of the insistent counter-pastoralism that characterised much of the social investigation in rural England over the previous forty years, and it remained the first duty of many investigators to assert that the appeal of 'Back to the land' was unsubstantiated in the context of the existing conditions of rural life.

If the problem of poverty as defined and measured at the end of the nineteenth century was the central concern of the investigators described in this chapter, they none the less all found that the long tradition of rural social inquiry continued to exert a powerful influence. J. A. Spender, planning a book based on the survey of the aged poor, found himself inexorably drawn to earlier studies. Writing to Booth in 1894, he explained:

> When I began to read backwards, I was taken from one step to another from the Poor Law Commission to Cobbett thence to Eden [and] thence to Arthur Young. . . . I am particularly impressed with the importance of the last thirty years of the [eighteenth] century if one wishes to understand certain aspects of village life as it is now, [and] the causes which have led to the so-called rural exodus.[104]

He began writing up the first part of the planned book, consisting of 150 pages on the 'history of the English Village & the various enquiries bearing upon it, drawn chiefly from Young, Eden, Cobbett, the Poor Law Commission, the Women and Children Enquiry, the Richmond Commission, with something about the census returns [and] the rural exodus question'.[105] (The manuscript of this book was lost, and it was never published.)[106] Spender

---

101 Ibid. 149.
102 Spender, *State and pensions*, 42–3.
103 Mann, 'Agricultural village', 173, 175.
104 Spender to Booth, 16 Sept. 1894, Charles Booth papers, MS 797 I/6045, reproduced in Freeman, 'Social investigation', 285–6.
105 Ibid.
106 J. A. Spender, *Life, journalism and politics*, London 1927, i. 60–1.

could not fully emerge from the long shadows cast by the great investigations of the previous century and by the history of economic and social change in the English countryside; and the Booth-Spender inquiry was supplemented by historical research on the enclosure movement carried out by Gilbert Slater at the London School of Economics.[107] Davies's book begins with a long (if uneven) historical treatment of Corsley, reflecting both the Fabian preoccupation with institutional history – she paid particular attention to the poor law in the parish – and the more general development of rural historiography in this period, especially the historiography of the labourer and the enclosure movement. Investigators were encouraged to examine the relationship of historical circumstances and processes to social conditions in the present. The *Edinburgh Review*, reviewing *Life in an English village* together with Wilhelm Hasbach's *History of the English agricultural labourer* under the title 'The English peasant', remarked that

> it is impossible to understand these changes, or even the present position of the English peasantry . . . without some knowledge of the history of this class in remoter times. We cannot separate the past from the present, and to form a fair judgement upon modern movements and schemes is impossible, unless we know in some degree at least how the present state of this class has been reached. . . . Many legislative mistakes would have been avoided, and many disappointments prevented, if the currents which have produced social results had been more accurately measured.[108]

Although the surveys of Mann and Davies did not result directly in any legislation, let alone 'legislative mistakes', they did contribute to a greater awareness of rural social problems, and they fed their concerns for the present into a developing contemporary interest in the problems of the English rural past.

The communities surveyed by Mann and Davies were small enough to be investigated as complete entities, and in theory at least to enable the collection of much more detailed information about each household than would have been possible in Rowntree's York survey. Gilbert Slater thought Davies had achieved 'a fulness and accuracy which could not possibly be attained in an urban survey'.[109] In York, although Rowntree achieved reasonably complete coverage, his paid investigator, according to a recent calculation by Peter Kaim-Caudle, may have enjoyed an average of only seven minutes in the company of each working-class informant, during which time a substantial questionnaire had to be filled out and a series of impressions obtained and recorded.[110] Davies, on the other hand, achieved a more intensive perspec-

---

107 Gilbert Slater, *The English peasantry and the enclosure of the common fields*, London 1907.
108 *Edinburgh Review* ccxi (1910), 338–9.
109 *Sociological Review* iii (1910), 170–1.
110 Peter Kaim-Caudle, 'Misleading data', unpubl. paper cited in Jonathan Bradshaw, 'Preface', to B. Seebohm Rowntree, *Poverty: a study of town life* (1st edn 1901), Bristol 2000, p. xxvi n. 6.

tive on the lives of the Corsley population, and as one admiring commentator remarked, 'Miss Davies has evidently spared no pains to get at the home life of the labourer, and she seems to have looked in upon him at meal times and seen with her own eyes how he fared'.[111] In this context both Mann and Davies emphasised the importance of a more intensive and intimate knowledge of the people under investigation than could could be obtained by a simple house-to-house survey, even if basic factual information was to be obtained accurately. Remembering the Ridgmount inquiry some fifty years later, Mann remarked on

> the failure of the so-called 'census' method of getting accurate data except for the simplest facts, such as the relative number of males and females, the size of families, or the age structure of the population. When one attempted to get data as to economic position, a census enumerator would be apt to get answers to his questions which would be far from an accurate presentation of the facts. In other words, it is only when the investigator is closely in touch with the people, and is quite familiar with their background that the data obtained are likely to be correct.[112]

Both Mann and Davies were careful to point out that they had received the full co-operation of the local inhabitants, and were familiar with their respective theatres of inquiry prior to commencing work.[113] Nevertheless, Davies relied at various points on second-hand information about the Corsley population; and she proposed a modified version of the informant method of inquiry, arguing in her book on school care committees that the most trustworthy evidence on working-class life was to be obtained from 'those who live not very differently from the working classes themselves, and yet are enough removed from their social sphere to be free from the petty spites and jealousies, that too often poison the imaginations and tongues of neighbours'.[114] Dissenting ministers, for example, made better informants than the 'aristocratic' district visitors who worked under Church of England auspices.

Davies used informants to deliver moral assessments of the working-class subjects of inquiry, making full use of a rather ambiguous 'person who knew the parish intimately', for example.[115] She claimed that her investigation divested her of her many misconceptions derived from the superficiality of her prior knowledge of the village, but many of the opinions expressed in *Life in an English village* savour of the manor house from which Davies came: she swept into her own working-class backyard, inquiring into the habits of the poor with an air of moral judgementalism which was not wholly redeemed by the outwardly sympathetic approach adopted at other stages of the inquiry.

---

111 *Standard*, 7 Feb. 1910, 6.
112 Mann, *Social framework*, 22–3.
113 Idem, 'Agricultural village', 164–5; Davies, *English village*, 104.
114 Davies, *School care committees*, 44.
115 Idem, *English village*, 102.

Nowhere was this made more clear than in her investigation of 'Character and its relation to poverty', in which the 'character' of 162 households (excluding the artisan population, who were known for their thrift and temperance, and were not thought to require investigation under this heading) was described by 'various persons likely to be well informed'.[116] The importance in this inquiry of the households' 'Promptness in paying debts and thrift generally' reflected the cultural standpoint of Davies and the bulk of her informants. It is not always clear from whom the reports on the adult population were taken, but the information on the children was derived from the reports of the parish schools. Sometimes two views were obtained for a household, one of them often from the employer of the head of household. Except where the informant was the employer, the source was not usually cited. This selection gives a flavour of the reports:

> Man gives no trouble. Wife inclined to drink; respectable otherwise. Son out of work; was bad at getting up in the mornings some time back.[117]

> [A widow's household:] Don't know much about her; used not to bear good character. 'Eldest son lazy, drunken, little beggar.' Those young men generally in any mischief going.[118]

> Very respectable people. Informant had once seen him with 'a little beer' and then very quarrelsome. A man scarcely ever seen at public-house.[119]

> (1) Very decent man. Wife a bad woman; would do any one harm if she got the chance.
> (2) Very nice, hard-working man; wife not so good as he is (tongue).[120]

The last example is a case where two reports were obtained for one household. In this instance, the reports concurred, but in other cases the two opinions could differ. One household, for example, was summarised briefly and inconclusively by two informants: '(1) Respectable. (2) *Employer:* Very nice man; wife dirty and untidy.'[121] These assessments, whether accurate or not, came from one class, and were not counterbalanced by any working-class opinion. Even when the working-class population was asked, through the method of the questionnaire (see appendix), to give information about itself, the responses were checked by a reliable informant; and in any case the questions asked gave little or no scope for the expression of opinion, and Davies counselled her readers that some of the answers given were unlikely to be an unbiased reflection of the truth.[122]

---

116 Ibid. 154.
117 Ibid. 159.
118 Ibid. 165.
119 Ibid. 181.
120 Ibid. 179.
121 Ibid. 159. Original emphasis.
122 Ibid. 101.

Davies positioned her work very deliberately within the 'national efficiency' debate, concluding her survey by drawing together the themes of rural
depopulation and urban degeneration, and expressing the hope that Corsley
would in future 'bring up an increased number of sons and daughters, more
healthy, vigorous, and efficient than their elder brothers and sisters of the
past, and ready to renew the less generous blood of the towns, or to recruit the
Army and Navy'.[123] As her school care committee work in London demonstrates, she was especially interested in problems of child life, and in the
Corsley survey she located the problem of primary poverty among children
within broader concerns about physical and moral deterioration. Thus in her
table of household 'character' she highlighted those families where 'one or
more children show characteristics which might be the result of poverty and
insufficient feeding. These marks of *deficiency* are dulness, nervousness, lazi-
ness, "strangeness" or "peculiarity" of disposition, dirtiness of disposition'.[124]
She emphasised that such 'deficiency' was widespread 'even in a rural district
where every advantage of good air and healthy surroundings is obtained'.[125]
The 'scientific' investigation of rural life, then, however intensive the rural
theatre of inquiry enabled it to be, was carried out within a moral and cultural
framework that was explicitly operational on the working-class population
with which it was concerned. Davies's 'view from above' was shaped by the
moral preoccupations associated with her own social position; it was ultimately as impressionistic as any other mode of investigation. E. P. Hennock
has pointed out that, for all the scientific pretensions of the Booth and
Rowntree surveys, their evaluation of household circumstances was ultimately based on a count of 'impressions, carefully cross-checked with other
impressions insofar as they were available'.[126] Where Rowntree's investigator
was told to look for 'obvious want and squalor',[127] Davies looked for those
'obviously living in want'.[128] Karel Williams has characterised this kind of
assessment of poverty as having 'only operationalised stock responses to the
working class';[129] and Mann admitted to a degree of cultural determination in
his count of the numbers in poverty: 'In deciding whether a particular household is to be classed as poverty-stricken, the personal feeling of the enumer-
ator also affects the results considerably.'[130] If the investigator went to the
village looking for deterioration, degeneracy and deficiency, he or she was
likely to find it. In doing so, the use of the survey method involved the
imposition of middle-class definitional categories and cultural values onto a

[123] Ibid. 290.
[124] Ibid. 152. Original emphasis.
[125] Ibid. 153.
[126] Hennock, 'Measurement', 208, and 'Concepts', 194. See also his 'Poverty and social
theory', 74.
[127] Rowntree, *Poverty*, 115.
[128] Davies, *English village*, 145.
[129] Williams, *From pauperism to poverty*, 348.
[130] Mann, 'Agricultural village', 185.

population that had neither the economic nor the cultural resources to conform to the behavioural patterns expected of them by these investigators.

The intensive methods of inquiry used in the poverty survey, then, did not entail an abandonment of the use of informants as moral authorities, and nor did it signify a democratisation of the investigative agenda, which remained determined by elite perceptions of the rural population and its role. The middle-class perceptions of these investigators were likely to be at variance with what the working-class subjects of inquiry actually experienced. Twenty years earlier, Thomas Hardy had delivered an indictment of just the kind of approach taken by Mann and Davies:

> The happiness of a class can rarely be estimated aright by philosophers who look down upon that class from the Olympian heights of society. Nothing, for instance, is more common than for some philanthropic lady to burst in upon a family, be struck by the apparent squalor of the scene, and to straightway mark down that household in her note-book as a frightful example of the misery of the labouring classes.[131]

Hardy disapproved of cultural judgements made on the basis of middle-class standards of cleanliness, for example, arguing that 'slovenliness' was not always 'accompanied by unhappiness',[132] and even identified tactics used to outwit the unwary social investigator. One woman apparently told him that 'I always kip a white apron behind the door to slip on when the gentlefolk knock, for if so be they see a white apron they think ye be clane'.[133] These points were affirmed by some of the investigators examined in the next chapter, Stephen Reynolds arguing that middle-class sensibilities could not appropriately be brought to bear on working-class social conditions, the life-styles of the two classes being essentially incomparable using the same yard-stick:[134] the 'judgment of one class by the standards of another' was essentially unfair.[135] As one aggrieved working-class woman remarked to her parson, '[i]t's no use Mrs Mitford measuring my corn with her bushel'.[136] Moreover, the investigation of domestic budgets, and the reduction of the complex and often unformulated subsistence strategies of working-class households into a quantifiable 'balance sheet' – or, in the case of Rowntree and Kendall, tabu-lating budgets and assessing their nutritive deficiences – located consumption in a context far removed from the experience of those from whom the infor-mation was gathered. Appending a descriptive 'monograph' to each tabulated budget may have helped to retrieve some of the proper context, but the

---

131 Hardy, 'Dorsetshire labourer', 255.
132 Ibid. 256.
133 Ibid. 255.
134 Stephen Reynolds, *A poor man's house* (1st edn 1908), London 1909, 88–95.
135 Stephen Reynolds, Bob Woolley and Tom Woolley, *Seems so! A working-class view of politics* (1st edn 1911), London 1913, 27.
136 R. L. Gales, *Studies in Arcady, and other essays from a country parsonage*, London 1910, 96.

process was geared towards the objectivisation of the sphere of consumption, often, as in the case of Rowntree and Kendall, within the context of physical and national efficiency. Similarly, the cultural preoccupations attached to the garden and allotment were not necessarily shared by those who actually worked such resources.

The methods used to gather information were questionable on the grounds of reliability and ethical practice. For the collection of her budgets, Davies asked a selection of families in Corsley to keep diaries of expenditure and consumption, some of which proved more reliable than others; while Rowntree and Kendall, having tried the diary method and found it unreliable, derived their information from face-to-face 'cross-questioning' of housewives.[137] Joseph Ashby adopted a similar strategy, personally visiting cottages, where (as his daughter somewhat unconvincingly claimed) 'a woman who had never made a note of what she spent would tell him precisely what had become of her weekly ten shillings for several weeks back'.[138] Not only was the accuracy obtainable from these methods questionable – various motives for giving a false or incomplete account of the domestic economy suggest themselves – but there may have been an understandable suspicion as to the uses to which the information given might be put. To take an urban example: when describing the collection of budgets from housewives for a Fabian Women's Group investigation in Lambeth, Maud Pember Reeves listed some of the amusing spelling mistakes and other basic errors to which her informants were prone;[139] and although done with sympathetic humour, this section of her report reads patronisingly and suggests an undercurrent of judgementalism that must have compromised the interpersonal relationships she claimed her investigators enjoyed with the local population. The reports of some of Rowntree and Kendall's interviews sound like stiff interrogations: one informant was asked, successively, '[h]ow much does your husband get with piece-work and overtime? . . . Still, you're well off compared with many. . . . Do you have to buy wood? . . . How about the clothing? . . . How much will shoes cost you a year? . . . Are you very heavily in debt?'[140] Cross-examination may have been necessary to obtain the detailed information that was sought, but it reflected a fundamentally unequal relationship between investigator and investigated. Both Rowntree and Davies collected evidence on individual households from their neighbours, a strategy that seems almost calculated to provoke resentment on the part of those who were subjected to it, although Davies did recognise the moral difficulties involved.[141] Unsurprisingly, perhaps, her book caused some bad feeling in Corsley, as, despite her attempts to anonymise the households, some were able to recognise them-

---

137 Rowntree and Kendall, *How the labourer lives*, 37.
138 Ashby, *Joseph Ashby*, 149.
139 Maud Pember Reeves, *Round about a pound a week*, London 1913, 12–15.
140 Rowntree and Kendall, *How the labourer lives*, 262–5.
141 Davies, *School care committees*, 22.

selves and their neighbours in it:[142] social inquiry was not a one-way process, and information had to be both obtained and used with care.

The rural population, then, was viewed by these investigators as essentially passive objects of social inquiries prompted by the problem of rural depopulation and carried out within the discourses of national efficiency that lay behind much of the investigative impulse of the 1900s. The national efficiency panic encapsulated the problems of an industrial nation experiencing relative economic decline coupled with imperial military setbacks and a threatened intensification of political conflict dominated by issues of class. Rural England, which offered a potential cultural counterpoise to the sense of urban industrial malaise, was proffered, as in earlier times, as a site of potential salvation, and inquiries like those of the 1890s and 1900s which showed this malaise afflicting rural communities as badly as the towns gave a serious jolt to any lingering complacency that may have surrounded dominant perceptions of rural life. Thus Harold Mann's conclusion to his survey of Ridgmount expressed unequivocally the futility of what one historian has called the 'pastoral impulse':[143] 'the outcry against the depopulation of the country . . . must remain little more than a parrot-cry', he argued, until something was done to improve the material condition and outlook of the agricultural labourer.[144] 'Scientific' surveys like Mann's, whatever their contestability on methodological or other grounds, appeared to show incontrovertibly that poverty was as widespread in rural communities as in the towns and cities, and in doing so set an agenda for further investigation and a framework for future social reform. Their aim was to separate the functions of social knowledge and cultural understanding in order to allow the developing scientific methods of inquiry, as pioneered by Booth and Rowntree, to evolve unhindered by impressionism and sentimentality. However, as we have seen, even the most detached and ostensibly scientific investigator was ultimately unable to operate outside either the cultural framework that surrounded the English countryside or the moral structures that conditioned middle-class responses to working-class behavioural norms in both urban and rural theatres of inquiry. The inherently contestable concept of poverty was applied to rural life only within a series of constructions derived from the literary tradition and from the previous century of social investigations of the countryside, and therefore the methodological difficulties associated with the execution of a quantitative poverty survey in a rural community were compounded by the ideological significance of resources such as payment in kind and domestically produced food. The problems of transmitting accurate and unbiased information about rural labouring life were thereby transferred to a new mode of social investigation.

---

142 Idem, *English village*, 103; information from John d'Arcy, Wiltshire Record Office.
143 Marsh, *Back to the land*.
144 Mann, 'Agricultural village', 192–3.

5

'The Challenge of Silence': Cultural Inquiry and the Rural Poor

The imposition of methods of social inquiry derived from the urban experience onto rural communities may have placed rural sociology on an apparently firm and assured statistical footing, but the techniques employed by the investigators examined in the last chapter by no means wholly supplanted the tradition of personal social observation of rural life. Indeed, as John Fraser has remarked, in addition to a growing vogue for 'scientific' social inquiry, the Edwardian period also saw 'a marked increase both in a concern with the interior life of the labouring people and the mechanics of their relationships with other classes, and in an awareness of how these things could best be conveyed to the reader'.[1] Just as urban England, invaded by social statisticians, continued to produce resident investigators of working-class life such as Florence Bell in Middlesbrough and Martha Loane in Portsmouth, so rural England supported a similar group. The investigators who form the subject-matter of this chapter lived in the midst of the rural poor and recorded their impressions, acting in the tradition of resident investigation of which Augustus Jessopp and Richard Jefferies were the best known and most prolific late nineteenth-century exemplars, although they differed methodologically and conceptually from them. Their observations were neither systematic like those of Harold Mann and Maud Davies nor widespread like those of Rider Haggard and other special correspondent journalists; rather they represented a parallel and developing *genre* of social inquiry in which the achievement of effective and meaningful communication with the rural working classes was the primary methodological concern. They grew out of a literary tradition, influenced by Jessopp and Jefferies, rather than a sociological one, but nevertheless conveyed information of sociological value and played a significant role in shaping popular perceptions of rural life. At any rate, their books and articles were more widely read, on the whole, than was the rural work of Mann, Davies and even Rowntree. As such, they formed part of the same 'passion for inquiry' that generated the classic urban and rural social surveys, and viewed themselves, in some respects at least, as fulfilling the same social need. Indeed, although many were critical of 'sociological' methods of inquiry, they took some pains to position themselves with regard to the

---

1 Fraser, 'George Sturt', 193.

Booth–Rowntree school of social surveys; and contemporaries did not assess their work in isolation from other kinds of social investigation.

The best known of these writers was George Sturt (1863–1927), a Farnham schoolmaster and wheelwright, who in 1891 moved to the nearby village of the Lower Bourne, the scene of most of his social observation. Sturt published a succession of books on rural life: *The Bettesworth book* (1901), consisting of discussions with his gardener, 'Bettesworth' (Frederick Grover); *Memoirs of a Surrey labourer* (1907), telling of the last days of Bettesworth, his failing health and his struggle to avoid the workhouse; and *Change in the village* (1912), a broad description of the village and the social changes and class tensions within it. These were all published under the pseudonym of 'George Bourne'. Sturt has been viewed as the most significant literary chronicler of the vanishing 'organic community' associated with rural pre-industrial life,[2] but he is no less important as a social investigator whose work gave unusually complete treatment to an individual, Bettesworth, and to a community, the Lower Bourne. Sturt's books, especially *Change in the village*, are regularly used by rural historians, but Sturt himself has been subjected to comparatively little scrutiny by historians, being viewed largely as a literary figure.[3] Yet he provides some interesting commentary on participant observation methodology, and as such is an important exemplar of a tradition of social investigation into which Stephen Reynolds also fitted. Reynolds (1881–1919),[4] born in Devizes in Wiltshire and, like Rowntree, educated in chemistry at Owens College, Manchester, began his career as a novelist – he corresponded with Joseph Conrad and Edward Garnett[5] – but in the early 1900s began an association with the fisherman Bob Woolley and his family at Sidmouth in Devon. Living and working with the fishermen, he experienced working-class life to a degree perhaps unrivalled by any other writer of the period. His experiences resulted in many articles in various journals and newspapers, and a string of books, most notably *A poor man's house* (1908), which has been called 'an almost Orwellian analysis' of the fishing family's life,[6] *Alongshore* (1910) and *Seems so! A working-class view of politics* (1911),

---

[2] Leavis and Thompson, *Culture and environment*; Denys Thompson, 'A cure for amnesia', *Scrutiny* ii (1933), 2–11.

[3] For recent treatments see David Gervais, 'Alive or dead? George Sturt (George Bourne), 1863–1927', *Cambridge Quarterly* xxvii (1988), 397–403, and 'Late witness'.

[4] This chapter was written prior to the appearance of Christopher Scoble's exhaustive biography, *Fisherman's friend: a life of Stephen Reynolds*, Tiverton 2000, which includes many of the quotations used in this chapter. Reference to this biography will be made only where it has added to, or amended, information from other sources.

[5] Various correspondence in *The collected letters of Joseph Conrad*, ed. Frederick R. Karl and Laurence Davies, Cambridge 1983, iii–v; J. D. Osborne, 'Stephen Reynolds: a biographical and critical study', unpubl. PhD diss. London 1978, appendix; *The letters of Stephen Reynolds*, ed. Harold Wright, London 1923, passim.

[6] J. D. Osborne, 'Introduction', to Stephen Reynolds, *A poor man's house* (1st edn 1908), London 1980, p. vii. Subsequent references to *A poor man's house* will be to the 1909 edition (see p. 130 n. 134 above).

the last of which was published under the joint authorship of Reynolds, Bob Woolley and his brother Tom. *Seems so!* was an extended version of a series of articles that originally appeared in various periodicals including the *Spectator* and the *Nation*. Reynolds was interested in both fishing and the navy, publishing a series of articles and a book on *The lower deck* (1912); and in 1912 was appointed to the Departmental Committee on Inshore Fisheries, as a result of which he obtained further employment as Adviser on Inshore Fisheries to the Development Commission. He died in 1919.

It might be objected that, alone among investigators considered in this book, Reynolds was not concerned with agricultural labourers; and indeed, it would be wrong to assume that all his conclusions would be applicable to them. However, it can equally be objected that, given the diversity of agricultural conditions across the country, the conclusions drawn by investigators in one part of the country were not necessarily applicable elsewhere. Fishermen were different from workers in agriculture, but the Norfolk labourer was just as different from the Dorset labourer or the Northumberland hind. In any case, Reynolds considered that the seafarer and labourer in agriculture were in some respects comparable:

> Like the agricultural labourer on the land, who belongs to the original stock of English industry, and on whom, in the end, we are all dependent for food, [the seaman] receives least recompense and esteem, I suppose for much the same reason, because his function is general and ancient, not new and specialised.[7]

To the seaman were attached cultural preconceptions similar to those pinned upon the agriculturist.[8] One biographer of Reynolds has remarked that his methods 'have so many parallels with such writers as . . . George Sturt that the inclusion of his name with theirs is unavoidable';[9] and his contemporaries tended to bracket him with rural writers. The *Times Literary Supplement*, for example, reviewed *A poor man's house* together with a book on the Devon countryside by Lady Rosalind Northcote;[10] and one scholar at the University of the Punjab delivered a series of lectures on Reynolds and Sturt in 1912,[11] rightly seeing many parallels between the two men, who also corresponded with each other intermittently.[12] Another biographer notes that Reynolds

---

[7] Stephen Reynolds, *The lower deck: the navy and the nation*, London 1912, 20.

[8] See Major Ernest Gambier-Parry, *Allegories of the land*, London 1912, 21–3, which remarked that both the countryman and the seaman spent their working lives 'fighting unseen forces'.

[9] Osborne, 'Stephen Reynolds', 263.

[10] *Times Literary Supplement*, 18 Feb. 1909, 61.

[11] Reynolds to Maurice Macmillan, 10 Jan. 1912, correspondence of Stephen Reynolds with Macmillan and Company, Macmillan archive, BL, MS Add. 54965, fo. 204, amended in Scoble, *Fisherman's friend*, 428, 747 n. 28.

[12] *Letters of Stephen Reynolds*, 141–9.

had worked very briefly on a farm, which was 'handy in boosting his credentials as a "country" writer'.[13]

Between them Sturt and Reynolds attracted much admiration and exerted a wide influence. The fruit farmer Ronald George Hatton, for example, using the pseudonym 'Christopher Holdenby' (which is used in the following discussion), dressed up as, and lived the life of, a farm labourer, the experiences giving rise to his memoir *Folk of the furrow*, published in 1913. Holdenby, a Balliol man, aimed, through his one-man meeting of 'Oxford and rural England', at familiarity with the labourers' 'home life, moral conduct, religion, hopes, fears, [and] material well-being'.[14] His concern, although not his method, was shared by R. L. Gales, vicar of Wanborough, near Guildford, who commented on rural life for a variety of journals, and contributed reviews of country books to the Liberal *Nation*. His main publications were two volumes of *Studies in Arcady* (1910 and 1912) – echoing Augustus Jessopp in his ironic comment on English rural life in his title – and *The vanished country folk* (1914). He judged that his personal experience in visiting and lodging in working-class homes gave him some personal authority to comment on the life of the poor. Other writers, whether directly influenced by Sturt and Reynolds or not, such as W. H. Hudson, Major Ernest Gambier-Parry, L. P. Jacks, P. H. Ditchfield and Walter Raymond, all presented similar kinds of accounts of rural labouring life which together form a substantial Edwardian *genre* of country literature, which had a significant impact on prevailing views of rural life and culture. The value of their accounts as sociological or anthropological documents varied: few had as much to offer as Reynolds or Sturt, but most acknowledged the personal influence and wider importance of the two men.

These investigators presented a different kind of information from that obtainable from the social surveys. Ross McKibbin has contrasted the work of three female investigators at work in the 1890s and 1900s with the surveys of Booth, Rowntree and Bowley.[15] He has argued that '[m]uch of what we understand by social and mental life cannot be examined by sampling techniques',[16] and that Florence Bell, Helen Bosanquet and Martha Loane all tried to supply a cultural understanding of the lives of the (mostly urban) poor, by taking a more anecdotal approach, and concentrating in their discussions of methodology on the difficulties of actually communicating meaningfully with the classes under investigation. He has shown how these women, in taking on the role of the cultural sociologist, offered the Edwardian reader a very different form of social study from that of the distributional social surveys; moreover, he argues that these works 'are in many ways more inter-

13 Scoble, *Fisherman's friend*, 77.
14 Christopher Holdenby, *Folk of the furrow*, London 1913, 139, 18.
15 McKibbin, *Ideologies of class*, 169–96. See also Cohen, 'Life and works of M. Loane', and 'Miss Loane, Florence Nightingale, and district nursing'.
16 McKibbin, *Ideologies of class*, 168–9.

esting to the historian than the work of, say, Bowley'.[17] Certainly the concerns of the modern social historian to understand the internal dynamics of the household and family, for example, or the attitudes of a particular working-class community to a political movement or institution, would normally be frustrated by a reliance on the distributional social survey. By contrast, Martha Loane's intensive contact with a rural household enabled her to obtain a better understanding of the complexities of its domestic economy than would have been obtainable from a short visit; and along these lines Paul Johnson has argued that '[s]ocial surveys tell of the hierarchical structure of credit and thrift agencies in a particular community, and how they were used by different groups. Autobiographies and interviews reveal the way in which different types of saving and borrowing were carried on by individuals simultaneously to meet different problems'.[18]

Moreover, in reducing social analysis to largely economic considerations, the social survey did not deal with many of the things that really mattered to those under investigation, and consequently presented an incomplete picture of working-class life. Indeed, Olive Dunlop, the historian of the agricultural labourer, made the point that reports of social investigators often overstated the miseries of the labourer, on the grounds that 'much of human happiness lies in personal relationships, and even in the worst times the labourer had that source of happiness open to him'.[19] The survey method reduced the complexities of the lives of the individuals under investigation to a mass of economic and statistical aggregations. Stephen Reynolds, one of its fiercest critics, argued that 'one of the vices of modern social and political thought [is that it] reduces the uncalculable to the bogus calculable, and proceeds to argue therefrom . . . if it hasn't the facts, it invents them, and that which cannot be expressed in facts and figures, it ignores'.[20] Rowntree and Kendall, in their book on *How the labourer lives*, recognised this in their attempt to 'give the reader the sense of intimate contact with facts which statistics alone do not always convey'[21] and to portray 'the meaning of inadequate wages in terms of sober reality'[22] rather than simply to demonstrate the extent of the problem. There was always a danger that the social survey, while arguably invaluable as a tool of the social reformer, could blind its readers with numbers; and it could give little indication of the social relationships which lay behind the problem of poverty with which it was primarily concerned. Furthermore, it provided only a static snapshot of the conditions it revealed,

---

[17] Ibid. 188.
[18] Freeman, 'Social investigation', 187; Paul Johnson, *Saving and spending: the working-class economy in Britain, 1870–1939*, Oxford 1985, 5.
[19] Olive Jocelyn Dunlop, *The farm labourer: the history of a modern problem*, London 1913, 5.
[20] Reynolds, *Lower deck*, 73–4. See also Reynolds and others, *Seems so!*, passim.
[21] Rowntree and Kendall, *How the labourer lives*, 6.
[22] Ibid.

and was at best clumsy as a means of illustrating social processes.[23] A more truly social inquiry would deal with a much wider range of material. For example, embarking on their attempt to explain 'The labourer's outlook', Rowntree and Kendall asked: 'Is his attitude one of content or discontent, of pure lethargy, of patient endurance, or of hope? A great many people outside his own sphere are thinking a great deal about him, but what is *he* thinking, and what is he feeling?'[24]

This echoes Victor Branford's plea in 1914 for a more cultural type of social study, in direct contrast to the kind of sociology epitomised, for him, by Booth's survey of *Life and labour of the people in London*:

> While the Booth type of survey is admirable in giving a picture of the economic and material conditions of the family it remains deficient . . . in the difficult task of describing the family's life of leisure, its spiritual condition. . . . Here the problem is to discover some method of observing and recording what the French call the *état-d'âme*, i.e. the thoughts and emotions, the habit of mind and life, of persons in their interior relations with their surroundings. The sort of question that this more intensive survey has to put before itself is – How can we decipher and record people's ideals, their characteristic ideas and culture, and the images and symbols which habitually occupy their minds?[25]

McKibbin has argued that Bell, Bosanquet and Loane were beginning, in the Edwardian period, prematurely to answer Branford's questions, and to pioneer an 'unselfconscious cultural anthropology' which relied on 'communications' for its effectiveness and was descriptive, anecdotal and impressionistic in both aim and outcome.[26] Building on this, Susan Cohen and Clive Fleay have shown how Loane enjoyed intensive and extended contact with the poor which taught her much that could not be learned from superficial and fleeting acquaintance. Loane 'made critical assessments of [the poor's] standard of living, and provided penetrating insights into their beliefs, attitudes, language and behaviour'.[27] Thus in addition to her awareness of the complexities of the structure of the domestic economy of working-class households (especially in the countryside), she was able to describe and analyse changing patterns of speech, attitudes to marriage and children, responses to illness and to her own role as a nurse, and even to identify a strong religious sense among the poor which, although not expressed in church attendance or other outward signs (such as Booth may have gathered for the religious influences series of *Life and labour*), was reflected in a powerful belief in the efficacy of

---

[23] See Webb, *My apprenticeship*, 253, 256; Mark Freeman, 'The provincial social survey in Edwardian Britain', *Historical Research* lxxv (2002), 73–89.
[24] Rowntree and Kendall, *How the labourer lives*, 314. Original emphasis.
[25] Victor Branford, *Interpretations and forecasts: a study of survivals and tendencies in contemporary society*, London 1914, 71–2; mostly quoted in McKibbin, *Ideologies of class*, 169.
[26] McKibbin, *Ideologies of class*, 188, 176–8.
[27] 'Introduction', to M. Loane, *The queen's poor: life as they find it in town and country* (first edn 1905), ed. Susan Cohen and Clive Fleay, London 1998, p. viii.

prayer. Cohen and Fleay, along with many of Loane's contemporaries, have defended her 'reliance on anecdotal evidence' from academic critics; indeed, they argue that this was 'authentic and revealing . . . [and] both underpinned and enlivened her texts'.[28]

Indeed, although now often marginalised by historians of social surveys, and although sometimes the target of contemporary dismissiveness, more generally within the culture of Edwardian social investigation and commentary, at a time when the internal and external boundaries of sociology were not clearly defined, studies like Loane's were regularly bracketed with the social survey as one manifestation of a developing interest in the investigation of working-class life. Investigators like George Sturt saw themselves as engaged in the same project as Booth and Rowntree, but were content to approach the task from a different perspective. In *Change in the village* Sturt drew a contrast between a 'scientific' study and one like his own, suggesting that they were appropriate to different aspects of working-class life. Thus on the matter of domestic income and expenditure, he admitted that his random and haphazard account could do the subject little justice:

> I must try to give some account of the ways and means of the villagers, although, obviously, in a population so heterogenous, nothing short of a scientific survey on the lines pursued by Sir Charles Booth or Mr Rowntree could be of much value in this direction. The observations to be offered here pretend to no such authority. They have been collected at random, and subjected to no tests.[29]

On the other hand, in his next chapter, on 'Good temper', he identified among the villagers 'a quiet and cheery humour, far indeed from gaiety, but farther still from wretchedness' and added that 'in matters like this one's senses are not deceived'.[30] These things could not be analysed statistically, and were amenable to literary description; but this did not necessarily detract from their value. A similar distinction was drawn by Horace Plunkett, in his introduction to Holdenby's *Folk of the furrow* in 1913: 'The main purpose of the book is to reveal to us the heart and mind of the folk. . . . Mr Holdenby's literary sense adorns but does not obscure the analysis he makes of the labourers' activities, and his study has a true kinship with Mr Rowntree's survey of their domestic economy.'[31] This notion of 'kinship' suggests that both kinds of survey were viewed as contributing to the sum total of knowledge and understanding of rural labouring life, and that the distinctions drawn between the two kinds of social study, although important, do not mean that they must be considered in isolation. Indeed, contemporaries recognised that in the 'sociology' of their period there was room for a variety of approaches.

---

28 Ibid. p. xx, and 'Fighters for the poor', *History Today*, January 2000, 36.
29 George Sturt, *Change in the village* (1st edn 1912), Dover, NH 1984, 52.
30 Ibid. 66.
31 Holdenby, *Folk of the furrow*, p. x.

Reginald Bray, himself an investigator of some repute,[32] reviewing *A poor man's house* in the *Sociological Review*, defended Stephen Reynolds's inclusion in the sociological canon:

> W[e] are in an age which desires exact knowledge; and that desire, in its craving after satisfaction, takes many forms. It may find its fulfilment in long columns of statistics; it may see itself realised in an intricate chain of reasoning; or it may win its goal in a series of impressionist studies. . . . Any one of these deserves the epithet scientific, provided the result is an accurate picture of facts.[33]

It is doubtful that Reynolds was grateful for this endorsement, which was forthcoming despite his own insistence that he should not be considered as an investigator.[34] Reynolds's approach may best be characterised as literary or anthropological rather than sociological,[35] but however it is classed it had a relationship with the social surveys of the period,[36] even if it resulted from a different series of ambitions and clashed with both the findings and the spirit of the distributional social survey.

The cultural approach to social inquiry, based as it was on close personal contact with the poor (by which, as McKibbin explains, was 'almost certainly meant the majority of wage-earners'),[37] entailed a rejection of traditional informant methods of investigation. Reynolds in particular had little patience with this kind of inquiry, arguing that for a realistic picture of conditions one should consult the poor directly, or at very least those closest to them. Thus in his forceful conclusion to *Seems so!* he quoted Loane's memorable exhortation from her book *The queen's poor*:

> Is it reasonable to ask the club doctor if the lower classes are healthy, to ask the coroner if they are sober and know how to feed their children, the police magistrate if they are honest and truthful, the relieving officer if they are thrifty, the labour master if they are industrious, the highly orthodox clergyman if they are religious, and then call the replies received, KNOWLEDGE OF THE POOR?[38]

Reynolds added the comment: 'Yet such, of course, has been the usual procedure!'[39] Reynolds, by contrast, emphasised that he lived among the poor

[32] See Reginald A. Bray, *The town child*, London 1907.

[33] *Sociological Review* ii (1909), 196.

[34] Reynolds, *Poor man's house*, p. x; Reynolds and others, *Seems so!*, 228.

[35] Osborne, 'Stephen Reynolds', 257, 260, 270.

[36] David Englander and Rosemary O'Day appear to have recognised this with the inclusion of *Seems so!* in their bibliography to *Retrieved riches*, although there is no mention of Reynolds in the text of the collection.

[37] McKibbin, *Ideologies of class*, 177.

[38] Reynolds and others, *Seems so!*, 290, quoting Loane, *Queen's poor*, 26. Original capitalisation.

[39] Reynolds and others, *Seems so!*, 290.

'neither as parson, philanthropist, politician, inspector, sociologist nor statis-tician'.[40] The imposition of an investigative agenda driven by the moral concerns of these groups of outsiders, reinforced by the rigid adoption of an informant method, would yield little of interest or importance about the poor man's life, and was likely to result in well-intentioned but ineffective and possibly offensive social reform legislation. What this really meant was that the poor should be investigated on their own terms rather than according to an agenda imposed by external authorities; indeed, for Reynolds, sociological inquiry as it was usually practised dehumanised the investigated population: 'Sociology and efficiency are right enough in their places, but for actual dealing with human beings, patience and charity are still of more avail.'[41] Sturt expressed the distinction in a less declamatory way. Wishing to 'get down' (the terminology is intriguing) and 'understand village life' from the point of view of those who lived it,[42] he gave much thought to methods of inquiry and to the kinds of information that could and should be sought. In a passage in his journal, written in September 1907, which has been seized upon by a number of commentators,[43] he drew a distinction between two contrasting methods:

> From speculating how the world looks to [labourers], I have come to discern that there are two quite diverse modes of studying them. One – an 'objective' method – views them with biologist eyes, as though they were animals whose ways were to be observed wholly from the outside; and this method seeks all explanation of their condition and behaviour in the formative influences of environment. How does bodily fatigue affect them; or their privation from luxuries? What are the results upon them, of their weekly tenancy of their cot-tages, of their employment by the hour; of the division of labour which makes them mere drudges; of the absence of economic relations with one another; of class distinctions and the fact that they wear peculiar clothes? . . . The 'subjec-tive' method on the other hand would seek in the labourer himself and his emotional life the chief formative influence – thwarted, of course, by the con-ditions enumerated, yet in spite of them preserving its essential characters. What are his hopes and ambitions? What his ideas of momentary happiness, or of life-long success? Upon what does he pride himself; and what are his views for his children? are some of the directions along which the 'subjective' stu-dent of labour would push his investigation.[44]

The 'objective' approach can be broadly equated with the social survey and the informant method, while the 'subjective' approach has its echoes in the

---

40 Reynolds, *Poor man's house*, p. x.
41 Ibid. 29.
42 Quoted by Arnold Bennett, preface to George Sturt, *A small boy in the sixties*, London 1927, p. ix.
43 See, for example, Keith, *Rural tradition*, 155–6; W. A. Ward, 'Poor old Grover!', *Cambridge Quarterly* iii (1967), 86–8.
44 *The journals of George Sturt, 1890–1927: a selection*, ed. E. D. Mackerness, Cambridge 1967, ii. 540–1.

concerns of the respondent inquiry, especially the interest in the more intangible aspects of the labourer's life. W. J. Keith has identified *The Bettesworth book* as a 'subjective' study; and by way of contrast he cites Richard Jefferies's letters to *The Times* in 1872 as an example of the 'objective' approach.[45] Unlike the rather unsympathetic Jefferies, Sturt and his contemporaries were able to obtain access to a number of insights into village life which would elude the 'objective' – and the non-resident – investigator.

The information they conveyed was dependent on the areas of working-class life which they were able to investigate 'subjectively'. Sturt, in *Change in the village*, was able to describe many of the social activities of the Lower Bourne, and analyse the 'temper' of the villagers,[46] describing their social interactions, their attitude to drinking, their attitude to work and so on. He was able to contrast the boldness of the middle-class village children with the 'timorousness' of their working-class counterparts;[47] and he also offered an analysis of the literary tastes of the adults, much as Florence Bell had done in Middlesborough.[48] Christopher Holdenby's main achievement was his depiction of the work in which he participated. (Alun Howkins has seen the developing understanding of the skills required for agricultural labour as one of the factors behind the shifting perceptions of the labourer in this period, and Holdenby as one of those who advanced this understanding.)[49] Reynolds, likewise, was able to describe with exactness many of the operations of the occupation in which he worked, as well as the home, the eating habits, the sleeping patterns and so on, of the Woolley family. Gales, as a clergyman, did not share the labourers' work, but was able to confirm the non-receptiveness of the bulk of the labouring classes to religious doctrine and (on the other hand) their attachment to the church as a village institution; as a regular house-visitor, he could remark on cooking and eating, and, like Loane, on the speech of the labourers, which sounded to him 'joyless' and 'anaemic'.[50] (He was, again, echoing Augustus Jessopp on this point.)[51] Close connection with the working classes often resulted in a refusal to condemn outright many of their ostensibly less endearing qualities: in presenting a fragment of talk overheard at a labouring family's dinner table, which sounded callous and uncaring to the sensitive middle-class ear, Gales remarked on 'the grimness of the outlook of the labouring poor, the little room which the imperious necessity of getting food leaves for sentimental and humanitarian considerations'.[52] He refused to preach abstinence from

45 Keith, *Rural tradition*, 156.
46 Sturt, *Change in the village*, ch. vii.
47 Ibid. ch. xii.
48 Ibid. 179–80; Lady [Florence] Bell, *At the works: a study of a manufacturing town*, London 1907, 142–70.
49 Howkins, 'From Hodge to Lob', 226, 228–9.
50 R. L. Gales, *The vanished country folk, and other studies in Arcady*, London 1914, 66.
51 See pp. 66–7 above.
52 Gales, *Studies in Arcady*, 130.

alcohol, arguing that the poor could not in any case afford to drink very much, and that it enabled them 'to forget for an hour the wretched conditions of their life'.[53] Sturt, similarly, took a view rather sympathetic than otherwise to the drinking habits of both Bettesworth in particular and the community in general.[54]

Sturt's intensive knowledge of working-class life in his village rested largely on his intimacy with one individual, Bettesworth, unusual because the 'relative positions of master and man are not generally conducive to friendly intercourse'.[55] In his particular case, however, he argued that because his economic relationship with Bettesworth was fundamentally non-exploitative – Sturt's garden was not a profit-making enterprise – no 'false inequality' sprang up between the two men.[56] In the sequel to this book Sturt described the 'intimacies' that sprung up, almost subconsciously, when working together in the garden.[57] However, if the relationship between the two men was unusual, it might be asked how far Sturt was qualified to comment on the life of the village as a whole. Karen Sayer has seen Bettesworth as Sturt's point of access for the rest of the community. As she points out, '[t]he social distance between Bettesworth and rural men and women was much less than that between [Sturt] and his country case studies, therefore the gardener constantly pointed out things to his employer that the latter had missed entirely'.[58] Once death had removed Bettesworth from the scene (in 1905), and thus severed Sturt's closest connection with labouring life, it could be argued that he became once more a middle-class villager, differing from the other villa-dwellers only in his political convictions and his Ruskinian temperament. He certainly became less convinced of the possibility of achieving a genuine cultural understanding of labouring life. By September 1907 his conclusions, as expressed in his journal (on the day on which he set down his thoughts about the 'objective' and 'subjective' methods), were pessimistic:

> No one knows the labourer. Nor is it easy to conceive such a true intimacy being set up. For my own part, at least, I find it more and more difficult to get upon terms of *cameraderie* with my working-class neighbours. Between my mind and theirs a great gulf widens . . . my brain activity is of a dissimilar order.[59]

One scholar has argued that 'these lines serve to emphasise the difficulty of

53 Ibid. 91.
54 [George Sturt], *Memoirs of a Surrey labourer: a record of the last years of Frederick Bettesworth* (1st edn 1907), London 1930, 128, and *Change in the village*, 45–50.
55 [George Sturt], *The Bettesworth book: talks with a Surrey peasant* (1st edn 1901), London 1902, 5.
56 Ibid. 5–6.
57 Idem, *Memoirs*, 234–5.
58 Sayer, *Women*, 150.
59 *Journals of George Sturt*, ii. 540.

any observer in comprehending how a person so very different from himself feels and thinks. The difference of outlook between himself and his neighbours extends much deeper than to factual discussions . . . and makes Sturt's assumptions on the sensitivity of the labourer all the more suspect'.[60] Sturt was a participant in the everyday life of the village, which gave him a longer-term and more intensive perspective than would be possible for the fleeting visitor, but the perspective was one gained as a member of the local social elite. Furthermore, Sturt was less successful in his penetration into the home lives of the villagers: Lucy Bettesworth, for example, the wife of his gardener, remained a shadowy figure for him even after he had written a long essay about her life.[61] Reynolds, arguably, was in a better position than Sturt. While Sturt's illustrations of the home lives of the Lower Bourne poor are limited, Reynolds shared both the work and the domestic life of the Woolley family. As John Fraser has argued, 'Reynolds can write even more from the inside than Sturt – from the kitchen as well as from the garden (i.e. boat)'.[62] He was able to describe their domestic habits in such great detail as to justify amply Peter Keating's categorisation of him as an anthropologist.[63] Only through the effacement of his middle-class identity, which Sturt never really shed, could Reynolds discover and convey the rigid psychological class barriers which posed almost insoluble problems for those who would communicate with the poor.

The main charge to which the work of both men lay open was that of generalising from the particular, and, in Reynolds's case, the unusual. Reynolds's experience of working-class life was confined to a limited geographical area (Sidmouth) and an atypical occupation (fishing). His Devonians had certain special qualities of independence, intensified no doubt by their self-employment and unusually dangerous occupation. In both *A poor man's house* and *Seems so!* Reynolds anticipated some criticism on this score. In the latter, he suggested that there were two possible ways to approach the poor: the extensive and the intensive (which corresponded roughly to Sturt's objective and subjective approaches). The former was analogous to scratching the surface of a field, while the latter was like digging a hole in just one part of the field, in order to obtain a better impression of the soil that lay beneath.[64] Reynolds saw himself as part of a group of writers, in different parts of the country, who commented with the authority of long association and sympathy on the thoughts and outlook of the poor in their

[60] Anthony Lister, 'George Sturt: a study of his development as a writer and his conception of village life', unpubl. MA diss. Manchester 1961, 176–7.

[61] He despaired of knowing very much about her: 'One or two incidents, one or two chance allusions to her by her husband – that is all the foundation one has on which to build up an account of her life': [George Sturt], *Lucy Bettesworth*, London 1913, 6.

[62] Fraser, 'George Sturt', 224.

[63] Keating, *Into unknown England*, 29–30; Osborne, 'Stephen Reynolds', 259–60.

[64] Reynolds and others, *Seems so!*, pp. xiv–xv.

midst. He was particularly impressed by the work of Sturt and Loane.[65] In a letter to G. W. Prothero, the editor of the *Quarterly Review*, he was pleased to note that other writers tended to corroborate the substance of his own conclusions:

> It has very much pleased me in reading the books you have sent down (Bourne's Bettesworth books are wonderful), to find that so much of what I've said of 'the poor' I know is said, sometimes in almost the same words but in different dialects, by other writers of those they know. One of the criticisms levelled at me [with reference to *A poor man's house*] was that I didn't know enough poor in sufficiently separate parts of the country. But 'tis apparently the intimacy with which one knows some typical 'poor' that really matters.[66]

Reynolds's defence of the typicality of his section of the working classes did not satisfy everybody, however. The reviewer of *Seems so!* in the *Times Literary Supplement*, for example, found Reynolds unconvincing on this point, remarking that 'Mr Reynolds would be the first to admit that he and his friends are investigators in one corner of the field only, whose conclusions are liable to modification in view of results obtained elsewhere.'[67]

What Reynolds's work lacked in coverage it made up for in intensiveness of contact; and the story of how this contact was obtained is a classic account of participant observation research. In *A poor man's house*, Reynolds described his early frustration at the difficulties in being admitted into the confidence of the Woolley family, who were reluctant to receive the 'gen'leman' into their lives without a show of respectfulness which hampered intercourse on an equal footing: 'They know intuitively . . . that one is thinking more than one gives voice to; putting two and two together; which keeps alive a lingering involuntary distrust and a certain amount, however little, of ill-grounded respectfulness.'[68] The barriers to intercourse could be overcome only with a long association on grounds of equality. By working with the fishermen, day in, day out, Reynolds found that some of these barriers were lowered;[69] but one of the main themes of *A poor man's house* is the constant working-class wariness of speaking to strangers from a different class. Thus in one of his best-known lines Reynolds expressed the class divide as it existed for the social investigator in terms that held little comfort for those who enjoyed only fleeting contact with the subjects of inquiry: 'There is not one high wall, but two high walls between the classes and the masses, so-called, and that erected in self-defence by the exploited is the higher and more difficult to climb.'[70] If *A poor man's house* provides a detailed portrait and analysis of the tensions inherent in the social relationships that shaped Reynolds's research,

---

65 Ibid. 297, 301–12.
66 Reynolds to Prothero, 5 Oct. 1909, in *Letters of Stephen Reynolds*, 126–7.
67 *Times Literary Supplement*, 23 Nov. 1911, 474.
68 Reynolds, *Poor man's house*, 80.
69 Ibid. 75; Reynolds and others, *Seems so!*, 190.
70 Reynolds, *Poor man's house*, 81.

in *Seems so!* he attempted to put his own experiences into a wider theoretical context. In his provoking remarks on 'Labour and brainwork', he described the conflicting social positions attached to each kind of work:

> in the need for personal experience of both brain work and labour, we are met by this difficulty: it is rare enough for a man to do both kinds of work, as work, day after day; but it is far rarer for a man to occupy at once the two social positions corresponding with the two kinds of work. . . . Everybody unites to drive him into the one social position or the other. It is astonishing how strong and persistent those forces are.[71]

Reynolds, then, argued that a dual process – economic on the one hand, social on the other – sundered manual from non-manual workers, and considered that he, unusually, had the occupational and social experience necessary to understand fully the labourer's life and grievances. Through this experience he also claimed to have obtained a fresh perspective on middle-class life; and here his findings parallel those of C. F. G. Masterman. Masterman, temporarily 'dropping out' of middle-class society, went to live in a working-class district of London, experiences described in his book *From the abyss*; and this perspective shaped the ideas which bore fruit in the classic statement of Edwardian radical Liberalism, *The condition of England*, which in turn drew on both Sturt and Reynolds for evidence on working-class life and opinion.

What Reynolds claimed to have obtained was an understanding of the thoughts and opinions of the Sidmouth fishing families, and in conveying some of this understanding, albeit gained in an atypical environment, he was fulfilling what was perceived as a deficiency in contemporary sociological knowledge. In the age of 'the rule of democracy',[72] when working-class opinion (at any rate male working-class opinion) could actually have a direct effect on the way the nation was governed, it was important to understand how the labourer approached politics. *Seems so!*, subtitled 'A working-class view of politics', attempted to express political opinion from the point of view of the working-class electors themselves. In particular, Reynolds described the impact of the Tariff Reform controversy, to which he attributed much of the resurgence of working-class interest in party politics, an attribution confirmed by Sturt in *Change in the village*, which identified a developing political awareness among the agricultural workers of Surrey prompted by the tariff question and the Edwardian interest in social reform.[73] As earlier investigators had recognised, and as contemporaries of Reynolds and Sturt agreed, it was especially difficult to 'get at' the political views of the rural population.[74] Reynolds, taking this a stage further, argued that not even the tradi-

71 Reynolds and others, *Seems so!*, 191–2.
72 Élie Halévy, *The rule of democracy, 1905–1914* (1st French edn 1932), London 1952.
73 Reynolds and others, *Seems so!*, ch. xv; Sturt, *Change in the village*, 200–2.
74 Caroline Gearey, *Rural life: its humour and pathos*, London 1899, 168–9.

tional channels through which working-class political views were expressed could really explain much about working-class political opinion: 'no means exist of gathering together working-class opinions. Neither elections nor newspapers do it'.[75] Party preferences were polled at elections, and Reynolds argued that party opinion and political opinion were distinct; the only way for the outsider to gain access to the frequently unformulated political opinions of the rural working classes was through sympathetic and patient personal contact.

One way to make this contact was to adopt clandestine techniques of investigation, much as Richard Jefferies had done in his preparation for writing *Hodge and his masters*. The tradition of dressing up as a tramp, to experience the workhouse casual ward and the open road, was a long-standing one,[76] and Christopher Holdenby employed these techniques of participant observation among agricultural labourers. Faced with 'the challenge of silence'[77] presented by the rural workers, and the difficulty of 'penetrat[ing] below the surfaces',[78] Holdenby 'determined to get as near to the labourers as possible – to become one of themselves'.[79] Working together, as Reynolds had found, was the quickest way to break down the social barriers which existed between him and them. Holdenby believed that, 'to a very large extent, one can only really get to know the countryman by working with him, week in, week out. Then the reserve and suspicion gradually die, and class is forgotten. The countryman is willing to forgive class if one can meet him across the plank of "work" '.[80] Holdenby was no socialist: an employer himself, he reminded his readers that the men respected a generous landlord or farmer with a human face,[81] and certainly did not consider conflict an inevitable feature of rural social relations.[82] However, he found himself in a position similar to Reynolds's, able to identify and explain much of the resentment felt among the labouring classes to investigation from outside. Parsons, for example, deeply suspected by the villagers as it was, made matters worse by visiting cottages infrequently and at inconvenient times.[83] (Flora Thompson's recollections of the visits of the parson and his daughter to her Oxfordshire cottage of the 1890s bear out Holdenby's remarks.)[84] The perspective of the village elite could only be denied through a conscious shedding of the investigator's identity as part of that social elite, and this is what Holdenby and Reynolds went some way towards achieving.

[75] Reynolds and others, *Seems so!*, 22.
[76] See Freeman, 'Journeys', for an examination of this mode of social investigation.
[77] Holdenby, *Folk of the furrow*, ch. i.
[78] Ibid. 1.
[79] Ibid. 15.
[80] Ibid. 138.
[81] Ibid. 226.
[82] Ibid. 139.
[83] Ibid. 217.
[84] Thompson, *Lark Rise to Candleford*, 220–2.

They were certainly influential. Sturt's work in particular – especially *The Bettesworth book* and *Memoirs of a Surrey labourer* – clearly made an impression on a number of country books which appeared in the years before the Great War, and which purported to represent a vanishing rural population, usually through descriptive accounts of individual rustics, many of whom bear more than a passing resemblance to Bettesworth. Their chroniclers were representative of a widespread attempt to convey, however crudely, information about and understanding of rural working-class life and its meanings through a predominantly literary medium, and although it is difficult to include such writers in a canon of social investigation that would undoubtedly include Sturt and Reynolds, they nevertheless contributed to contemporaneous perceptions of rural life, and most were concerned to some extent to emphasise the closeness of their own contact with the poor and to give some indication of how they achieved it.[85] Now-forgotten writers such as L. P. Jacks – who wrote a somewhat embellished and highly condescending account of a shepherd of his acquaintance, 'Snarley Bob'[86] – and Major Ernest Gambier-Parry (a Gloucestershire man who claimed an almost unrivalled intimacy with the elderly poor of his district)[87] were clearly influenced by Sturt, as was W. H. Hudson, known more for his nature writing than his representations of labourers, but whose influence on the Edwardian view of country life should not be underestimated.[88] Like Sturt, Reynolds influenced these writers: both Hudson and Gambier-Parry visited the beach at Sidmouth in the early 1910s, evidently attracted by the fame of the author of *A poor man's house*.[89]

R. L. Gales was another admirer of Reynolds. Gales was conscious of the importance of crossing the gulf which lay between him and his working-class parishioners, and believed that the country clergyman was in about the best position to communicate effectively with the rural poor.[90] However, he admitted that the really close association which Reynolds had achieved was denied to him.[91] Gales approved of Sturt, recommending both *Memoirs of a Surrey labourer*[92] and *Lucy Bettesworth*.[93] However, Reynolds was better still. Reviewing Reynolds's book of short stories, *How 'twas* (1912), in the *Nation*, Gales enthused:

[85] For a more detailed examination of many of these writers see Fraser, 'George Sturt', ch. vi.
[86] L. P. Jacks, *Mad shepherds, and other human studies*, London 1910.
[87] Major Ernest Gambier-Parry, *The spirit of the old folk*, London 1913, and *Allegories of the land*.
[88] See, espescially, W. H. Hudson, *The land's end: a naturalist's impressions in west Cornwall*, London 1908; *Afoot in England*, London 1909; and *A shepherd's life*, London 1910.
[89] Reynolds to Sir Frederick Macmillan, 20 Jan. 1911, and to George Macmillan, 26 Sept. 1912, Reynolds–Macmillan correspondence, MS Add. 54965, fos 169, 259.
[90] Gales, *Studies in Arcady*, 71.
[91] *Nation* xi (1912), 553; Gales, *Vanished country folk*, 105.
[92] R. L. Gales, *Studies in Arcady, and other essays from a country parsonage, second series*, London 1912, 59.
[93] Idem, *Vanished country folk*, 11ff.

Mr Reynolds is, in fact, the one living English writer who shows us working-class life from the inside. This is a very different thing to the writing of
those who are, indeed, in close touch with working-class life, but, after all,
remain outside it. Anyone, so to speak – at least anyone with some power of
observation and sympathy – can get into close touch with working people, and
then come away and, in an altogether different atmosphere, record his impressions; but Mr Reynolds appears to have merged himself in the life of the working classes. Hence, one looks upon him with the somewhat uncomfortable
veneration with which one regards a mystic. Mr Bourne comes nearest to him;
but Mr Bourne lives in a Surrey village, and writes about the people – with
admirable discernment and sympathy, no doubt – while Mr Reynolds lives in a
Devon village, amid fishermen, and lives the life of the people. He shares their
work and food.[94]

Gales's main point of disagreement with Reynolds and Sturt arose from the
marginalisation in their accounts of the place of religion in rural
working-class life. Reynolds was criticised by a Congregationalist minister in
his home town of Devizes, who accused him of depicting 'a godless home, and
a godless life', characterised by bad language, materialism and spiritual emptiness; and although, as Reynolds pointed out in his own defence, his entire literary output was 'one long protest against materialism either in politics, in
sociology, or in religion',[95] Gales was similarly concerned about the apparent
absence of religion in Reynolds's work. For this reason he was even more
impressed with L. P. Jacks's book on *Mad shepherds*:

> The veil which hides the life of the inarticulate peasant from the outside world
> has been somewhat lifted for us of late years by writers like Mr Stephen
> Reynolds and Mr George Bourne. Mr Jack [sic] sees further into the life of the
> rustic poor than even these writers do, because he possesses a religious sense
> which they lack. They, for instance, report the expression of the peasant's hos-
> tility to parsons, and so far, perhaps, they report truly enough; but how much
> more there is in his attitude to religion than that! . . . The mad shepherds,
> mystics or atheists, emerge from the dim background of the ordinary life of the
> country poor, and show . . . Mr Jacks their hearts.[96]

Gales clearly disliked Reynolds's fiercer indictments of organised religion,
and was also quick to praise his fellow clergyman P. H. Ditchfield whose
stream of books on rural life were generally of more immediate interest to the
antiquarian than to the sociologist, but which described in some detail the
superstitions of the rural poor with whom he claimed familiarity.[97] However,
the importance of these assessments lies in the fact that they were based
almost wholly on the degree of first-hand contact with the labouring popula-

94 Ibid. 96–7, and *Nation* xi (1912), 552. This is wrongly attributed to H. W. Massingham in
Scoble, *Fisherman's friend*, 446.
95 Quoted in Scoble, *Fisherman's friend*, 429–30.
96 Gales, *Studies in Arcady*, 111.
97 Ibid. 101–2.

tion that Gales believed these contemporaries to have enjoyed. The efforts of
these investigators to establish their credentials for commenting on the rural
poor by describing the intricacies of their social interaction with them
demonstrate a respect for any view of 'the poor man's country' which
appeared to come from the inside. Reviewing each other's work and referring
to each other regularly, these writers, for all their differences, represent a
distinctive group active within the Edwardian investigative culture.

What really united them was their obsession with class relationships.
McKibbin has concluded from his study of Bell, Bosanquet and Loane that
'their observation was anchored to a central organizing theme – social class –
which gives unity to a material which would otherwise appear antiquarian
and discrete'.[98] They remarked on the social relationships which they
observed, and as often as not played a part in these relationships themselves,
in their capacity as house-visitor, charitable patron or nurse. The same was
true of their rural counterparts. Faced with an apparently hostile set of
subjects, they were methodologically preoccupied with surmounting social
barriers; and these social barriers are described in detail in their published
reports. Thus they all devoted a large proportion of their output to explaining
the hostility which existed among the working-class population to members
of the middle classes interfering in their lives, and to the air of superiority
which was frequently adopted. For example, Reynolds made much of the
Woolley brothers' resentment towards the behaviour of middle-class tourists
who rode in their fishing boats at Sidmouth,[99] while Sturt echoed
Bettesworth's bitterness at the inquisitiveness and patronising behaviour of
middle-class visitors.[100] In pointing to the resentments engendered by
middle-class behaviour – behaviour which they, who knew better, did not
imitate – these writers were engaged in a degree of self-promotion: they
signalled themselves as the fortunate few with access to cultural understanding, who had been able to overcome the barriers they encountered. In
doing so, they were fulfilling a widely articulated contemporary need, in their
attempt to understand and overcome the alienation of the rural working
classes from the middle-class-dominated society in which they lived. This
alienation was in itself a barrier to investigation; circuitously, it was also the
finding of much of it.

The ethnographic insights with which the work of these investigators is
littered reflect the wider development in this period of a more sophisticated
set of anthropological techniques among folklore collectors, with whom they
had obvious similarities.[101] This is particularly evident in their concern for
the everyday occurrence, and commonplace talk, which they claimed could

98 McKibbin, *Ideologies of class*, 189.
99 Stephen Reynolds, *Alongshore: where man and the sea face one another*, London 1911,
ch. x.
100 Sturt, *Memoirs*, 77.
101 Freeman, 'Folklore collection'.

reveal much about the way country people viewed themselves and their relationships with their surroundings. For Sturt, listening to the 'almost
unheeded talk' of the villagers could give the careful listener indications of a
folk memory that was an 'instrinsic . . . part of the endless life of England's
country districts';[102] and his own relationship with Bettesworth was such that
'[t]his kind of chatter . . . is as endless as weeds in a hedgerow'.[103] Sturt
preferred the ordinary and everyday to the unusual, subverting traditional
ideas of what was historically significant, and emphasising the permanence
and even grandeur of rural labouring life. Similarly, Reynolds believed that
the commonplace sayings of the poor were a better point of access to their
opinions than their more thoughtfully formulated statements made before an
interrogator.[104] Major Gambier-Parry was also convinced of the value of the
everyday saying, many of which he had heard casually dropped during his fifty
years of acquaintance with agricultural labourers.[105] This insistence on the
value of the commonplace crossed over to the activities of folklore collectors,
who were also shifting their focus from a primarily informant method of
inquiry to an approach which emphasised the value of close and patient association with the rural working-class population.[106] As Alun Howkins has
shown, this also reflected a 'reconstruction' of the labourer: no longer the
dull, empty-minded and occasionally insolent Hodge, he had become, in the
eyes of many who wrote of country matters in the Edwardian years, 'Lob', a
repository of lore, 'the bearer of Englishness' and the possessor of a culture
wholly superior to that of his debased urban counterpart.[107]

Sturt, Reynolds and Holdenby all contributed to this reconstruction of the
countryman by imposing their own views of the value of the rural population
onto those about whom they wrote. While it is easy to contrast them with,
say, Rider Haggard, they entered their projects with just as many strongly-
held preconceptions about rural life as he did. All held the ruggedness of rural
and seafaring life in high regard, and portrayed the rural working classes as
the bearers of a folk wisdom which was somehow superior to the values of the
urban-educated middle classes from which they themselves came, and this
gives their descriptions of their working-class friends a hagiographic quality
that can sometimes detract from the otherwise valuable content of the texts.
Sturt, for example, identified men like Bettesworth as the true bearers of an
ancient Englishness which was threatened, if not debased, by the cultural
forms associated with urban (and, in Surrey, suburban) life; while Reynolds
claimed to have experienced 'the presence of a wisdom that I know nothing
about . . . and that I suspect to be largely the traditional wisdom of the folk,

---

102 Sturt, Lucy Bettesworth, 149.
103 Idem, Bettesworth book, 191–2.
104 Nation xiv (1914), 896–8; Osborne, 'Stephen Reynolds', 226–7.
105 Gambier-Parry, Allegories of the land, 173–6, 176 n. 1.
106 Freeman, 'Folklore collection'.
107 Howkins, 'From Hodge to Lob'.

gained from contact with hard fact, slowly accumulated and handed on through centuries'.[108] Other commentators also subscribed to this ennobling view of the rural population: C. F. G. Masterman, for example, reviewing *A poor man's house* in the *Nation*, remarked that Reynolds would probably find fewer of the virtues he so admired among the poor 'in the difficult darkness of the cities, where Fear, rather than Courage, is the driving force of common humanity'.[109] Reynolds himself was prone to exaggeration to labour his point: 'I am often asked why I have . . . made my home among "rough uneducated" people. . . . The briefest answer is, that it is good to live among those who, on the whole, are one's superiors.'[110] His belief in the 'magnificent courage' of the rural poor was seconded by Holdenby, who claimed that it was the countryman's 'dependence on supplying his own needs with good simple stuff, and on storing and husbanding it, which has given him so many fine qualities and a rare position on the earth'.[111] Both Reynolds and Holdenby subscribed to the contemporary vogue for Bergsonian philosophy – Bergson's *L'Evolution créatice* was published in 1907 and in an English edition in 1911 – and consequently in their analyses of working-class consciousness valued 'instinct' more highly than 'intelligence'.[112] This entailed a fundamentally anti-positivistic approach to social research, challenging the empiricist and quantitative obsessions epitomised by investigations of the Rowntree type; but it also invited criticism on the grounds that they were bringing untenable preconceptions to their study of the rural poor. Lob may have been more worthy of respect than Hodge, but the lionisation of the labourer did not necessarily reflect an achievement of empathy any more than had the reduction to an unflattering stereotype.

On the other hand, some of their comments on the rural poor were as critical as those found in the writings of Richard Jefferies or Rider Haggard. Although Holdenby respected the intuitive wisdom of the labourers with whom he worked, he still employed much of the animalistic imagery used to characterise Hodge: 'Both men and women take their cue from the beasts of the field. . . . I do not think they have any conception of a higher relationship.'[113] On political matters, although Hodge was to some extent now the master, the implications of the franchise had not yet come home to him: 'Though they "have the vote", they do not realise that they are "government", and I think the proportion of my country friends who vote with any intelligent understanding of the issues involved is very small.'[114] Nevertheless, he could point to an awakening of political sensibility among the rural

---

108 Reynolds, *Poor man's house*, 80.
109 *Nation* iv (1908), 249; Masterman, *Condition of England*, 117.
110 Reynolds, *Poor man's house*, 314.
111 Ibid. 263; Holdenby, *Folk of the furrow*, 53.
112 Holdenby, *Folk of the furrow*, 221, 282–3 and passim; Reynolds, *Poor man's house*, 80, 118–22, 258–74 and passim; Henri Bergson, *Creative evolution*, London 1911.
113 Holdenby, *Folk of the furrow*, 148–9.
114 Ibid. 263.

poor. Similarly, Reynolds found it necessary to distinguish between three different 'stages' of political awareness. Quoting Augustus Jessopp, who had suggested in the 1880s that '[i]t must be a long time before the vote of the agricultural labourers can represent anything better than the views of those who happen to dominate over them for the time being',[115] Reynolds found many who still deferred on political matters to what 'gen'lemen' told them, although there were others who took a more independent approach. The illogicality of the poor man's mind, as Sturt pointed out, was increasingly inappropriate to the conditions of modern life. The intuitive mental process of earlier peasant generations did not suit the 'new thrift', which 'has found the villagers unequipped with any efficient mental habits appropriate to the altered conditions'.[116] Indeed, not all resident investigators of the period were as sensitive as Sturt and Reynolds. For example, Caroline Gearey, a south-eastern Primrose League activist, while she admired the Mitfordesque characters who populated her village and presented them in an attractive if patronising way, and while she appreciated the instinctive deference of the poor to a socially benevolent squire and parson, regretted the rise of the spirit of socialism in rural communities, and thought the labourers, who too gullibly believed what they were told by radical agitators, needed to be taught who were 'their true friends'.[117] It was still possible to portray the labourer in terms that retained vestiges of the Hodge stereotype, emphasising his ignorance and dependence. Thus Gales suggested that the villager's mind was usually vague on subjects that lay outside its immediate surroundings;[118] while at the local reading room, the labourers 'do not care for the news and games, or even for the gossip, unless they can wash all down with a glass or two of beer'.[119]

Like the investigators of the 1880s, these writers still approached the poor from an essentially middle-class perspective, and were speaking to a middle-class audience. For all their sympathy with the villagers among whom they lived, Sturt and Holdenby, as local employers, and Gales as a country parson, were identifiably members of village elites, and were unable wholly to shed their middle-class identity. We have only their word that intimacy was established with those whose views they purported to represent, and we are left with accounts only of those about whom they chose to write. Many found that their agenda was not necessarily shared by their working-class neighbours. Gales, aware of the delicacy of his position as a clerical house-visitor and a social investigator, was conscious that many of the Wanborough poor, rightly suspicious of his intentions, had 'a dim inkling that "copy" may be made of their remarks'.[120] Sturt pointed out that he was careful to hide from

---

115 Reynolds and others, *Seems so!*, 161, quoting Jessopp, *Arcady*, p. xviii; also quoted at pp. 68–9 above.
116 Sturt, *Change in the village*, 133.
117 Gearey, *Rural life*, 168 and passim.
118 Gales, *Studies in Arcady*, 72.
119 Idem, *Studies in Arcady . . . second series*, 59.
120 Ibid. 22–3.

Bettesworth the fact that he had been made the subject of a book;[121] and there are also indications that their strange relationship was the source of some comment and even resentment in the Lower Bourne.[122] Reynolds was reluctant to let the Woolley family know that they featured in *A poor man's house* until close to the date of publication;[123] and he fell out with Tom Woolley over the contents of the book.[124] The readers of books like this could also react angrily to their representation in them. Tom Woolley himself suffered a physical attack by a group of Sidmouth men who disapproved of *Seems so!*, on the title page of which his name appeared.[125] Similarly, when Eleanor Hayden, a Berkshire vicar's daughter, published the personal stories of some of her villagers in *Travels round our village* (1901), a copy was passed around the village, arousing such anger that she was 'hissed and hooted' as she walked down the street, and prompting one villager to shout "Ere cooms yon graäde big lee-er!'[126]

The rural poor, aware of their status as objects of inquiry, were often alert to the investigative spirit of the Edwardian middle classes, and realised that they were rarely viewed as genuinely equal partners in the research process. Even Reynolds's self-appointed role as 'amanuensis' for the Sidmouth fishermen begs significant questions about the relationships that shaped his representations of them. However, Reynolds did provide some of the ammunition for a subversion of the investigative process. This subversion would transcend the simple dialogue between informant and respondent methods of inquiry, and entail the proposition of an egalitarian social research agenda. One academic sociologist in the 1980s, arguing for 'research from the underside', suggested that 'for the top-down model to be completely reversed, the socially deprived should study the rich . . . why should not the poor examine the habits and conditions of the powerful, of cabinet ministers, business executives, barristers?'[127] In Edwardian Britain this reversal was delivered through satire: Reynolds, for example, delivered some biting satirical representations of middle-class behaviour from what he claimed was a working-class point of view.[128] This often turned on the unfairness of the standards applied by middle-class investigators to working-class life and behaviour. Another investigator who admired Reynolds's work,[129] F. E. Green, suggested that

---

121 Sturt, *Memoirs*, p. vii.

122 Ibid. 126–7.

123 Osborne, 'Introduction', p. xiii.

124 Idem, 'Stephen Reynolds', 125–6.

125 Reynolds to George Macmillan, 3 Dec. 1911, Reynolds–Macmillan correspondence, MS Add. 54965, fo. 196.

126 P. H. Ditchfield, *The parson's pleasance*, London 1910, 217–18, probably referring (but not by name) to Eleanor G. Hayden, *Travels round our village: a Berkshire book*, London 1901.

127 Bob Holman, 'Research from the underside', *British Journal of Social Work* xvii (1987), 682.

128 See, for example, Reynolds, *Alongshore*, 90–1.

129 F. E. Green, *The awakening of England*, London 1912, 303.

'when the poor begin to write about the manners of the upper classes, we should have satire of a new and wonderful order';[130] and Green illustrated this potential himself by pointing to the unfairness of the inclusion of non-monetary remuneration in official agricultural wage statistics:

> Surely only a middle-class bureaucracy could be mean enough to take into account a gallon or two of beer, a truss or two of straw, a bag of potatoes, a bucket of separated milk, or a bundle or two of faggots – often a gift of charity on the part of the farmer – as part payment of a labourer's wage. Imagine a schedule being drawn up of the average earnings of managing directors of city companies in which invitations to a champagne lunch, a box of expensive cigars, a barrel of oysters, a first-class season ticket, a first-class cabin on an ocean liner, all given for business purposes, were taken into account![131]

Working-class opinion was rarely incorporated into the social research strategies adopted by social investigators in this period, even those who adopted the respondent method of inquiry; and it was left to writers like Reynolds and Sturt to express the working-class responses to investigation, albeit in an imperfect way.

Partly as a result of this approach, both Reynolds and Sturt tended to represent the poor man's attitude to politics in terms of opposition to the activities of the governing classes. They made very few if any proposals for specific legislative or other reforms, and Reynolds's 'working-class view of politics' was largely confined to announcements as to whether the poor approved or, more usually, disapproved of particular legislative measures, and why. The 'Seems so!' articles, featuring fictionalised characters discussing political issues, attacked the police and magistracy, the reports of the poor law commissioners, the 'Children's charter', the licensing laws and, most controversially of all,[132] the education system. These were all indicative of a 'survey' attitude that treated the labouring classes as objects of inquiry or legislation. The Fabian Society and other 'intellectuals' – memorably characterised as 'so well-intentioned, so merely logical, so cruel'[133] – were a particular target for criticism; and the collectivist assumptions that underlay much of the social reform of the Edwardian period were caricatured, often through the use of machine metaphors. Thus Reynolds was scathing about the proposals contained in the minority report of the poor law commission, which 'waken in me the same sort of horror as a huge piece of machinery which, should one have the misfortune to tumble into it, will go on grinding and crush one's vitals out'.[134] The National Insurance Act – which its proponents had advertised as 'ninepence for fourpence', was condemned as 'Ninepence for

130 Ibid. 304.
131 Idem, *The tyranny of the countryside*, London 1913, 227.
132 On this controversy see Scoble, *Fisherman's friend*, 386–8.
133 Reynolds and others, *Seems so!*, p. xxv.
134 Ibid. 298.

Fourpence at a cost of Sixpence'.[135] Reynolds approached the poor as individuals rather than as a statistical aggregation, and this had implications for the kind of proposals that he might endorse. McKibbin has suggested that the non-distributional social studies of Bell, Bosanquet and Loane, based on 'a kind of cultural archaeology dependent upon imaginative and apparently informed observation', implied an essentially individualist political conclusion that entailed non-collectivist solutions to the problem of poverty.[136] These investigators defined poverty as a cultural phenomenon, focusing on issues of individual moral choice and the social transmission of behavioural patterns. Sturt and Reynolds, no less culturally preoccupied than Bell, Bosanquet and Loane, differed from them in finding generally more of value in the working-class cultures they encountered; but the focus on the individual rather than the mass tended to make them similarly sceptical of 'top-down' social action. Virtually no practical measures were proposed (except practical reforms suggested by Reynolds aimed at improving efficiency and conditions in the fishing industry), and the same goes for Gales, whose main suggestion was the provision of beer at Christmas in workhouses.[137] Holdenby could only report the ambiguous conclusion that the countryman 'knows not what to make of "Them there new Ac's", except that they have the power both to ameliorate and to sting'.[138]

As these investigators did not set out to propose specific measures of social reform, the ambivalence of their proposals is unsurprising; and the real value of their output lay in the human corrective it supplied to the often reductive approaches of the social-scientific mode of investigation and the official inquiry. This value is enhanced for the historian of social investigation by the illumination of certain features of the investigative process that could only be shown at the 'micro' level. Most important of all, as Eileen Yeo has recognised, Reynolds's books in particular provide an insight into working-class attitudes to social inquiry: although some evidence of the response of the organised working classes to the activities of social investigators is available from other sources (from the agricultural trade union press, for example), for Yeo '[t]he biggest challenge to the historian is to get beyond the organized working class and tap the reservoir of sensibility of working people who never joined an organization, in order to sample their reaction to the middle-class social scientific offensive',[139] and this is what Reynolds's work allows the historian to do. Yet however insistent Reynolds may have been that he should not be considered a social investigator, neither he nor the other writers examined in this chapter lacked an awareness of the potentials and pitfalls of the

135 *Pall Mall Gazette*, 12 Feb. 1912, 4; Reynolds to George Macmillan, 9 Feb. 1912 and 17 Feb. 1912, Reynolds–Macmillan correspondence, MS Add. 54965, fos 209–11.
136 McKibbin, *Ideologies of class*, 168, 190.
137 Gales, *Studies in Arcady*, 433–40.
138 Holdenby, *Folk of the furrow*, 264.
139 Yeo, *Contest*, 242.

participant observation method, and all were motivated by the desire to investigate and report. Perhaps the most interesting aspect of their work is the pattern of social relationships that lay behind it: Sturt and his fellow investigators all approached the poor from the perspective of the local social elite, and theirs was the 'survey' method in the sense of coming socially from above. This is of redoubled importance given that they were just the sort of people who might themselves figure as sources of information within the informant method of inquiry. (Even Reynolds was eventually drawn into the realm of the official investigation, serving as a member of the Departmental Committee on Inshore Fisheries.) They represent an important strand of Edwardian social inquiry, showing that there was a significant diversity of modes of representing the lives of the rural (and seafaring) poor; at the same time, and no less important, their cultural preoccupations demonstrate that even the most sympathetic investigator was constrained by a certain conception or series of conceptions of the countryside which set a peculiarly rural framework for the representations of working-class life which resulted. If they present the historian with an alternative perspective on rural working-class life to that obtained from the official inquiry or the social survey, it should be remembered that they were no less subject to fierce contestation than these other forms of social investigation.

6

Continuing Contests:
Housing, Wages and Land

Although the social survey represented a new way of investigating working-class life, especially the measurable problem of poverty, and although the cultural anthropology practised by Sturt, Reynolds and others represented a deeper penetration into the cultural lives of the rural poor, appearing to some observers to transcend the simple investigation of observable and quantifiable aspects of labouring life, many of the older approaches to social inquiry in the English countryside also survived into the Edwardian period. Not even in the midst of the panic over rural depopulation in the 1890s had the 'passion for inquiry' been manifested in such an extent and variety of investigations of rural life. Interest peaked between 1912 and 1914 in what F. E. Green called the 'rural literary Renaissance': a flurry of books and articles representing a culmination of the previous forty years of investigative activity.[1] The awareness of older traditions of social inquiry was reflected in the flourishing historiography of the agricultural labourer in this period, empirically grounded in the accounts of Arthur Young and James Caird and the reports of the official inquiries of the 1840s and 1860s.[2] These histories focused on the experience of conflict, especially the 'Swing' riots and the agricultural trade unionism of the 1870s – almost all saw 1872 as an important watershed – and in so doing they remind the reader of the conflicts that shaped the sources upon which they are based. Many inquiries were carried out along similar lines to those seen in earlier decades: in particular, special correspondent journalism continued to be a feature of social investigation in the countryside, especially in the context of the problems of rural housing. Yet the period also saw the 'passion for inquiry' taking new directions, in both urban and rural theatres of inquiry. The mechanisms of official investigation of working-class life and social conditions were being improved under the influence of key civil servants, especially in the Labour Department of the Board of Trade,[3] for which Arthur Wilson Fox's investigations of rural wages were carried out in 1900 and 1905. Like earlier inquiries of this

1 Green, History, 178.
2 See, for example, Dunlop, Farm labourer; Slater, English peasantry; J. L. Hammond and Barbara Hammond, The village labourer, 1760–1832: a study of the government of England before the Reform Bill, London 1911; Prothero, English farming; W. H. R. Curtler, A short history of English agriculture, Oxford 1909.
3 Davidson, Whitehall and the labour problem.

type, these surveys provoked a fierce debate on the nature of agricultural remuneration. Above all, the social investigation of the period was informed, and arguably dominated, by the issue of land, which, as Asa Briggs once remarked, was predominant in the political and social discourse of the period to an extent often overlooked by historians.[4] As the Liberal government battled with the House of Lords over the taxation of land values, the reports of the Land Enquiry Committee were published, initiating an intense debate which was curtailed only by the outbreak of war in 1914. This chapter examines these various manifestations of the 'passion for inquiry' in the Edwardian period, in particular the issues of housing, wages and land.

Nowhere was the contestability of the practice of social inquiry more evident than in the investigation of rural housing. Housing had never lain far from the concerns of social investigators, and it was touched on by almost all those examined elsewhere in this book. Housing had been thoroughly investigated on a regular basis by medical officers of health – the reports by Dr H. J. Hunter in the 1860s have proved a particularly useful source for rural historians[5] – and the tied cottage system had been one of the many grievances aired by the National Agricultural Labourers' Union in the 1870s.[6] Special correspondent journalism had proved a particularly effective means of spreading information about the undoubtedly poor stock of rural housing; and the cottage question was invested with a new importance by the acceleration of rural depopulation in the 1890s, which many observers blamed in part on questions of housing quality, availability and tenure. Even after the progress of depopulation had thinned out the rural population, there was still a chronic housing shortage in many places, to which, for example, the assistant commissioners of the Royal Commission on Labour had repeatedly drawn their readers' attention.[7] The Housing of the Working Classes Act of 1890 sought to remedy the situation, but in the late 1890s and 1900s the surface of the problem had barely been scratched.[8] A variety of investigative methods were brought to bear on the subject in this period, the most widely read of which were those of the special correspondents. In 1899 Clement Edwards and George Haw wrote a series of articles in the *Daily News*, a paper long interested in rural problems, Haw exploring London and Edwards the rural south-west; and in 1900 Haw claimed credit for the *Daily News* in making the housing question 'the chief social question of the hour': 'Not only in London,

---

[4] Briggs, *Seebohm Rowntree*, 67. The omission of the land question from the historiography of the period has since been addressed by a number of historians, most recently in Ian Packer, *Lloyd George, Liberalism and the land: the land issue in party politics in England, 1906–1914*, Woodbridge 2001, which was published too late to be drawn upon in the preparation of this chapter.
[5] Burnett, *Social history of housing*, 127.
[6] Ibid. 133; Selley, *Village trade unions*, 89. It was also an important issue for the trade unionists of the Edwardian period: see, for example, Groves, *Sharpen the sickle!*, 125–6.
[7] *RC on Labour: assistant commissioners' reports*, i. 11; ii. 33–4; iv. 14; v. 15.
[8] Burnett, *Social history of housing*, ch. v.

where the need for reform is greatest, but in country villages and provincial towns, there has been a great awakening to the want of room to live.'[9] The *Daily News* articles were one of many results of this awakening: from the late 1890s, a variety of housing inquiries were carried out by a diverse range of investigators. It was increasingly emphasised that housing was often as bad in rural as in urban districts: an investigation in 1897 of 4,179 cottages in 78 villages found that a quarter were 'bad' or 'extremely bad', and another study of 240 different villages found 'bad' cottages in half of them.[10]

The counter-pastoral literary strategy of contrasting the attractive exteriors of cottages with squalid conditions inside was still powerful, and most investigators used it at some point. The period was one during which the charm of rural England was being feted in country literature in response to the problems of urban England[11] – Helen Allingham's attractive pictorial representations of country cottages were one notable example[12] – and many social investigators felt a duty to explain to their readers how idealised representations of country life hid the miserable social realities and bitter political conflicts that lay beneath. E. N. Bennett remarked on the eve of the Great War that

> [t]he casual visitor to our rural districts is frequently led by the picturesque exteriors of our country cottages to ignore the existence of the damp and squalid accommodation within. Mrs. Allingham's charming sketches . . . must not blind us to the fact that the general standard of rural housing is disgracefully low.[13]

Other investigators, as diverse as Clement Edwards and Christopher Holdenby, pointed out that the worst cottages were often those at some distance from the main road, which might mislead the visitor who was unfamiliar with a district.[14] Hugh Aronson, a Hertfordshire barrister and journalist, contrasted the 'village from without' – 'the delightful old village that we rush through on our modern contrivances of petrol or of steam'[15] – and the 'village from within', where the reports of inspectors were testament to the poor quality of country homes.[16] The rural location of this poor housing still had an ideological power, especially significant in the context of depopula-

---

9 George Haw, *No room to live: the plaint of overcrowded London*, London 1900, p. viii.
10 W. Walter Crotch, *The cottage homes of England: the case against the housing system in rural districts* (1st edn 1901), 2nd edn, London 1901, 7–8.
11 Walter Raymond, *English country life*, London 1910; Marsh, *Back to the land*; Howkins, 'Discovery'.
12 Helen Allingham and Stewart Dick, *The cottage homes of England*, London 1909.
13 Bennett, *Problems of village life*, 70.
14 Clement Edwards, 'Bad housing in rural districts', in Fabian Society, *The house famine and how to relieve it* (Fabian Tract ci), London 1900, 4–5; Holdenby, *Folk of the furrow*, 48–50.
15 Hugh Aronson, *Our village homes: present conditions and suggested remedies*, London 1913, 5.
16 Ibid. ch. ii.

tion, capable of undermining efforts at reform. For example, William G. Savage, medical officer of health for Somerset, well aware of the poor standards of cottage accommodation and the inadequacy of existing laws for the purpose of remedying them, still pointed out (in 1915) that urban populations were on the whole less healthy than the rural,[17] and that migration to towns was a cause of 'national ill-health'.[18] The exposure of the conditions of rural housing was clearly related to the wider question of 'national efficiency'. As Hugh Aronson explained, '[n]ational efficiency is vital to the welfare of the State; and national efficiency can never be secured without that national health which is being steadily undermined by bad housing'.[19]

The subject had another political dimension. The tied cottage system, a long-standing grievance among many agricultural labourers, was criticised by many investigators. Indeed, the report of the Royal Commission on the Housing of the Working Classes had pointed out that security of cottage tenure was more important to the labourers than the physical surroundings of the home.[20] Complaining about the conditions in which they lived was difficult for labouring families, as tied cottages established a barrier to the discovery of the truth about housing conditions. F. E. Green, a land reformer who concerned himself particularly with the 'tyranny' of the tied cottage system, inspected cottages in his own Surrey village and found that he needed to visit at night so that local farmers and landlords could not see that their tenants were revealing to him the inadequacy of their accommodation.[21] Green claimed that his efforts at reform were thwarted by the opposition of local farmers on the parish council.[22] Clement Edwards made a point of speaking to labourers about tied cottages, finding that they condemned them and the insecurity of tenure that resulted.[23] It was also argued that the political and financial influence of landowners could frustrate efforts at housing reform. Another contributor to the substantial literature on rural housing, the campaigning journalist Walter Crotch, suggested that even medical officers of health, supposedly the most independent of investigators, were subject to pressures from vested interests in the countryside. They had private practices in addition to their public duties, and Crotch claimed that he had 'known of cases where the fear of losing a valuable part of an income from a big country magnate has induced an officer to see fewer gross insanitary evils on that person's estate than actually existed'.[24] One investigator in an unnamed southern village, who gave information to a Fabian Society committee of investigation, found that whereas a poor law official

---

[17] William G. Savage, *Rural housing*, London 1915, 245.
[18] Ibid. 268.
[19] Aronson, *Village homes*, 101.
[20] Burnett, *Social history of housing*, 133.
[21] Green, *Tyranny*, London 1913, 30, and *Awakening*, 271.
[22] Idem, *Tyranny*, 30–1, and *The Surrey hills*, London 1915, 23–4.
[23] Edwards, 'Bad housing', 5.
[24] Crotch, *Cottage homes*, 153.

condemned the local housing as 'disgraceful', the local medical officer of health was reluctant to criticise the landlord, 'being dependent upon him, and living in one of his houses'.[25]

The social and political implications of these vested interests could be encountered and assessed within the official structure of local housing investigation, to which, theoretically, every member of the rural community had access. The restructuring of local government in 1888 and 1894, along with the 1890 Act, had established a process by which complaints about the quality or supply of housing in a particular district could initiate an official inquiry with a view to the construction of cottages by the local authority. These official inquiries, no less than those of freelance investigators such as F. E. Green, often became scenes of bitter conflict. There were substantial pressures on the labourers housed in squalid conditions to refrain from complaining about their condition to official inquiries. Hugh Aronson, writing in 1913, described a local inquiry held near his home village of Chipperfield in Hertfordshire under the provisions of the 1890 Act. Very many of the villagers 'would not attend to make their voices heard for very fear';[26] and one expert witness, a sympathetic parish councillor, said that people were afraid to give him information, in the belief that it would find its way back to their landlords and make trouble for them.[27] The obstacles in the way of building houses under the provisions of the act were in any case immense: the construction of just six cottages at Penshurst in Kent in 1899, for example, was the result of four separate inquiries held over a period of three years.[28] As Walter Crotch reported, at the colliery village of Wales in Yorkshire, despite 'overwhelming' evidence of the need for new cottages at an inquiry in 1898, the local inquiry had to be adjourned for six months in order to ascertain the willingness of landowners in the area to cooperate.[29] Vested interests were invariably lined up against the labourers, who if fortunate were assisted by well-meaning social reformers, such as Jane Escombe at Penshurst or Walter Crotch at Wales. Only through the efforts of sympathetic investigators such as these could the manifest inequalities that characterised the processes of investigation be at least partially addressed.

One investigator who was particularly interested in the cottage question was Constance Cochrane of Huntingdonshire. Cochrane explored cottages herself, and also carried out a large-scale investigation in the course of which she sent circulars to nearly 3,000 potential informants (more than 500 of which were returned), and sent deputies to inspect seventy villages in thirteen different counties.[30] Of 141 returns which gave sufficient details to judge

[25] Henry D. Harben, *The rural problem*, London 1913, 129–30.
[26] Aronson, *Village homes*, 15.
[27] Ibid. 18.
[28] Crotch, *Cottage homes*, ch ix.
[29] Ibid. 66.
[30] Constance Cochrane, *Papers on rural housing: the present condition of the cottage home of the agricultural labourer*, St Neots 1901, 12–13.

from, 96 described 'bad' or 'very bad' cottages, 25 'fair' and only 20 'good'.[31] Cochrane found that her findings were borne out by the reports of medical officers of health, local government reports and 'blue books'.[32] There is little evidence of the social make-up of her informant base, but in a report prepared for the Fabian Society in 1900 she cited returns from three parish councillors, a rural district councillor, a clergyman, a clergyman's wife, a sanitary inspector, a labourer and, curiously, a baker.[33] The new organs of local government had created a new class of supposedly trustworthy informants – councillors and their paid officials – while the more traditional informants were also drawn upon. While vested interests were disproportionately represented on rural district and parish councils, those consulted were presumably relatively sympathetic towards the labourers' discontents, as their reports bore out Cochrane's views on rural housing; the high non-response rate suggests that many did not share her views or approve of her independent investigations. Cochrane persistently attempted to expose the vested interests that she believed hid the condition of the labourer's cottage from the view of the outside investigator. Having shown Rider Haggard some poor cottages at Eltisley in Huntingdonshire in 1901, she wrote to her cousin, Arthur Cochrane, explaining the barriers encountered by the investigator of rural housing:

> I want just once more to impress upon you & Mr. Haggard the great difficulty of finding out the truth about the cottages when you are in different villages. The outside appearance is a most unsafe & misleading guide. The people themselves will oftener than not tell any amount of untruths to a *stranger*, for fear of being 'turned out', or because they have been threatened with high rents if they complain. The farmers will hardly ever tell the truth, as many of them are on Rural District Councils, & are afraid of the rates. . . . Owners very often do not know, & oftener do not care & they do not hear the *truth* from their agents. If Mr. Haggard had been taken to Eltisley by anyone about here except me, he [would] not have been able to gain any idea of the conditions of the cottages & san[itary] arrangements except where they *looked* bad from the outside.[34]

Local vested interests, then, were not only obstacles in the way of reform, but also barriers to social investigation. Cochrane emphasised the need for personal knowledge of an area, and the winning of confidence among the cottagers themselves: they needed to be sure that their complaints would not result in eviction or other forms of victimisation. The accurate and sensitive investigation of housing appeared to require the perspective of a resident.

---

31 Ibid. 13.
32 Ibid. 14.
33 Constance Cochrane, 'Laborers' [*sic*] cottages', in Fabian Society, *House famine*, 7–8.
34 Constance Cochrane to Arthur Cochrane, 18 May 1901, Rider Haggard papers, MS 4692/25 (Cambs.). Original emphases.

If housing was one important concern among social investigators in rural England in this period, the subject of agricultural wages was no less intensely discussed than in earlier decades. F. E. Green, remarking in 1920 on the variety of books on the condition and history of the agricultural labourer published in the years before the Great War, noticed that '[t]he crop was a big one, yet it was significant that every investigator's hand had found its way to the one upstanding thistle which he grasped with unpleasant prickings, and that was the lowness of the labourers' [sic] wage'.[35] Within this sphere of inquiry, the conflicts between users and advocates of the informant and respondent methods remained very much in evidence. The debates coalesced around the investigations carried out in 1900 and 1905 under the auspices of the Board of Trade by Arthur Wilson Fox, veteran of the Royal Commission on Labour and other official inquiries;[36] and these were followed in 1910 by George Askwith's report on the earnings and hours of labour in agriculture, which formed one part of the Board of Trade's 'wage census', and was carried out on a larger scale than Wilson Fox's surveys.[37] In the footnotes of official inquiries and freelance social investigations, a vigorous debate was instigated around the methodology of the investigation of the rural wage. Wilson Fox was commissioned by the Board of Trade – which, as E. P. Hennock has pointed out,[38] was active in social investigation in the Edwardian period to a degree often overlooked by historians – to discover the average cash wages and weekly earnings (inclusive of perquisites) in each of the counties of Britain, and to describe other conditions of employment such as the terms of the labourer's hire. He also attempted to gain some insight into the domestic economy of labouring families, and to describe their patterns of consumption. Wilson Fox was engaged in freelance investigations at the same time – he read a paper on agricultural earnings during the previous fifty years to the Royal Statistical Society in 1903[39] – but it was only with the support of the official machinery of the state that a realistic attempt at a nationwide survey could be attempted. As Francis Heath, referring to Wilson Fox's surveys, pointed out, '[o]nly the resources of a great Government department . . . with its army of correspondents in all parts of the kingdom, could enable us to give a rapid survey, which would be at the same time simultaneous'.[40]

Wilson Fox's inquiries were one manifestation of the development of labour statistics under the auspices of the Labour Department of the Board of

[35] Green, History, 178.

[36] Report by Mr Wilson Fox on the wages and earnings of agricultural labourers in the United Kingdom, with statistical tables and charts, PP 1900, Cd. 346; Second report by Mr Wilson Fox on the wages and earnings of agricultural labourers in the United Kingdom, with statistical tables and charts, PP 1905, Cd. 2376.

[37] Report of an enquiry by the Board of Trade into the earnings and hours of labour of workpeople of the United Kingdom, V: agriculture in 1907, PP 1910, Cd. 5460.

[38] Hennock, 'Measurement', 216–19.

[39] Wilson Fox, 'Agricultural wages'.

[40] Heath, British rural life and labour, 56.

Trade, which had been established in 1893 to succeed the Labour Bureau, itself created in 1886. The activities of the Labour Department in social investigation, under the direction of Hubert Llewellyn Smith, himself a veteran of Charles Booth's inquiry, were indicative of the growing professionalisation of social inquiry in this period, and have been examined in detail by Roger Davidson.[41] The collection of labour statistics had been initiated partly as a result of pressure from the Royal Statistical Society, with which men like Wilson Fox and Llewellyn Smith were themselves associated, and had developed in the context of the industrial conflicts in the period of the 'new unionism'. The board's expenditure on the collection of labour statistics expanded enormously between 1886 and 1914,[42] while the more complex analysis required in the context of the fiscal problems and concerns over national efficiency in the 1900s resulted in the employment of experts on a part-time basis to undertake specific statistical tasks.[43] Although, as Davidson shows, the labour statistics produced by the board remained deficient in many respects down to 1914, the growing concern for the collection of accurate and reliable data on social conditions was clearly reflected in the expanding activities of the Labour Department. In a rural context, the department had initiated some systematised data collection in 1894, from which date the chairmen of rural district councils had supplied information on wages, and by 1902 about 300 farmers were in regular contact with the department and were used as sources of information in Wilson Fox's inquiries.[44] Davidson argues that the board's inquiries tended to serve a conservative purpose: the 'Tory progressive' Wilson Fox and his colleagues at the board 'viewed labour statistics as a means of cementing social relations and diverting working-class discontent into constructive channels'.[45] The methods used in the rural inquiries were similarly conservative, reflecting the traditional structure and concerns of the official inquiry and the social and political backgrounds of those who carried them out.

To obtain his information on wages in England in 1905 – and the methods used in 1900 were very similar – Wilson Fox consulted a large number of individuals. Information on weekly cash wage rates was taken from the chairmen of rural district councils, from the usual contacts in the farming community and from 'a large number' of farmers who disclosed the wages they had paid in 1902. In 1900 Wilson Fox had explained that some of the council chairmen had brought the inquiry to the attention of council meetings, and that others who were not themselves directly involved in agriculture had consulted 'representative farmers' in their districts.[46] In order to obtain information on

---

[41] Davidson, *Whitehall and the labour problem*.
[42] Ibid. 104–6.
[43] Ibid. 106, 215–20.
[44] *Second report by Mr Wilson Fox*, 7.
[45] Davidson, *Whitehall and the labour problem*, 118–19.
[46] *Report by Mr Wilson Fox*, 4.

earnings, including extra cash payments and allowances in kind, Wilson Fox sent forms out to about 10,500 farmers in 1903, of which about 3,200 were returned and useable; these related to about 28,000 labourers, including those who were absent from work for part of the year, but excluding casual labourers.[47] Certain farms were examined in more detail, again using information chiefly supplied by the employers.[48] One of the clearest features to emerge from Wilson Fox's reports was the wide regional diversity in the pay and conditions of agricultural labourers, a long-standing feature of the rural labour problem. The highest average earnings in England in 1902 were 22s. 2d. in Durham, and the lowest 14s. 6d. in Oxfordshire.[49] Not only did earnings vary markedly from place to place, but the structure of remuneration also differed widely, and no one county could be taken as typical: the excess of earnings (as calculated by employers) over wages varied from 4s. in Hampshire to 1s. 7d. in Leicestershire and Rutland.[50] In some counties, the availability of piece-work could significantly improve the labourer's earning potential, while in others free cottages and potato ground were common, and elsewhere free cider or beer was given. The emphasis on regional variations was illustrative of the perennial problem facing the investigator of rural life: to avoid the charge of generalising from the particular, a wide geographical area had to be investigated, but the variety of conditions that such a survey would reveal made meaningful generalisations extremely difficult. In any case, county averages concealed significant variations within counties. Harold Mann, in his brief contribution to this debate, argued that Wilson Fox's average wage of 15s. 5d. for Bedfordshire, the county with which Mann was most familiar, was too high, as Wilson Fox had overestimated the numbers of 'higher grades' of labourers;[51] moreover, wages varied considerably within Bedfordshire. While money wages in Ridgmount were higher than Wilson Fox's estimate of the money wages in Bedfordshire as a whole, the position was reversed when additional payments were included in the figures.[52]

The most important area of disagreement, however, was in the informant method that Wilson Fox had adopted. As an official investigator, his choice

[47] Second report by Mr Wilson Fox, 7. The inquiry of 1900 received usable replies from 1,857 farmers, relating to 18,069 labourers; and George Askwith's inquiry was based on nearly 15,800 referring to over 78,000 labourers. The returns received for 1907 seem to represent smaller farms: the average employed on each farm was just over five, whereas for Wilson Fox's report in 1900 it was nearly ten, and for 1905 the figure was just under nine. The implications of these discrepancies require further investigation.
[48] Second report by Mr Wilson Fox, 46–64. Eight of these farms were in Lincolnshire, two in Herefordshire, and one each in Northumberland, Cumberland, Northamptonshire, Suffolk, Sussex, Wiltshire and Somerset.
[49] Second report by Mr Wilson Fox, 28–9.
[50] Ibid. 28–9, 34.
[51] Mann, 'Agricultural village', 192.
[52] Ibid. 191.

of method was naturally constrained, but he employed a similar approach in his inquiry for the Royal Statistical Society. For this investigation, he collected information from 125 farmers on which to base his analysis,[53] while the historical material in the paper was taken from inquiries such as the poor law commission reports of 1843 – which according to Wilson Fox took evidence from 'reliable witnesses such as medical men and the clergy'[54] – and from the published work of James Caird and Frederick Clifford.[55] In his 1905 survey Wilson Fox did try to investigate the domestic economy of labourers' households, and drew on a wide range of correspondents including 'land-owners, Local Government Board inspectors, members of Local Authorities, farmers, clergymen, relieving officers, village tradesmen, and labourers',[56] and he claimed to have met some labourers personally in the course of the investigation.[57] However, rural elites evidently formed the dominant group of informants, and it was on these grounds that Wilson Fox attracted the most criticism. Hugh Aronson, commenting on the 1905 report, was certain that the wage figures erred on this high side, because 'the information was obtained solely from employers, and there is no doubt that they estimated the value of allowances at a higher figure than was justified and considerably higher than the men would have valued them at had they been consulted'.[58] Similarly, the historian Wilhelm Hasbach, the English translation of whose history of the agricultural labourer was published in 1908, concluded that 'too much faith must not be rested on [Wilson Fox's] data, seeing that they mostly come from farmers, though some, and in particular the figures for the money-wages, are from the chairmen of Rural District Councils'.[59] Even the latter group were often farmers themselves, although in giving evidence to Wilson Fox they tended not to comment very much on the really contentious aspects of the agricultural wage structure. E. N. Bennett, who noted that Wilson Fox did not make deductions for wet weather and short-time working,[60] thought that the reports' 'careful statistics . . . would have been even more reliable had they not been based so largely on returns made by employers',[61] and argued that the perquisites which Wilson Fox incorporated into his wage calculations were simply an excuse used by farmers to pay low wages, and concealed the 'economic facts of village life' from observers.[62] F. E. Green also put little faith in Wilson Fox's figures, noting the 'very doubtful cash value' of payments in kind, and declaring:

[53] Wilson Fox, 'Agricultural wages', 273.
[54] Ibid. 301.
[55] Ibid. 303, 314.
[56] Ibid. 274.
[57] Ibid. 289 n. 23.
[58] Hugh Aronson, *The land and the labourer*, London 1914, 53 n. 10.
[59] Hasbach, *History*, 317.
[60] Bennett, *Problems of village life*, 158.
[61] Ibid. 9.
[62] Ibid. 67.

It is only human nature that all farmers, desiring to appear as generous as possible, should put down sums against allowances in kind which are very far from being accurate. Indeed, I doubt whether Farmer Giles, who perhaps has never had an account book to keep during his whole life, would retain anything like accurate figures in his head as to the cash equivalent of many of these 'allowances'.[63]

Even Francis Heath, whose 1911 survey was largely based on the Board of Trade reports, remarked on the inferiority of the cider supplied to labourers in lieu of wages in the west of England, and on this basis thought its value 'rather over-estimated' by employers.[64]

Even if the potential for farmers to exaggerate the real earnings of their employees was overstated – and it should be borne in mind that Wilson Fox pointed out that payments in kind, which had the most contestable cash value, were relatively rare and formed only a small proportion of the total earnings[65] – the information obtained by the Board of Trade inquiries could be challenged on the grounds that only the more generous employers were represented in the informant structure. As the Fabian investigator Henry Harben pointed out in 1913, the figures in official reports like Wilson Fox's

> were calculated from information supplied by a small and picked minority of employers, under whom conditions of labour are probably most free from reproach. The method employed has been to send schedules to farmers who are known to the Department and to the Local Authority; all of these are employers who would have least reason to avoid answering questions about their workpeople.[66]

Employers whose labourers were poorly paid and worked under unfavourable conditions were less likely to respond to a Board of Trade questionnaire, and were also unlikely to become regular correspondents of the increasingly professionalised statistical wing of the Labour Department. However confident the Edwardian governmental bureaucracy may have been in its ability to obtain a generally accurate and representative view of conditions across a wide range of industries and districts, even the superficially simple question of wages continued to baffle investigators as it had done half a century earlier.

If many of the same problems were being identified by social investigators in the early twentieth century as had been described by their predecessors (and in some cases by themselves) in the 1870s, the most striking feature of the inquiries of the 1900s and early 1910s was that they were always informed

---

[63] Green, *Tyranny*, 226. Green did not share the belief of many investigators that the labourer was inclined to undervalue his earnings: he considered that the labourer, when questioned, would be embarrassed to disclose the true extent of his impoverishment, and would thus also overvalue his remuneration: *History*, 105.

[64] Heath, *British rural life and labour*, 35.

[65] *Second report by Mr Wilson Fox*, 22–3.

[66] Harben, *Rural problem*, 8.

by, and often structured around, the land question.[67] The importance of land reform to the architects of the 'New Liberalism' brought a new and important dimension to the debate on rural England, the stirrings of which had been felt in the 1890s. The land question seemed to unite the concerns of 'national efficiency',[68] as articulated most forcefully by Rider Haggard, and the 'condition of England', as explored by social commentators such as C. F. G. Masterman,[69] and to merge them together in a distinctive approach to social reform. Although the issue was politically contentious, both Conservatives and Liberals found merit in certain proposals for land reform. Haggard and Henry Chaplin came to support smallholdings as the basis for a re-creation of the old yeoman class;[70] and on the other side of the party divide, Henry Campbell-Bannerman, in a speech at the Albert Hall during the general election campaign of 1905–6, expressed his party's desire 'to colonise our own country': 'We wish to make the land less of a pleasure-ground for the rich, and more of a treasure-house for the nation.'[71] It was the Liberal party that took the most proactive approach to land reform, its spokesmen relating landownership directly to economic and social deprivation. This was the Edwardian legacy of the Victorian drive towards land reform that had been manifested in the activities of groups such as the English Land Restoration League. As H. J. Perkin has explained:

> There was scarcely a social problem, from rural hovels and village pauperism to the slums, drunkenness and moral degradation of town life, which reformers did not place at the landlords' door. The landlords had driven the people from the soil, and therefore they were responsible for the consequences: the loss of prosperity and self-respect, the dependence on an insecure wage, the lack of steps in the form of allotments and smallholdings by which the landless man could climb to a farm, and [what the land reformer James Beal called] 'all the vast and unnumbered social sores connected with pauperism and rural degradation'.[72]

The link between social problems and the land became firmly established in the investigative culture of the period. By 1908 the Fabian investigator D. C. Pedder could write of 'the great plea of LABOUR *versus* LAND which

---

67 For examples of other books on the land question which are not considered here see L. Jebb, *The small holdings of England: a survey of various existing systems*, London 1907; George Cadbury and Tom Bryan, *The land and the landless*, London 1908; Joseph Edwards (ed.), *Land and real tariff reform, being the land reformers' handbook for 1909*, London 1909; Joseph Hyder, *The case for land nationalisation*, London 1913.

68 See Searle, *Quest for national efficiency*, 172.

69 Masterman, *Condition of England*.

70 See pp. 76–7 above.

71 Quoted in Douglas, *Land, people and politics*, 135, and Offer, *Property and politics*, 356.

72 H. J. Perkin, 'Land reform and class conflict in Victorian Britain', in J. Butt and I. F. Clarke (eds), *The Victorians and social protest: a symposium*, Newton Abbot 1973, 188.

is now going on in our midst',[73] while, as noted above, Seebohm Rowntree insisted in the early 1900s that 'the most important factor in determining social conditions was the tenure of land'.[74]

Edwardian preoccupation with the land gave rise to a conception of rural life which tended to accentuate the non-wage aspects of rural poverty and the monotony and hopelessness of rural existence. This cultural poverty would be ascribed to different causes: the land reformer would generally cite the persistence of unaccountable private landownership and its stultifying effect on village democracy and independence, which deprived the labourer of a healthy democratic village life and a chance to advance on the land; the Conservative was likely to point to the demise of paternalist social relations, the pernicious influence of the cash-nexus and the emergence of class politics in the countryside. Liberal and socialist commentators blamed the dullness of village life on the 'tyranny' of parson and landowner and the limited access of agricultural labourers to the land. Pedder, admitting that the decline of the old village gentry had contributed to the dullness of village life,[75] and regretting the increasingly embittered social relations in the English countryside,[76] firmly endorsed Henry George's view that land monopoly was the root cause of poverty,[77] and advocated the creation of a class of small independent cultivators who would have a personal attachment to the land.[78] Another Fabian investigator, Henry Harben, believed that the labourer's social position was not far removed from serfdom, and condemned the tied cottage system which engendered 'servility and dependence' on the labourer's part.[79] Even where allotments were provided to give the labourer a measure of independence, many were of poor quality and were often situated a long way from the labourer's home.[80] For these investigators, although the labourer's horizons were broadening as a result of improved education and increased contact with the non-rural world,[81] his lack of opportunity to advance on the land and to participate in organised village activities contributed to the exodus from the countryside. The Liberal government's endorsement of the potentially popular cause of land reform led the Conservative opposition to frame their own proposals: their approach, as E. H. H. Green has explained, was 'driven by a more general effort to broaden the electoral appeal of Conservatism after 1906', and was symptomatic of a 'growing desire to identify themselves as a

[73] D. C. Pedder, *Where men decay: a survey of present rural conditions*, London 1908, p. v. Original capitalisation.
[74] See p. 124 above.
[75] Pedder, *Where men decay*, ch. i, and *Secret*, 13.
[76] Idem, *Where men decay*, 32–7.
[77] Idem, *Henry George and his gospel*, London 1908, 86.
[78] Idem, *Secret*, 17–19.
[79] Harben, *Rural problem*, 4–5.
[80] Ibid. 12.
[81] See, for example, Pedder, *Secret*, 8.

party of land reform'.[82] Conservative policies were based on the development of smallholdings as a bulwark against the socialist threat – one commentator remarked in 1909 that '[w]hen the land is in the hands of but few it is powerless to defend itself against the attacks of fantastic and predatory doctrines'[83] – and as a means of improving the economic outlook of the agricultural labourers and, ultimately, keeping more of them on the land as efficient producers. Ultimately, as Avner Offer has shown, the land reformers in the main parties did not so much differ on the need for reform, as on the best means of effecting and managing it,[84] although the backwoodsmen who were to come to prominence in the attack on the 'People's Budget' and the land campaigners were more intransigent in their insistence on the maintenance of the *status quo*.[85] The widespread desire for reform reflected both the economic imperatives of the period and social and cultural changes. As Alun Howkins has explained, 'the question was not solely or even mainly one of politics or economics but one of the transformation of a whole culture'.[86]

Rooted in the new historiography of rural England which emphasised the landlessness of the labourer and the superiority of pre-industrial social relationships, and overlaid by a pastoral tradition that continued to represent the countryside as a potential reservoir of a manly Englishness vastly superior to debased working-class and effete middle-class urban cultural forms, the evidence for cultural decline (the concomitant of the obvious economic and demographic decline of the English countryside) was drawn on fully by the popular nostalgic country literature of the period, which often portrayed an urgent need to re-create the kind of paternalist village community that had supposedly characterised the pre-enclosure (and pre-Puritan) countryside. It was not just economic advancement that the labourer needed, but social and cultural opportunities as well. Thus, for example, the antiquarian and country parson P. H. Ditchfield, who published widely on the cultural and customary life of rural England, was in no doubt that depopulation would be decelerated by the revival of old village sports and pastimes, and that a knowledge of local history would add interest and colour to country-dwellers' lives: 'The death of the old social customs which added such diversity to the lives of our forefathers tends to render the countryman's life one continuous round of labour unrelieved by pleasant pastime, and if innocent pleasures are not indulged in, the tendency is to seek for gratification in amusements that are not innocent or wholesome.'[87] Ditchfield admired the village communities of Tudor and Stuart England,[88] and derived some of his information on the mid-nineteenth

82 Green, *Crisis of conservatism*, 218.
83 See ibid. 219, 210 for Henry Chaplin's endorsement of this view. See also Offer, *Property and politics*, 352–3.
84 Offer, *Property and politics*, 356–7.
85 Ibid. 367–9.
86 Howkins, 'Discovery', 69.
87 P. H. Ditchfield, *Vanishing England*, London 1910, 375.
88 Idem, *Old village life, or glimpses of village life through all ages*, London 1920, pp. vii–viii.

century from Miss Mitford, citing for example her descriptions of village cricket matches;[89] while, to take another example, the veteran commentator Augustus Jessopp claimed in 1914 that although 'England's peasantry' were undoubtedly better fed, better educated, better housed and less overworked than a century earlier, their ancestors had nevertheless '*enjoyed* their lives much more than their descendants [and] had incomparably more laughter, more amusement, more real delight in the labour of their hands', which were the true 'constituents of happiness'.[90] As Offer and others have shown,[91] this nostalgic literature fed directly into, and in some respects shaped, contemporaneous debates on the land question, whether the remedy proposed was feudal, co-operative or socialistic in ambition.

The special correspondent journalists of the Edwardian period found themselves increasingly polarised around the land question. One good example of the contestability of the morality of the landholding system and its effects on the labouring population is to be found in the differing responses of special correspondents to their visits to Lord Salisbury's estates in Hertfordshire. In 1901, while Salisbury was still prime minister, Rider Haggard and the *Express* remarked on 'The Lucky Fortune of Those who Chance to be Tenants of Lord Salisbury', and described the good cottages, all built by workmen on the estate.[92] On the other hand, when Robert Outhwaite, a correspondent of a very different political complexion – he was a prominent land reformer and famously won the Hanley by-election for the Liberals in 1912[93] – visited Hatfield in 1909, he compared the conditions unfavourably with a London slum. Under the headline 'Hatfield and the hovels', he recognised that the worst cottages were not actually owned by the then Lord Salisbury (the premier's successor to the title), but argued that 'his ownership of almost every vacant acre is the cause of such conditions existing'.[94] Similarly, in 1912 Harold Spender, a noted journalist and lecturer, reported for the *Daily News and Leader* on 'Landlord-ridden Cornwall',[95] and in a series of articles laid the blame for poor housing firmly at the door of the land monopolists.[96] Another example was W. B. Hodgson, yet another *Daily News* special correspondent, who in the mid-1900s began a tour of Devon and the west, which was completed after his death by C. F. G. Masterman.

These correspondents continued to stress the different character of information and opinion obtainable from different standpoints, and emphasised the value of the testimony taken from the informants they chose. Masterman,

[89] Idem, *The cottages and the village life of rural England*, London 1912, 147.
[90] Jessopp, *England's peasantry*, 40–1. Original emphasis.
[91] Offer, *Property and politics*, chs xx–xxi; Howkins, 'Discovery'.
[92] *Daily Express*, 26 July 1901, 4.
[93] Douglas, *Land, people and politics*, 157–9.
[94] R. L. Outhwaite, *Peer or peasant? The ruin of rural England and the remedy*, London 1909, 25.
[95] *Daily News and Leader*, 19 Sept. 1912, 4.
[96] Ibid. 30 Sept. 1912, 7; 1 Oct. 1912, 7; 2 Oct. 1912, 7.

for example, obtained useful information from Mr Weaver, chairman of Castle Morton parish council in the Malverns, 'a sturdy Radical yeoman of the old school',[97] while Outhwaite spoke to an artisan at Petworth in Sussex (on Lord Leconfield's land), who claimed to be fearful of reprisals if he was caught talking to a Liberal correspondent.[98] In the north of Scotland, Outhwaite travelled across the duke of Sutherland's estate: Sutherland, he pointed out, was a prominent Tory, president of the Tariff Reform League, whereas Outhwaite took as his guide Mr Joseph McLeod, organising secretary of the Inverness Liberal Association, and long active in the Highland Land Reform movement.[99] Unsurprisingly, the views expressed in his columns reflect those of McLeod (who still bore a grudge against the landlord for his grandfather's eviction over a century earlier), as well as the natural political sympathies of a *Daily News* journalist. Similarly, when Hodgson talked to a Norfolk landowner, he was told that the labourers could get cottages, but that they were not given them because their children were dirty and prone to break windows;[100] but from another perspective, Mr Weaver told Masterman that they were fortunate to have no resident landlord at Castle Morton,[101] and Masterman, like George Millin nearly two decades earlier, contrasted the open 'free' village with the closed 'feudal' one.[102] The labourer in the 'free' village was independent, and not subject to the 'tyranny' of parson and squire. Like their predecessors, these men leaned towards the evidence of the labourers and Dissenters. Outhwaite found the perfect witness in the Vale of Aylesbury: Mr Foat, 'a member of the Aylesbury Board of Guardians, a man of independent means, a leader of Primitive Methodism, and so knowing the life of the villages, and not afraid to speak his mind'.[103] Foat was a respectable man, in positions of authority, but also in close touch with the villagers, who gave him much of his information. He believed that the labourers only stayed on the land at all because of allotments; and that farmers on the small hold-ings committee of the county council frightened the labourers out of applying for this form of access to the land.[104] The special correspondent, then, in this period, was increasingly concerned with the politics of the land question, and these politics were again reflected in the informant structure he chose to adopt.

If the tradition of the rural special correspondent was adapted to the exam-ination of the land question, the most notable result of its prominence was a series of large-scale inquiries conducted by various bodies concerned in some

97   C. F. G. Masterman, W. B. Hodgson and others, *To colonise England: a plea for a policy*, London 1907, 76.
98   Outhwaite, *Peer or peasant?*, 11.
99   Idem, *Deer and desolation: the Scottish land problem*, London 1912, 24–5.
100   Masterman and others, *To colonise England*, 54.
101   Ibid. 75, 80.
102   Ibid. 91; Millin, *Life in our villages*, 106–13.
103   Outhwaite, *Peer or peasant?*, 20–1.
104   Ibid. 21–2.

way with the politics of land. The Rural Land League, the Central Land Association, the Land Agents' Society and other bodies all carried out their own inquiries, as did the Conservative party, the Labour party and the Fabian Society, but without doubt the most important was the two-volume report of the Liberal party's Land Enquiry Committee, which deserves extended consideration as one of the most important and large-scale investigative ventures of the period.[105] As will be seen, the Land Enquiry Committee's activities provoked intense debate, and spawned hostile counter-investigations by other bodies. The committee was appointed by the Chancellor of the Exchequer, David Lloyd George, in 1912, and had a membership of twelve. The chairman was Arthur Acland, and the honorary secretary Charles Roden Buxton. R. L. Reiss was head organiser of the Rural Enquiry, and the committee also included Richard Winfrey, Liberal MP for South-West Norfolk from 1906 (who had assisted C. F. G. Masterman with his investigations in Norfolk for the *Daily News*)[106] and Seebohm Rowntree. It was thus rather unfair of the committee's critics to suggest that the chairman was 'the only member who could claim any knowledge of agriculture':[107] Rowntree's exhaustive investigations of Belgian agricultural conditions, at any rate, gave him some authority as a rural investigator, and Gilbert Slater thought his co-written volume on *How the labourer lives* was 'practically a companion volume to the Land Report'.[108] Slater agreed that the committee's report 'suffers . . . from the fact that it is to a great extent the work of town-dwellers', but argued that 'these town-dwellers are conscious of the disability under which they have laboured, and have taken exceptional pains to get at the thoughts, the feelings and the fundamental realities of [the] life of the rural worker'.[109] There is no doubt that, as appointees of Lloyd George, the inquirers approached their task with a predetermined agenda of radical land reform,[110] but to marshal evidence in support of this agenda they conducted an investigation on an impressive scale. The committee employed seventy people, and Rowntree regularly spent four days a week over a two-year period working on the inquiry in London.[111]

The committee reported in two stages: the rural volume of its findings was

[105] For accounts of the Land Enquiry Committee and the land campaign see Douglas, *Land, people and politics*, 158–66; Offer, *Property and politics*, chs xxii–xxiii; Bentley B. Gilbert, 'David Lloyd George: the reform of British landholding and the budget of 1914', *Historical Journal* xxi (1978), 117–41; Briggs, *Seebohm Rowntree*, 64–73.

[106] On Winfrey see Howkins, *Poor labouring men*, ch. v.

[107] Charles Adeane and Edwin Savill, *The land retort: a study of the land question with an answer to the report of the Secret Enquiry Committee*, London 1914, p. ix.

[108] *Sociological Review* vii (1914), 177.

[109] Ibid. 175.

[110] See Chris Wrigley, *Lloyd George*, Oxford 1992, 26–7, 44–6, 48, 54–6; Bentley B. Gilbert, *David Lloyd George, a political life*, II: *Organizer of victory, 1912–1916*, Columbus, Ohio 1992, 55–66, 81–93.

[111] Briggs, *Seebohm Rowntree*, 65–6.

published in 1913, and the urban volume in 1914. While the latter was concerned only occasionally with conditions of working-class life in towns, the rural inquiry examined the condition of the agricultural labourer in great detail, and the discussion here focuses on this aspect of the committee's work. For the purposes of the rural inquiry, England and Wales were divided into twelve districts, and a head investigator was appointed for each.[112] Schedules of questions were sent out to informants selected by the head investigators. Schedule A, 2,759 of which were received, was mainly concerned with wages and conditions of labour, housing and allotments, 'and related to matters of fact rather than of opinion'.[113] Schedule B dealt with more directly agricultural matters; 866 of these were filled in.[114] Anonymity was assured for informants, an aspect of the inquiry which provided grounds for criticism.[115] Other information was obtained from the reports of independent investigators, including Rowntree, Harold Mann and Maud Davies,[116] and two opponents of the Liberal government, Daniel Hall[117] and Rider Haggard.[118] Official inquiries were freely quoted throughout the report; and Thomas Hardy's evidence to Haggard's inquiry was cited in the section on tied cottages.[119] The rural report, then, is a good example of the intermingling of different aspects of social investigation in this period, and was a means of drawing different kinds of evidence together. The committee emphasised that as broad a range of informants as possible had been consulted in the preparation of the report: although schedule B was necessarily mainly the province of farmers, agents and landowners,[120] schedule A was filled in by 'men of all classes, including landowners, large farmers, shopkeepers, labourers, small holders, clergy and ministers of all denominations', and occasionally by a local committee formed for the purpose.[121] Like Charles Booth's inquiry into old age in villages, the committee's investigations were supplemented by a historical account written by Gilbert Slater.[122]

---

112 There was a separate inquiry for Scotland (Scottish Land Enquiry Committee, *Scottish land, rural and urban: the report of the Scottish Land Enquiry Committee*, London 1914); and, although the Land Enquiry Committee covered parts of Wales, a separate rural report was also prepared by the Welsh Land Enquiry Committee (*Welsh land, rural: the report of the Welsh Land Enquiry Committee*, London 1914).
113 Land Enquiry Committee, *The land: the report of the Land Enquiry Committee*, I: *Rural*, London 1913, p. xiv.
114 Ibid. i, pp. xv–xvi.
115 Adeane and Savill, *Land retort*, p. x.
116 Land Enquiry Committee, *The land*, i, pp. xliii, 23–9.
117 Ibid. i. 39, 160, 231, 233–5.
118 Ibid. i, pp. xxxii, xlvii–l, 138, 150.
119 Ibid. i. 150.
120 For the urban inquiry solicitors, architects, surveyors and others with direct experience of urban land problems were generally used: Land Enquiry Committee, *The land: the report of the Land Enquiry Committee*, II: *Urban*, London 1914, p. xxiv.
121 Ibid. i, p. xvi.
122 Ibid. i, pp. lxi–lxxxiii. See also p. 126 above.

Partly because of the committee's interest in the condition of the agricultural labourer, the informant structure of the rural inquiry reached further and more frequently down the social pyramid than did the urban investigation. Of thirty-three rural informants whose evidence to the urban inquiry on the subject of the farmer and the rating of improvements was quoted, eighteen were farmers (two of them county councillors), and there were also three 'yeoman farmer[s]', two builders, a 'tenant farmer', a 'gentleman farmer', a county councillor, a rate collector, a landowner, a willow merchant, an overseer, a surveyor and a 'Chamber of Agriculture'.[123] On the other hand, when the rural inquiry came to consider the question of objections to tied cottages, a subject on which it was not to be expected that farmers would give views which were shared by the Liberal investigators, the evidence used was supplied by a variety of informants including a mason, a boot repairer, a shopkeeper, a railwayman, a postman and a number of labourers.[124] Some farmers were quoted on the subject, but only those who agreed with the committee's criticisms of the system.[125] (In any case, it is unlikely that many farmers who disagreed with the objectives of the inquiry would have agreed to submit written evidence.) The committee had a stated aim of taking evidence from lower down the social scale than official inquiries had done in the past. The choice, as they expressed it, was between the methods of Booth and Rowntree – that is, 'to employ investigators who would go from place to place and obtain information on the spot, either personally or through local helpers'[126] – and the royal commission method of cross-examining witnesses in a metropolitan headquarters. In general, the Booth–Rowntree approach was adopted, and the report explained:

> Royal Commissions are . . . apt to hear only the bigger people. Thus, the witnesses before the Commissions on Agriculture were mainly large farmers, landlords and agents, the small farmer and the labourers, speaking generally, did not appear before them. Moreover, cross-examination by a Committee is more of an ordeal to the small man. He is less expert at putting his case, and the knowledge that his name, as well as a verbatim report of all he says, will be published, must inevitably prevent him, very frequently, from referring to matters which intimately affect him, and regarding which it is essential to learn his true opinion. It is true that some Royal Commissions have appointed assistant commissioners to visit and report on specific areas. These assistant commissioners obtained information from the smaller men, but they gave only

---

123 Land Enquiry Committee, *The land*, ii. 525–30. One informant's background was not stated.
124 Ibid. i. 138–42; cf. Land Agents' Society, *Facts about land: a reply to 'The land'*, *the report of the unofficial Land Enquiry Committee*, London 1916, 119, which notes that only one of the 37 informants quoted on pp. 138–43 of the report (including three informants from Wales) was designated specifically as an 'Agricultural Labourer'. The others are designated simply as 'Labourer'.
125 Land Enquiry Committee, *The land*, i. 148–9.
126 Ibid. i, p. xiv.

their own reports to the Commission, with the result that no first-hand information was available from the small farmers and labourers.[127]

Acland, the committee's chairman, therefore recognised the possible conflicts between different grades of informant; and, perhaps uniquely, he conceived and expressed these conflicts in terms of two identifiable points of view – the 'social' and the 'economic' – which were apt to polarise debate on the condition of agriculture and rural life.[128] The employer and the landowner thought in terms of their own self-interest, which necessitated the adoption, generally, of the 'economic point of view', while the social reformer was liable to overlook this perspective in favour of his more directly 'social' concerns. This division clearly had implications for the methods of investigation that were to be adopted. Acland argued that neither approach, uncritically adopted, could really solve the immense problems that were facing rural life.[129] Thus the labourer, it was argued, needed access to land 'from a social point of view',[130] but smallholdings were also 'extremely desirable from an economic point of view'.[131] The committee repeatedly attempted to justify their proposals on both social and economic grounds: thus, for example, they argued that labour was cheaper (because more efficient) where it was better paid.[132] Nevertheless, the subjects considered under the general heading of the 'economic point of view' were 'agriculture as an industry', the 'position of the landowners' and the 'position of the farmer';[133] while the 'social point of view' considered the wages and conditions of the agricultural labourer.[134] To describe and assess each 'point of view' necessitated the collection of different kinds of evidence from different sources, and thus the notion of potentially conflicting economic and social imperatives was paralleled in the conflicts between the informant and respondent methods of inquiry.

The methods adopted, and the findings and policy recommendations they were used to justify, were certainly open to contestation. Avner Offer has contrasted the methods of the Land Enquiry with the Conservative Tariff Commission, which had taken the approach of the official inquiry and based its research on the public examination of witnesses.[135] Like the Tariff Commission, the Land Enquiry formed the basis of a popular campaign, the significance of which in some respects transcended political party boundaries (although both were certainly designed with party advantage in mind). The Land Agents' Society, in a counter-investigation whose impact was limited

127 Ibid. i, p. xiv.
128 Ibid. i, pp. xxiv–xxv.
129 Ibid. i, pp. li–lii, lvii.
130 Ibid. i. 169, 193
131 Ibid. i. 194.
132 Ibid. i. 56–60, 67.
133 Ibid. i, pp. xlv–li.
134 Ibid. i, pp. xxix–xlv.
135 Offer, *Property and politics*, 372.

through not being published until 1916, was in no doubt that the methods of investigation were unsatisfactory:

> The Report . . . bears on its face defects which are inseparable from the conditions of its preparation. The evidence is anonymous, unsifted, unverified, and often hearsay. It largely consists of the opinions, no doubt honestly entertained and expressed, of men who argue from a narrow range of information and experience. It is selected and marshalled by seven gentlemen, inexperienced in agricultural problems, who are prominently associated with one particular school of political thought, and draw inferences, which often seem unwarrantably large, from special instances reported to them by unknown informants. The result is, that the Report does not bear the stamp of an open-minded investigation of all the facts as the preliminary and necessary foundation for the proposal of remedies. It rather has the impress of a collection of material gathered in support of preconceived ideas and a predetermined policy.[136]

The use of evidence from tradesmen and other countrymen in non-agricultural employment was criticised by Charles Adeane and Edwin Savill, whose Land retort swiftly followed the 'land report': 'Selected evidence from landowners and farmers cannot be accepted as having any weight, and when on agricultural matters it is given by grocers, barbers, chemists, chauffeurs, schoolmasters, signalmen, fellmongers, cycle agents, still less are agriculturists likely to receive it with any respect'.[137] Adeane had been elected to the council of the Royal Agricultural Society of England in 1905, and the Land retort was a wide-ranging criticism of the methods and findings of the Land Enquiry Committee. In particular, Adeane and Savill disagreed with the committee's condemnation of the perquisite system, referring like the committee to Wilson Fox's reports and pointing out that payments in kind, 'of which such a pother is made', formed on average only ten pence of the labourer's wage, and in no county more than 1s. 2d.[138] They also disputed the committee's findings on the hours of labour, defended the system of tied cottages, and repeatedly pointed out that many farmers allowed old and infirm labourers to stay on rent-free in a tied cottage.[139] As in earlier years, spokesmen for the farming interest dwelled on the supposed generosity of farmers towards their employees, and drew on the authoritative knowledge of the organised body of agricultural opinion.

The response of the Land Agents' Society to the Land Enquiry, entitled Facts about land, was based on a detailed circular sent to the twenty-one provincial branches of the society asking for its members' opinions on ninety-nine separate conclusions and recommendations of the enquiry. Like Adeane and Savill, who were keen to emphasise that the Land Enquiry was

[136] Land Agents' Society, Facts about land, p. ix.
[137] Adeane and Savill, Land retort, p. x.
[138] Ibid. 10.
[139] Ibid. 11–13, 19–21, 49–50, 145.

'secret', the Land Agents' Society remarked on the 'unofficial' status of the Liberal investigation: although appointed by the Chancellor, the committee had no official status, and the Land Agents were more impressed by inquiries such as those carried out by the Board of Trade, although they noted that the findings even of these inquiries were based on insufficient data.[140] On the subject of land courts, which were recommended in the Land Enquiry Committee's report, the Land Agents preferred the trustworthy evidence of the 'public, official, and impartial' final report of the Royal Commission on Agriculture, published in 1897, which had condemned an earlier proposal to establish land courts.[141] Although admitting that land agents 'are personally interested in the maintenance of the existing system', and conceding that 'it would not be unreasonable to make some allowance for this unconscious bias',[142] the society launched a powerful assault on the Land Enquiry's conclusions, especially those relating to the earnings and housing of agricultural labourers. The links between these two features of the rural social landscape were emphasised, the society arguing that '[t]he difference between the rents that are actually paid [for cottages], and those which might be commercially charged, forms part of the total earnings of the agricultural labourer', and hence that the Land Enquiry (and other inquiries) had underestimated the real earnings of many labourers.[143] There was strong defence of the perquisite system: the Land Agents found no evidence for the Land Enquiry's assertion that it was 'resented' by labourers, and were particularly insistent on the value of the provision of milk.[144] As for the tied cottage, condemned almost unreservedly by the Land Enquiry Committee, while the Land Agents preferred direct letting, they argued that 'the evils of the existing system are exaggerated' and that labourers did not strongly object to it.[145] Indeed, it was one of the structures that continued to cement the benevolent paternalism of the agricultural community: 'a fairer presentment of the case [against tied cottages] would not omit the countless acts of sympathy and kindness which are done daily in every part of England and Wales by these . . . tyrants to the poorer friends and neighbours whom them employ'.[146] The detractors of the Land Enquiry Committee asserted that only one side of a complicated story was being told: like the denunciators of the 'agitators' in the 1870s, Adeane and Savill claimed that 'the inaccurate assertions in the Report are being unscrupulously used on public platforms, and . . . the country is to be flooded with a body of irresponsible young men who have been instructed like parrots to repeat what they are told'. In disseminating their own versions of the 'facts', these counter-investigations attempted to undermine the authority of

[140] Land Agents' Society, *Facts about land*, 10.
[141] Ibid. 270–5, 298 (quoted); Land Enquiry Committee, *The land*, i. 354–83.
[142] Land Agents' Society, *Facts about land*, p. iv.
[143] Ibid. 46 and passim.
[144] Ibid. 24–6.
[145] Ibid. 118–19.
[146] Ibid. 122.

the outwardly impressive volumes of information presented by the Land Enquiry Committee, attacking in particular the methods of investigation and the obvious political motivation that lay behind its report.

The 'public platforms' to which Adeane and Savill referred were being used as part of Lloyd George's land campaign, initiated to spread the findings of the Land Enquiry. At the core of the land campaign were the committee's proposals for minimum wages for agricultural labourers, standardised at the levels paid in the highest-wage districts, set and enforced by wages boards, which had been established for other low-wage industries in 1909. These wage increases would be paid for by farmers but funded through reduced rents, which were to be set by land courts. A by-product of this scheme was that labourers would be enabled to pay economic rents for their homes, which would in turn free them from the alleged tyranny of the tied cottage system. To supplement these proposals, the committee called for a Ministry of Land, which would be able to acquire land compulsorily for the provision of allotments and smallholdings. As we have seen, the committee's social diagnosis and its proposed remedies, with their explicit and implicit denunciations of the landed interest and the economic and social subjection of the labourer, attracted criticism from many quarters. However, whatever the methodological failings of the Land Enquiry Committee, the Conservative opposition was evidently wrong-footed by the land campaign, which attracted great publicity and widespread popular support, and different wings of the party responded in different, all largely ineffective, ways to the challenge that had been laid down. While the Unionist Social Reform Committee's agricultural subcommittee agreed in some measure with the reform of smallholdings legislation, and even supported the principle of minimum wages, the Central Land Association, which had produced its own scheme of reform in 1909,[147] was more antagonistic, and the 'Land Union' aggressively hostile, to accommodation with the reformists' aims.[148] Eventually, official Conservative policy came to support the establishment of yet another investigation, 'a new, impartial inquiry to establish the facts, propose remedies and lift the land question out of the realm of party politics',[149] reflecting the party's own inability to reach an agreement on the issue. Only the outbreak of war brought the land conflicts to a sudden halt; the Liberal party had to start all over again with a new land inquiry in the 1920s.[150]

Although the Land Enquiry Committee attempted to consult a broad range of informants, the adoption of a respondent method of inquiry did not necessarily entail the shedding of urban middle-class preconceptions about

[147] Christopher Turnor, Land problems and national welfare, London 1911, 297–9.
[148] Offer, Property and politics, ch. xxii.
[149] Ibid. 382.
[150] Liberal Land Committee, The land and the nation: rural report of the Liberal Land Committee, 1923–1925, London 1925, and Towns and the land: urban report of the Liberal Land Committee, 1923–1925, London 1926. See also Douglas, Land, people and politics, 190–5.

the agricultural labourer or a genuine penetration into what Seebohm Rowntree called the 'inner region of village thought and feeling, into which the casual visitor from the town or the official investigator can seldom hope to enter'.[151] Many of the assumptions and attitudes of the 'survey' method of inquiry found their way into the committee's report. Acland, for example, pointed to the importance of solving the problems of the countryside from a 'national efficiency' perspective,[152] while in the urban volume the report of the Interdepartmental Committee on Physical Deterioration was cited as evidence of the link between overcrowding and intemperance.[153] In the rural volume, similarly, reports from medical officers of health were used to illustrate the physical and moral effects of bad housing on the population.[154] The committee concurred with earlier observers who had pointed to the debilitating effects of the rural exodus, and remants of the old Hodge stereotype can still be discerned: as the best labourers left the land, those who remained were 'keeping down the standard of physical and mental development',[155] while one Norfolk farmer, contrasting conditions in his neighbourhood with those in high-wage Northumberland, was reported as telling the committee that the northerners were much better workmen – 'not that our people are slow in thinking, but much slower to act, the standard wage stultifies development'.[156] Even superficially sympathetic observers might represent the rural working classes in ways which were unlikely to reflect their own priorities. For example, in *The labourer and the land*, a pamphlet designed to spread the Liberal land reform gospel, Rowntree reported that he had talked to a schoolmaster, who complained that '[t]he problem . . . is not one of destitution, but of the general monotony and dreariness. These people have so little to live for. I am in the village myself, and I seldom leave it, but I have the world of books, they have not'.[157] The 'world of books', however, was not one to which the labourers necessarily aspired: they had their own cultural institutions, and understandably resented being judged by the standards of another class, which were as often as not unattainable from a position at the margins of poverty. Thus, although the Land Enquiry intended to integrate fully the views and aspirations of agricultural labourers into its social diagnosis, and attempted to devise a methodology of investigation which would enable this to be achieved, the perspectives of its members and, just as important, its chief propagandists, were fundamentally external to the cultural world of the classes whose condition and outlook they purported to represent.

---

151 Quoted in Briggs, *Seebohm Rowntree*, 65, and 'Seebohm Rowntree's *Poverty: a study of town life* in historical perspective', in Bradshaw and Sainsbury, *Getting the measure of poverty*, 16–17.
152 Land Enquiry Committee, *The land*, i, pp. xxxix–xl.
153 Ibid. ii. 34n.
154 Ibid. i. 92–107.
155 Ibid. i. 66.
156 Ibid. i. 58.
157 Rowntree, *Labourer and the land*, 24.

The report of the Land Enquiry Committee, then, is an appropriate subject with which to end the body of this book. It was a substantial attempt to investigate the conditions of life on the land, and if the bulk of the report was not directly related to labouring life, it dealt with enough contentious issues to initiate a vigorous debate on its methods and findings. In presenting a typical 'New Liberal' diagnosis of the problems of rural life, with an awareness of the contestable features of such a venture, and in involving those such as Buxton and Rowntree who had prior experience of investigating rural matters, it is good evidence of the state of rural social investigation on the eve of the Great War. It epitomised the various contests which were played out in the rural theatre of investigation, and which were also to be seen in the reports of housing reporters and investigators of the rural wage. Many of the old problems of rural life were still being identified in this period: this is testament both to the lack of success of social reformers' efforts to solve them and to the continuing vigour of political and social conflicts in the countryside. The continued vitality of the informant method of inquiry, as epitomised by the inquiry of the Land Agents' Society and the official reports of the Board of Trade, is evident even in a period in which the development of the respondent method and its application to the investigation of the land question was proceeding in the context of the growing political participation of the rural working classes. The desire among members of the Land Enquiry Committee to present their results as authoritative statements resulting from a professional approach to social inquiry echoes developments in the extent and practice of official investigation of working-class life in both town and country in this period. The official inquiries carried out by the Board of Trade established a regular system of consultation of farmers by official statisticians, and if this meant that the labouring classes were excluded from participation in the mechanisms of official investigation, there was enough evidence available from freelance investigators, especially on the subject of rural housing, to present an alternative point of view to the readers of newspapers, periodicals and pamphlets. These inquiries all took place in a context of party political conflict over the land issue and other aspects of rural life, and thus demonstrate the continuing contests that shaped the processes of social investigation in the English countryside.

Conclusion

Introducing *The revival of English agriculture* in 1899, Anderson Graham remarked that the broadness of his informant structure had been the chief joy of carrying out the investigation on which his book was based: 'After listening to the talk of a nobleman . . . it is like turning the handle of a kaleidoscope to get into familiar converse with a labourer.'[1] Graham's simile is as applicable to the range of social inquiries considered in this book, and as such it is difficult to draw general conclusions, especially from what has necessarily been a selective survey. What is clear is that a developing 'passion for inquiry' spawned a diverse range of approaches to social investigation throughout this period, shaped by changing economic and social imperatives and employed with a greater awareness of the methodological complexities of the task than would have been conceded by historians who once viewed the development of social investigation as the story of the progressive abandonment of the 'journalistic method' in favour of systematic quantitative social research. The royal commission of inquiry – characteristically employing special assistant commissioners in rural areas to gather information that was harder to obtain than in an urban context – together with the reports of special correspondent journalists, formed no less significant a part of the investigative culture in rural England than the poverty survey as pioneered by Booth, modified by Rowntree and improved by Bowley, and as applied in rural areas by Harold Mann and Maud Davies. Similarly, the intensive cultural investigation of rural working-class life, paralleled in urban theatres of inquiry by the accounts of women such as Florence Bell and Martha Loane, was a no less significant feature of social research in this period than the more widespread and systematic modes of inquiry. Taken together, these different strands of social investigation delivered frequently conflicting perceptions of rural working-class life to a largely middle-class urban readership which in turn generated the demand for social knowledge that fuelled the intensifying 'passion for inquiry'. This book has focused on the genesis of the documentary manifestations of this passion, and in particular on the methodological implications of different approaches to social investigation. This in turn may have implications both for the historian using the reports of social inquiries as primary source material, and for the history of the period in which they were produced. As Brian Harrison has explained with reference to the development of official investigation in the nineteenth century, '[t]his vast accumu-

---

[1]   Graham, *Revival of English agriculture*, 15.

lation of information has a double interest for the historian. It provides him with a wealth of raw material, but it is also an event in its own right'.[2]

This book has shown that what shaped this 'event', in the case of each social inquiry considered, was the process of interaction between researcher and researched, together with its specifically rural location. The practice of social inquiry in the countryside was clearly invested with features that differentiated it from investigation of aspects of urban life. On a practical level, the complexities of the agricultural wage structure, the importance of tied cottages, the wider availability of allotments and gardens and the nature of agricultural work made assessment of the standard of living much more difficult than would have been the case in an industrial town. On the other hand, where the rural community was made accessible to an investigator, very often a resident, the small size of the area under investigation made a more synoptic approach feasible, and it was arguably possible to avoid the reductive generalisations based on extensive quantitative research that characterised the distributional urban surveys carried out by Booth, Rowntree and Bowley. However, the remoteness of many rural districts made them difficult to visit, and the size of farms often meant that the workforce was dispersed and difficult to contact, especially given the long hours common in agrarian employment. The persistence of an exploratory tradition in the literature of rural social inquiry – the idea of exploration was implicit even in the activities and reports of official assistant commissioners – illustrates the perceived inaccessibility and even alienness of rural communities to the social investigator. Whereas, by the 1900s, the exploratory language of slum journalism had largely given way to a more sober descriptive style in the reports of urban investigators, except where the subjects of inquiry were vagrants or some other similarly inaccessible group, reports of the investigation of subjects such as rural housing or the land question were still frequently invested with the language of intrepidity that had characterised the output of men like the 'Amateur Casual' in the 1860s. The image of the colonial explorer pervaded the literature of rural social inquiry, the English countryside having been likened by Karen Sayer to 'a mini-empire within the borders of England, which had to be explored'.[3] These investigations, therefore, were initiated and executed across the 'town and country divide' that has characterised modern English history.[4]

It is arguably a tribute to the pervasiveness of this 'divide' that, despite the apparent advances in urban knowledge and understanding of rural life since the 1870s and the fundamental challenges made by the agricultural trade unions to the Hodge stereotype, the natives of the rural 'mini-empire', even in the early 1910s, were viewed by some urban observers as 'mere clods,

---

2 Harrison, *Peaceable kingdom*, 272.
3 Sayer, *Women*, 122. See p. 48 above.
4 Ian Dyck, 'The town and country divide in English history', in Chase and Dyck, *Living and learning*, 81–102.

without individuality and abject in their servitude'.[5] We find many echoes of the old Hodge stereotype in Edwardian portrayals of the agricultural labourer, thus reflecting the still insensitive approach of many urban commentators to the rural population. However, we also find more consistent challenges to these portrayals from a rural perspective. To take one example, A. H. Baverstock, writing in 1912, eagerly caricatured the activities of the social explorer who brought his urban preconceptions and prejudices to the investigation of rural life:

> Today the townsman reporter will visit some country village . . . find it very dull, and only amusing from its very dullness. A superficial article is penned which discourses lightly of 'Slocum-in-the-Marsh', and leaves an impression of 'Hodge' as a gaping booby with no object for his existence save to be laughed at. . . . The townsman comes to the country for his flying visit, and goes away to gibe, no wiser than he came. Ask him about the problems of the village community, the capacities and the needs of the farmer or the labourer, and he can tell you nothing of them. He has only learnt to give them nicknames![6]

The reports of social investigators were repeatedly challenged by residents of the countryside who resented what they viewed as the intrusiveness and double standards of the external, urban inquirer. In the same year that Baverstock delivered his indictment of the rural special correspondent, Alfred Williams rounded even more caustically on what he saw as the prevalent urban condescension of the English countryside:

> The poverty, or very often apparent poverty, of the countryside cottage stands out in greater relief, and is more readily observed by 'charitable' persons and intermeddlers than is that of urban districts; by setting about to remedy it in the spirit of 'I will force you to accept of my help, whether you will or not,' folk generally do ten times more harm than good. . . . If you want to find dirt, and filth, and squalor, and nakedness, and destitution, and starvation, and rags, and smut, and disease, and suffering, and misery, for Heaven's sake, look under your very noses, about the backyards and alleys of your own cities and towns, and do not come pestering us with official prying and inquisition![7]

Urban understandings of the 'rural labour problem', then, as far as many self-appointed spokesmen for the countryside were concerned, reflected a very imperfect sympathy among town-dwellers with the countryside and its inhabitants.

If the 'town and country divide' issued particular challenges to the investigator of rural life, the conflicts within rural society generated no less intense contestation around the processes and the reception of social investigation. The geographical remoteness of the rural areas under investigation was

---

5   *Sociological Review* vi (1913), 273.
6   A. H. Baverstock, *The English agricultural labourer*, London 1912, 1.
7   Alfred Williams, *A Wiltshire village*, London 1912, 162.

compounded by the social, political and cultural divisions within the rural social structure through which the information on rural labouring life obtained by investigators was mediated. The challenges issued to the dominant informant method of inquiry by the upheavals of 1872 and by subsequent social changes in the countryside were more than just methodological: they entailed a fundamental reassessment of the sources of social knowledge within rural communities and of the whole process of information-gathering that had underpinned the social investigation of earlier decades. The politicisation of the English countryside as a result of the spread of agricultural trade unionism and subsequent political developments invested with new meanings the much repeated mantra that 'knowledge is power'. The informant method survived – and remained the mainstay of parliamentary inquiries as well as the preferred approach of many independent investigators – but was always open to contestation from other sources, just as the adoption of the respondent method of inquiry provoked charges of untrustworthiness, unrepresentativeness and political bias. Although the first-hand consultation of those who were the subject of most of the investigations discussed in this book was on the whole more widespread by 1914 than in the mid-nineteenth century, there was no simple transition from one method to the other, and contemporaries were often aware of the epistemological controversies that their adoption of a particular method might provoke. Catherine Marsh has related the more widespread use of the respondent method, mainly with reference to urban theatres of inquiry, to the development of trade unionism, which was indicative of a more politically articulate working class.[8] Trade unions also gave investigators an institutional mechanism for the consultation of working-class people and their spokesmen, making the gathering of working-class opinion easier. This explanation certainly holds true for the English countryside, where the growth of trade unions encouraged many investigators to seek the reasons for social discontent through the first-hand consultation of agricultural labourers. Although agricultural trade unionism was a short-lived, often highly localised phenomenon, other political developments also contributed to new approaches to rural social inquiry. The concession of the franchise in the 1880s and the accumulating body of evidence for the 'rural exodus' in the 1890s both suggested that to understand the outlook of the labouring classes a more intensive degree of personal contact between investigator and investigated was desirable or necessary. This was achieved through the unsystematic approach to social inquiry adopted by resident investigators ranging from Augustus Jessopp to George Sturt, whose authority as social commentators rested on the intimacy of the social contact they were able to claim with the labouring population. This kind of social investigation, based on what might be termed participant observation methods of inquiry, was an important part of the range of inquiry

8   Marsh, 'Informants', 214.

that was brought to bear on the rural poor in this period. Indeed, its impor-tance reflects the development of the respondent method and hence of new understandings of rural working-class life, although, as we have seen, the employment of these intensive methods of social investigation was itself fraught with methodological difficulties and did not go uncontested, especially at the local level.

The production of social knowledge, then, was the result of negotiated interactions with a particular set of informants or respondents, selected according to the ideological stance of the investigator; and the context of these interactions shaped the collection and presentation of the information contained in the reports of social inquiries. Whether sought by 'stout and reli-able informants'[9] or by more sensitive participant observers, issues of stand-point epistemology impeded the collection of neutral 'social facts'. As Charles J. Hanser argued in 1965, '[t]he objective facts of a social situation are determined and interpreted from the special-interest viewpoint of the group, be it political party, trade association, union, church, or profession'.[10] Although Hanser believed that the format of the royal commission, comprising as it did 'members, of unquestioned integrity and competence, with least self-interest in the problem [under investigation], yet bringing to its consideration the viewpoints of important interests', could transcend these epistemological problems and deliver 'a closer approximation to social truth by balancing partial and conflicting perspectives',[11] this book's exami-nation of the official investigation in the period under consideration has shown that it was an inherently contestable instrument of governance, applying a politically determined series of methods to the investigation of the countryside and delivering verdicts with which other bodies were likely to disagree. There was conflict between different modes of social investigation as well as within the process of knowledge construction itself. In any case, although Hanser believed that the official inquiry supplied appropriate 'direc-tional guidelines' for political decision-makers and indeed for society as a whole,[12] the blue book as a guide to action in the period covered by this book was limited by its inaccessibility to the reader and by its claims to encyclopaedic authority and consequent unwieldiness as a tool of reform. Francis Heath explained in 1911 that the 'few monumental heaps' of blue books produced on the subject of rural life during the preceding half-century had been 'practically dropped still-born . . . . asphyxiated, by the mass of undi-gested, ill-arranged material obtained':[13] his point emphasises the restricted readership and questionable impact of the official investigation of rural life as a guide to action. However, at the same time, a dominant culture which

9 Idem, *Survey method*, 18.
10 Hanser, *Guide to decision*, 146.
11 Ibid. 148.
12 Ibid. 147.
13 Heath, *British rural life and labour*, p. v.

viewed the official inquiry as embodying an ideal of disinterested social research was unlikely to take much account of the unofficial investigation carried out by the special correspondent journalist or the resident investigator. It was not surprising, therefore, that men like Rider Haggard attempted to invest their inquiries with as many of the trappings of the royal commission as possible, in an attempt to enhance their perceived authority as social investigators. Moreover, although in this period the development of the distributional social survey appeared to suggest the possibility of a scientific representation of social distress untainted by the vagaries of the impressionistic account, even the most avowedly scientific investigators of rural life were unable to divest their work of the moral preconceptions that underpinned middle-class investigation of working-class life in both town and country; and their findings were consequently open to contestation. Given this level of potential disagreement between different kinds of investigator, it is perhaps unsurprising that few of the investigations considered in this book, whether official or unofficial, extensive or intensive in ambition and approach, can be seen to have had a direct impact on legislative responses to the problems of rural England. They evidently created a climate in which these problems could reach a prominent position in national political discourse, but the political contestability of the social investigation of the English countryside and its inhabitants, together with the powerful but often conflicting imperatives associated with ruralism and rusticity in this period, limited the practical impact that social investigation could have in terms of preparing the ground for political change.

In any case, a perspective which focused on the direct political impact of social investigation would be likely to fail to take account of the agency of the investigated population in the production and contestation of social knowledge; and would at the same time downplay the significance in itself of the 'event' of the genesis of these historical documents. This book has sought to keep in view the perspective of the working-class participants in the processes of social investigation, be they 'objects of scrutiny',[14] respondents or readers. Working-class perspectives on the 'passion for inquiry' are difficult for the historian to assess, as most of the surviving evidence presents the processes of social investigation from the investigator's point of view. Glimpses of working-class responses to inquiry were made available by Stephen Reynolds and other participant observers, but even these sources, as social investigations in themselves, can be seen to distort and arguably to misrepresent the lived experiences of those whom they describe. They could certainly be charged with being unrepresentative. Nevertheless, as we have seen, the direct challenges made by the English Land Restoration League to the findings of the Royal Commission on Labour, the adverse reaction of the St Neots labourers to the opinions of Tom Stone as reported by Rider Haggard, and the

14 Yeo, *Contest*, p. xvii.

impact of Reynolds's own books on the life of Sidmouth all illustrate the contestability of the methods of gathering and disseminating social knowledge. Even at the end of the period covered by this book, it was clear to many observers that the agricultural labourer, about whom so much had been written by social investigators since the 1870s, was in many respects as unknown as he had been in the years prior to the 'revolt of the field'. Although cast in a somewhat nobler light in view of the gradual (though not complete) effacement of the Hodge stereotype, the labourer remained a silent and inaccessible figure. As C. F. G. Masterman explained in 1909:

> The landlord, the farmer, the clergyman, the newspaper correspondent primed with casual conversation in the village inn, think that they know the labourer. They probably know nothing whatever about him. With his limited vocabulary, with his racial distrust of the stranger, and all of another class, with a mind which maintains such reticence except in moments of overpowering emotion, that labourer stands, a perplexing enigmatic figure alone in a voluble, self-analysis world.[15]

For Masterman, the poor of both town and country were 'as different from, and as unknown to, the classes that investigate, observe and record, as the people of China or Peru':

> Living amongst us and around us, never becoming articulate, finding even in their directly elected representatives types remote from their own, these people grow and flourish and die, with their own codes of honour, their special beliefs and moralities, their judgement and often their condemnation of the classes to whom has been given leisure and material advantage. The line is cut clean by both parties, neither desiring to occupy the territory of the other.[16]

The social investigator, then, remained an explorer of unknown territory, reporting on a class whose culture and experiences were so different from his own as to make the accurate and meaningful representation of them futile at worst, problematic at best. The rural poor inhabited a world arguably even more remote from the urban middle classes than did the city slum-dweller or the poor but respectable artisan; and they were also imperfectly understood by the rural elites among whom they lived. The divisions between country and town, and the nature of the social structure of rural communities, made the social investigation of rural England seem of paramount importance, and shaped the diverse and contestable ways in which it was carried out.

[15] Masterman, *Condition of England*, 195–6.
[16] Ibid. 112.

APPENDIX

Selected Questionnaires

1. ELRL Daily Report Form used in the 'red van' investigations

[Source: ELRL, *Special report, 1891*]

Are there any Allotments in the Parish?

If so, to what extent?

Allotment Rent per Acre? Farmers' Rent per Acre?

Names of largest Farmers in the Parish [State acreage and rent, if possible]

Any unoccupied Farms or uncultivated Lands? For what reason?

What is the rate of Agricultural Labourers' Wages?

Rent of cottages?

Is the Population diminishing? If so, what is the reason given locally for this?

Are there any large Mansions or Parks in the Parish

Name of Mansion, etc.   Name of Owner   Amount at which Assessed

Local Organisations [Labourers' Unions; Political or Social Clubs or Associations; Reading Rooms, etc.], with Secretaries' names and addresses

Remarks

2. Rider Haggard's questionnaire used in the preparation of his survey of rural England

[Source: Haggard's circular, Rider Haggard papers, MS 4692/25 (Devon)]

1. Have rents fallen in your district since 1875, and if so, how much per cent? What is the average rental now on average lands?

2. To what extent has the 'fee simple' value of land fallen since 1875?

3. Are there many resident landlords in your district?

4. Do farms let readily and are rents regularly paid?

5. Is labour plentiful or scarce? What is the average wage, with and without harvest and all other extras?

6. Are cottages plentiful or scarce? What is their average size and condition?

7. Do the young men stay on the land or migrate to the towns? If the latter, what is the cause of this movement? Has education anything to do with it? If so, do you think the system could be improved?

8. What is the general condition of the tenant farmer – of the landlord – and of the labourer, in your district?

9. Do you see any signs of a revival of the agricultural interests? Are you personally hopeful as to the future?

10. What do you think will be the effect on the farming industry and the country at large, of the desertion of the land by the labouring classes? Have you any remedy to suggest?

3. Charles Booth's questionnaire to the rural clergy used in his survey of old age in villages

[Source: Booth, *Aged poor*, 336]

The clergy were asked for the following information on each individual in their parishes over the age of 65:

Age

Sex

Occupation

Health

Sources of maintenance (viz. whether parish, charity, relations, earnings, or private means, or any combination of these)

Whether in a club

Rent

Whether having a garden or allotment

Family connections

General remarks on manner of life

4. Maud Davies's household questionnaire used
in her survey of Corsley

[Source: Davies, *English village*, 99–100]

Name

Age

Place of birth

Occupation

Name of employer (or state if on own account)

Wife's name

Wife's place of birth

Father's name

Father's occupation

Father's place of birth

Paternal grandfather's name

Paternal grandfather's occupation

Paternal grandfather's place of birth

Maternal grandfather's name

Maternal grandfather's occupation

Maternal grandfather's place of birth

Names and sex of all children born, and date of birth; marking those which are still living; and trade or occupation of those who have left school

Have any of your children left the parish? and if so, state where they went to, and what occupation they are following

How many rooms are there in the house that you occupy?

Does any one else, and if so, who, dwell in the house?

If occupying land state the number of acres

If employer, state occupation and number of persons employed, men, women, and young people

Bibliography

Unpublished primary sources

London, British Library
MS Add. 44487 correspondence between Augustus Jessopp and William Gladstone
MS Add. 54965 Macmillan archive, correspondence of Stephen Reynolds with Macmillan and Company

London, British Library of Political and Economic Science
Fabian Society archive

London, House of Lords Record Office
Herbert Samuel papers

London, University of London Library
MS 797 Charles Booth papers

Norwich, Norfolk Record Office
MS 4692/20–31 Rider Haggard papers

York, Borthwick Institute of Historical Research
B. Seebohm Rowntree papers

Official documents and publications (in chronological order)

Reports of special assistant poor law commissioners on the employment of women and children in agriculture, PP 1843, C. 510

Royal Commission on the Employment of Children, Young Persons, and Women in Agriculture: first report of the commissioners, PP 1867–8, C. 4068

Royal Commission on the Employment of Children, Young Persons, and Women in Agriculture: second report of the commissioners, PP 1868–9, C. 4202

Royal Commission on the Depressed Condition of the Agricultural Interest: assistant commissioners' reports, PP 1880, C. 2678; PP 1881, C. 2778 (ii), C. 2951; PP 1882, C. 3375 (i–iv)

Royal Commission on the Depressed Condition of the Agricultural Interest: minutes of evidence, PP 1881, C. 2778 (i), C. 3096; PP 1882, C. 3309 (i)

Royal Commission on the Depressed Condition of the Agricultural Interest: final report, PP 1882, C. 3309

Minutes of evidence taken before Her Majesty's Commissioners on Agriculture, volume III, PP 1882, C. 3309 (i)

Royal Commission on Labour: assistant commissioners' reports on the agricultural labourer, volume i: England, PP 1893–4, C. 6894 (i–vi, xiii)

Fifth and final report of the Royal Commission on Labour, part I: the report, PP 1894, C. 7421

Fifth and final report of the Royal Commission on Labour, part II: secretary's report on the work of the office: summaries of evidence (with index); and appendices, PP 1894, C. 7421 (i)

Report by Mr Wilson Fox on the wages and earnings of agricultural labourers in the United Kingdom, with statistical tables and charts, PP 1900, Cd. 346

Report of the Interdepartmental Committee on Physical Deterioration, PP 1904, Cd. 2186

Interdepartmental Committee on Physical Deterioration: minutes of evidence, PP 1904, Cd. 2210

Second report by Mr Wilson Fox on the wages and earnings of agricultural labourers in the United Kingdom, with statistical tables and charts, PP 1905, Cd. 2376

Report of an enquiry by the Board of Trade into the earnings and hours of labour of workpeople of the United Kingdom, V: agriculture in 1907, PP 1910, Cd. 5460

Newspapers and periodicals

Annals of Agriculture and Other Useful Arts
Athenaeum
Church Reformer
Contemporary Review
Cornhill
Daily Express
Daily News
Daily News and Leader
Economic Journal
Edinburgh Review
Fraser's Magazine
Journal of the Royal Agricultural Society of England
Journal of the Royal Statistical Society
Longman's Magazine
Macmillan's Magazine
Morning Advertiser
NAPSS Transactions
Nation
Nineteenth Century
Nineteenth Century and After
Pall Mall Gazette
Quarterly Review
St James's Gazette
Sociological Papers
Sociological Review
Spectator
Standard
The Times
Times Literary Supplement

Contemporary books and articles

Adeane, Charles and Edwin Savill, *The land retort: a study of the land question with an answer to the report of the Secret Enquiry Committee*, London 1914

'An agricultural labourer', *The position of the agricultural labourer in the past and in the future*, London [1885]

Alexander, William, *Rural life in Victorian Aberdeenshire*, ed. Ian Carter, Edinburgh 1992

Allingham, Helen and Stewart Dick, *The cottage homes of England*, London 1909

Anon, *A farmer's views on the agricultural labour question, by one of them*, Norwich 1873

—— *Other views on the trials of a country parson*, London 1891

Arch, Joseph, *Joseph Arch: the story of his life told by himself*, London 1898

Archer, Thomas, *The pauper, the thief and the convict: sketches of some of their homes, haunts and habits*, London 1865

—— *The terrible sights of London, and labours of love in the midst of them*, London 1870

Aronson, Hugh, *Our village homes: present conditions and suggested remedies*, London 1913

—— *The land and the labourer*, London 1914

Ashby, Joseph and Bolton King, 'Statistics of some midland villages: I', *Economic Journal* iii (1893), 1–22

—— 'Statistics of some midland villages: II', *Economic Journal* iii (1893), 193–204

Atkinson, J. C., *Forty years in a moorland parish: reminiscences and researches in Danby in Cleveland* (1st edn 1891), London 1892

Batson, Henrietta M., 'Hodge at home', *Nineteenth Century* xxxi (1892), 174–80

Baverstock, A. H., *The English agricultural labourer*, London 1912

Bear, William E., 'The principle of tenant right', *Contemporary Review* xli (1882), 645–55

—— 'The agricultural problem', *Economic Journal* iii (1893), 391–407, 569–83

—— 'Our agricultural population', *Economic Journal* iv (1894), 317–31

—— 'The land and the cultivator', in James Samuelson (ed.), *The civilisation of our day: a series of original essays on some of its more important phases at the close of the nineteenth century by expert writers*, London 1896, 1–25

Begg, Revd James, 'Houses of the working classes of Scotland: the bothy system', *NAPSS Transactions* (1858), 621–4

Bell, Lady [Florence], *At the works: a study of a manufacturing town*, London 1907

Bennett, E. N., *Problems of village life*, London 1914

Bergson, Henri, *Creative evolution*, London 1911

Besant, Walter, *The eulogy of Richard Jefferies*, London 1888

Booth, Charles, 'Enumeration and classification of paupers, and state pensions for the aged', *Journal of the Royal Statistical Society* liv (1891), 600–43

—— *The aged poor in England and Wales*, London 1894

—— (ed.), *Life and labour of the people in London* (1st edn 1889; 2nd edn 1892–7), London 1902–3

[Booth, Mary,] *Charles Booth: a memoir*, London 1918

Bosanquet, Helen, 'Wages and housekeeping', in Loch, *Methods of social advance*, 131–46

Bourne, H. R. Fox, *English newspapers: chapters in the history of journalism*, London 1887

Bowley, A. L., 'Rural population in England and Wales: a study of the changes of density, occupations and ages', *Journal of the Royal Statistical Society* lxvii (1913–14), 597–652

———— and A. R. Burnett-Hurst, *Livelihood and poverty: a study in the economic conditions of working-class households in Northampton, Warrington, Stanley and Reading*, London 1915

———— and M. H. Hogg, *Has poverty diminished? A sequel to* Livelihood and poverty, London 1925

Branford, Victor, *Interpretations and forecasts: a study of survivals and tendencies in contemporary society*, London 1914

Bray, Reginald A., *The town child*, London 1907

Brewer, J. S., 'Workhouse visiting', in [Maurice], *Lectures to ladies*, 262–83

Cadbury, George and Tom Bryan, *The land and the landless*, London 1908

Caird, James, *English agriculture in 1850–51* (1st edn 1852), London 1968

———— 'General view of British agriculture', *Journal of the Royal Agricultural Society of England* 2nd ser. xiv (1878), 271–332

Clayden, Arthur, *The revolt of the field: a sketch of the rise and progress of the movement among the agricultural labourers known as the 'National Agricultural Labourers' Union', with a reprint of the correspondence to the* Daily News *during a tour through Canada with Mr Arch*, London 1874

Clifford, Frederick, *The agricultural lock-out of 1874, with notes upon farming and farm-labour in the eastern counties*, London 1875

———— 'The labour bill in farming', *Journal of the Royal Agricultural Society of England* 2nd ser. xi (1875), 67–127

Cobbett, William, *Rural rides* (1st edn 1830), Harmondsworth 1967

Cochrane, C., 'Laborers' [sic] cottages', in Fabian Society, *House famine*, 7–9

———— *Papers on rural housing: the present conditions of the cottage home of the agricultural labourer*, St Neots 1901

The collected letters of Joseph Conrad, ed. Frederick R. Karl and Laurence Davies, Cambridge 1983

Cooper, A. N., *Our villages: another view: a reply to the special commissioner of the* Daily News, London 1891

Crotch, W. Walter, *The cottage homes of England: the case against the housing system in rural districts* (1st edn 1901), 2nd edn, London 1901

Curtler, W. H. R., *A short history of English agriculture*, Oxford 1909

Davies, David, *The case of labourers in husbandry stated and considered*, London 1795

Davies, M. F., *Life in an English village: an economic and historical survey of the parish of Corsley in Wiltshire*, London 1909

———— *School care committees: a guide to their work*, London 1909

———— 'Rural districts', in Clementina Black (ed.), *Married women's work, being the report of an enquiry undertaken by the Women's Industrial Council*, London 1915, 230–51

Defoe, Daniel, *A tour through the whole island of Great Britain* (1st edn 1724–6), Harmondsworth 1971

Dent, J. Dent [sic], 'The present condition of the English agricultural labourer', *Journal of the Royal Agricultural Society of England* 2nd ser. vii (1871), 343–65

Ditchfield, P. H., *The parson's pleasance*, London 1910

—— *Vanishing England*, London 1910

—— *The cottages and the village life of rural England*, London 1912

—— *Old village life, or glimpses of village life through all ages*, London 1920

Doyle, Martin, *The agricultural labourer, viewed in his moral, intellectual and physical conditions*, London 1855

Dunlop, Olive Jocelyn, *The farm labourer: the history of a modern problem*, London 1913

Eddowes, John, *The agricultural labourer as he really is, or village morals in 1854: a pamphlet for the present day*, Driffield 1854

Eden, Sir Frederick Morton, *The state of the poor; or, an history of the labouring classes in England, from the conquest to the present period*, London 1797

Edwards, Clement, 'Bad housing in rural districts', in Fabian Society, *House famine*, 3–6

Edwards, Joseph (ed.), *Land and real tariff reform, being the land reformers' handbook for 1909*, London 1909

ELRL, *Special report, 1891: among the Suffolk labourers with the 'red van'*, London 1891

—— *Special report, 1892: among the agricultural labourers with the 'red vans'*, London 1893

—— *Special report, 1893: among the agricultural labourers with the 'red vans'*, London 1894

—— *Special report, 1894: among the agricultural labourers with the 'red vans'*, London 1895

—— *Special report, 1895: among the agricultural labourers with the 'red vans'*, London 1896

—— *Special report, 1896: with the 'red vans' in 1896*, London 1897

—— *Special report, 1897: with the 'red vans' in 1897*, London 1898

Fabian Society, 'To your tents, oh Israel!', *Fortnightly Review* lx (1893), 569–89

—— *The house famine and how to relieve it* (Fabian Tract ci), London 1900

Fox, A. Wilson, 'Agricultural wages in England and Wales during the last fifty years', *Journal of the Royal Statistical Society* lxiv (1903), 273–359

Gales, R. L., *Studies in Arcady, and other essays from a country parsonage*, London 1910

—— *Studies in Arcady, and other essays from a country parsonage, second series*, London 1912

—— *The vanished country folk, and other studies in Arcady*, London 1914

Gambier-Parry, Major Ernest, *Allegories of the land*, London 1912

—— *The spirit of the old folk*, London 1913

Garnier, Russell M., *Annals of the British peasantry*, London 1895

Gavin, Hector, *Sanitary ramblings, being sketches and illustrations of Bethnal Green*, London 1848

Gearey, Caroline, *Rural life: its humour and pathos*, London 1899

George, Henry, *Progress and poverty: an inquiry into the cause of industrial depressions and of increase of want with increase of wealth*, New York 1880

Gilly, W. S., *The peasantry of the border: an appeal on their behalf* (1st edn 1842), ed. R. H. Campbell, Edinburgh 1973

Girdlestone, Edward, 'Landowners, land, and those who till it', *Fraser's Magazine* lxxviii (1868), 728–47

——— 'The agricultural labourer', *Macmillan's Magazine* xxvi (1872), 256–64

——— 'The National Agricultural Labourers' Union', *Macmillan's Magazine* xxviii (1873), 436–46

Graham, P. Anderson, *The rural exodus: the problem of the village and the town*, London 1892

——— *The revival of English agriculture*, London 1899

Green, F. E., *The awakening of England*, London 1912

——— *The tyranny of the countryside*, London 1913

——— *Everyman's land and allotment book*, London 1915

——— *The Surrey hills*, London 1915

——— *A history of the English agricultural labourer, 1870–1920*, London 1920

Greenwood, James, *In strange company, being the experiences of a roving correspondent*, London 1874

Haggard, H. Rider, *A farmer's year, being his commonplace book for 1898*, London 1899

——— *Rural England, being an account of agricultural and social researches carried out in 1901 and 1902*, London 1902

——— 'Agriculture and the unemployed question: an address', in Loch, *Methods of social advance*, 64–78

——— *The poor and the land, being a report on the Salvation Army colonies in the United States and at Hadleigh, England, with scheme of national land settlement and an introduction*, London 1905

——— *The days of my life: an autobiography*, London 1926

Hammond, J. L. and Barbara Hammond, *The village labourer, 1760–1832: a study of the government of England before the Reform Bill*, London 1911

Harben, Henry D., *The rural problem*, London 1913

Hardie, J. Keir, *The unemployed problem, with some suggestions for solving it*, London 1904

Hardy, Thomas, 'The Dorsetshire labourer', *Longman's Magazine* ii (1883), 252–69

Hasbach, Wilhelm, *A history of the English agricultural labourer* (1st German edn 1894), London 1908

Hatton, Joseph, *Journalistic London, being a series of sketches of famous pens and papers of the day*, London 1882

Haw, George, *No room to live: the plaint of overcrowded London*, London 1900

Hayden, Eleanor G., *Travels round our village: a Berkshire book*, London 1901

Heath, F. G., *The 'romance' of peasant life in the west of England*, London 1872

——— *The English peasantry*, London 1874

——— *The fern paradise: a plea for the culture of ferns*, London 1875

——— *The fern world*, London 1877

——— *Burnham Beeches*, London 1879

——— *Peasant life in the west of England*, London 1880

——— *British rural life and labour*, London 1911

Heath, Richard, *The English peasant: studies historical, local and biographic*, London 1893

Holdenby, Christopher, *Folk of the furrow*, London 1913

Hope, Revd Peter, 'On the right condition of an agricultural community', *NAPSS Transactions* (1860), 791–7

Hudson, W. H., *The land's end: a naturalist's impressions in west Cornwall*, London 1908
———— *Afoot in England*, London 1909
———— *A shepherd's life*, London 1910
Hutton, Revd Thomas, 'Agricultural gangs, their influence upon the morals and the education of the young', NAPSS *Transactions* (1864), 650–5
Hyder, Joseph, *The case for land nationalisation*, London 1913
Jacks, L. P., *Mad shepherds, and other human studies*, London 1910
Jebb, L., *The small holdings of England: a survey of various existing systems*, London 1907
Jefferies, Richard, *The gamekeeper at home: sketches of natural history and rural life*, London 1878
———— *The amateur poacher*, London 1879
———— *Wild life in a southern county* (1st edn 1879), London 1889
———— *Hodge and his masters*, London 1880
———— *A classic of English farming: Hodge and his masters* (1st edn 1880), London 1946
———— *Round about a great estate* (1st edn 1880), London 1894
———— 'The Wiltshire labourer', *Longman's Magazine* iii (1883), 52–65
———— 'After the county franchise', *Longman's Magazine* iii (1884), 362–75
———— *The life of the fields* (1st edn 1884), London 1899
———— *Red deer* (1st edn 1884), London 1900
———— *The open air* (1st edn 1885), London 1893
———— *The toilers of the field* (1st edn 1892), London 1907
———— *The hills and the vale*, London 1909
Jessopp, Augustus, *Arcady: for better for worse* (1st edn 1887), popular edn, London 1887
———— *The trials of a country parson*, London 1890
———— *England's peasantry, and other essays*, London 1914
Kebbel, T. E., *The agricultural labourer: a short summary of his position*, London 1870
———— (ed.), *Selected speeches of the late right honourable the earl of Beaconsfield*, London 1882
———— *The agricultural labourer: a short summary of his position: a new edition brought down to date*, London 1887
———— *The old and the new English country life*, London 1891
———— *The agricultural labourer: a short summary of his position*, 3rd edn, London 1893
———— *The agricultural labourer: a summary of his position*, 4th edn, London 1907
Kingsley, Charles, 'The country parish', in [Maurice], *Lectures to ladies*, 53–66
Land Agents' Society, *Facts about land: a reply to 'The land', the report of the unofficial Land Enquiry Committee*, London 1916
Land Enquiry Committee, *The land: the report of the Land Enquiry Committee*, I: *Rural*, London 1913
———— *The land: the report of the Land Enquiry Committee*, II: *Urban*, London 1914
Leighton, Baldwyn, William Morris and E. L. O'Malley, 'How may the condition of the agricultural labourer be improved?', NAPSS *Transactions* (1872), 393–416

Le Play, Frederic, *Les Ouvriers européens: études sur les travaux, la vie domestique et la condition morale des populations ouvrières de l'Europe; précédées d'un exposé de la méthode d'observation*, Paris 1855

Liberal Land Committee, *The land and the nation: rural report of the Liberal Land Committee, 1923–1925*, London 1925

—— *Towns and the land: urban report of the Liberal Land Committee, 1923–1925*, London 1926

Little, Herbert J., 'The agricultural labourer', *Journal of the Royal Agricultural Society of England* 2nd ser. xiv (1878), 761–802

—— 'Report on agricultural education', *Journal of the Royal Agricultural Society of England* 2nd ser. xxi (1885), 126–64

Loane, M., *The queen's poor: life as they find it in town and country* (1st edn 1905), ed. Susan Cohen and Clive Fleay, London 1998

Loch, C. S. (ed.), *Methods of social advance: short studies in social practice by various authors*, London 1904

Mann, H. H., 'Life in an agricultural village in England', *Sociological Papers* i (1905), 163–93

—— 'The untouchable classes of an Indian city', *Sociological Review* v (1912), 42–55

—— *The social framework of agriculture: India, Middle East, England*, ed. Daniel Thorner, London 1967

Marshall, William, *The rural economy of Norfolk, comprising the management of landed estates, and the present practice of husbandry in that county*, London 1787

—— *The rural economy of Yorkshire, comprising the management of landed estates, and the present practice of husbandry in the agricultural districts of that county*, London 1788

—— *The rural economy of Gloucestershire, including its dairy, together with the dairy management of north Wiltshire and the management of orchards and fruit liquor in Herefordshire*, Gloucester 1789

—— *The rural economy of the midland counties: including the management of live stock in Leicestershire and its environs*, London 1790

—— *The rural economy of the west of England, including Devonshire and parts of Somersetshire, Dorsetshire and Cornwall, together with minutes in practice*, London 1796

—— *The rural economy of the southern counties, comprising Kent, Surrey, Sussex, the Isle of Wight; the chalk hills of Wiltshire, Hampshire, etc. and including the culture and management of hops in the districts of Maidstone, Canterbury and Farnham*, London 1798

—— *The review and abstract of the county reports to the Board of Agriculture* (1st edn 1808–15), Newton Abbot 1969

Masterman, C. F. G., *The condition of England*, London 1909

—— W. B. Hodgson and others, *To colonise England: a plea for a policy*, London 1907

[Maurice, F. D. (ed.),] *Lectures to ladies on practical subjects*, Cambridge 1855

Mayhew, Henry, *London labour and the London poor: a cyclopedia of the conditions and earnings of those that will work, those that cannot work, and those that will not work*, London 1851

Mearns, Andrew, *The bitter cry of outcast London* (1st edn 1883), ed. Anthony S. Wohl, Leicester 1970

Miller, Thomas, *Rural sketches*, London 1839

———— *English country life*, London 1859

[Millin, G. F.], *Life in our villages, by the special commissioner of the* Daily News, *being a series of letters written to that paper in the autumn of 1891*, London 1891

Mitford, Mary Russell, *Our village: sketches of rural character and scenery* (1st edn, 5 pts, 1824–32), London 1863

Montgomery, Revd John, 'On overcrowded villages', NAPSS *Transactions* (1860), 787–90

Moore, E. W., *An address on the condition of the agricultural labourer and his cottage home, delivered at a meeting of the Oxford Farmers' Club*, London 1864

Moule, Henry, *Four letters to His Royal Highness Prince Albert, as president of the council of the duchy of Cornwall, on the dwellings and condition of eleven hundred of the working classes and poor of Fordington*, London 1854

———— *Eight letters to His Royal Highness the Prince Albert, as president of the council of the duchy of Cornwall*, London 1855

———— *Our home heathen: how can the Church of England get at them?*, London 1868

———— *The impossibility overcome, or the inoffensive, safe, and economical disposal of the refuse of towns and villages*, London 1870

Outhwaite, R. L., *Peer or peasant? The ruin of rural England and the remedy*, London 1909

———— *Deer and desolation: the Scottish land problem*, London 1912

Paul, C. Kegan, *Memories* (1st edn 1899), London 1971

Pedder, D. C., *The secret of rural depopulation* (Fabian Tract cxviii), London 1904

———— *Henry George and his gospel*, London 1908

———— *Where men decay: a survey of present rural conditons*, London 1908

Perkin, H. J., 'Land reform and class conflict in Victorian Britain', in J. Butt and I. F. Clarke (eds), *The Victorians and social protest: a symposium*, Newton Abbot 1973

Prothero, Rowland E., *English farming past and present*, London 1912

Raymond, Walter, *English country life*, London 1910

Reeves, Maud Pember, *Round about a pound a week*, London 1913

Reynolds, Stephen, *A poor man's house* (1st edn 1908), London 1909

———— *Alongshore: where man and the sea face one another*, London 1911

———— *The lower deck: the navy and the nation*, London 1912

———— Bob Woolley and Tom Woolley, *Seems so! A working-class view of politics* (1st edn 1911), London 1913

The letters of Stephen Reynolds, ed. Harold Wright, London 1923

Richards, Roger Charnock, 'The landlord's preferential position', *Fortnightly Review* liii (1890), 881–95

Rowntree, B. Seebohm, *Poverty: a study of town life* (1st edn 1901), London 1902

———— *Land and labour: lessons from Belgium*, London 1910

———— *The labourer and the land*, London 1914

———— and May Kendall, *How the labourer lives: a study of the rural labour problem*, London 1913

———— and Bruno Lasker, *Unemployment: a social study*, London 1911

Savage, William G., *Rural housing*, London 1915

Scottish Land Enquiry Committee, *Scottish land, rural and urban: the report of the Scottish Land Enquiry Committee*, London 1914

Scrivener, Scrivener C. [sic], *Our fields and cities, or misdirected industry*, London 1891

Shimmin, Hugh, *The courts and alleys of Liverpool described from personal inspection*, Liverpool 1864

Sinclair, Sir John, *The statistical account of Scotland; drawn up from the communications of the ministers of the different parishes*, Edinburgh 1791–9

Slater, Gilbert, *The English peasantry and the enclosure of the common fields*, London 1907

Smith, H. Llewellyn, 'Influx of population (East London)', in Booth, *Life and labour*, iii. 58–166

Somerville, Alexander, *The whistler at the plough* (1st edn 1852) ed. K. D. M. Snell, London 1989

'A son of the marshes', *With the woodlanders and by the tide*, ed. J. A. Owen, London 1893

—— *Drift from longshore*, ed. J. A. Owen, London 1898

Spender, J. A., *The state and pensions in old age*, London 1892

—— *Life, journalism and politics*, London 1927

—— *Men and things*, London 1937

Stevenson, Revd Nash, 'On statute fairs: their evils and remedy', NAPSS *Transactions* (1858), 624–31

—— 'On the rise and progress of the movement for the abolition of statutes, mops, or feeing markets', NAPSS *Transactions* (1860), 797–805

Stubbs, Charles William, *Village politics: addresses and sermons on the labour question*, London 1878

—— *The mythe of life: four sermons, with an introduction on the social mission of the Church*, London 1880

—— *The land and the labourers: facts and experiments in cottage farming and co-operative agriculture* (1st edn 1884), London 1893

—— *The church in the villages, principles and ideal: an address to the church council and wardens of the united parishes of Stokenham, Chivelstone, and Sherford*, Dartmouth 1887

—— *Charles Kingsley and the Christian social movement*, London 1899

[Sturt, George], *The Bettesworth book: talks with a Surrey peasant* (1st edn 1901), London 1902

—— *Memoirs of a Surrey labourer: a record of the last years of Frederick Bettesworth* (1st edn 1907), London 1930

—— *Change in the village* (1st edn 1912), Dover, NH 1984

—— *Lucy Bettesworth*, London 1913

—— *A small boy in the sixties*, London 1927

The journals of George Sturt, 1890–1927: a selection, ed. E. D. Mackerness, Cambridge 1967.

Thompson, Flora, *Lark Rise to Candleford* (1st edn 1945), Harmondsworth 1973

Tremenheere, H. S., *I was there: the memoirs of H. S. Tremenheere*, ed. E. L. Edmonds and O. P. Edmonds, Windsor 1965

Turnor, Christopher, *Land problems and national welfare*, London 1911

Twining, Louisa, 'Workhouses', NAPSS *Transactions* (1857), 571–4

—— 'The Workhouse Visiting Society', NAPSS *Transactions* (1858), 666–72

Webb, Beatrice, *My apprenticeship* (1st edn 1926), Harmondsworth 1971

—— and Sidney Webb, *Methods of social study*, London 1932

Welsh Land Enquiry Committee, *Welsh land, rural: the report of the Welsh Land Enquiry Committee*, London 1914

Whitehead, Charles, *Agricultural labourers*, London 1870

Williams, Alfred, *A Wiltshire village*, London 1912

———— *Life in a railway factory*, London 1915

Worthington, T. Locke, 'Proposal for rural university settlements', in J. A. Hobson (ed.), *Co-operative labour upon the land, and other papers: the report of a conference upon 'Land Co-operation and the Unemployed' held at Holborn Town Hall in October 1894*, London 1895, 111–16

'A Wykehamist', *The agricultural labourer*, London 1873

Yeames, Revd James, *Life in London alleys, with reminiscences of Mary McCarthy and her work*, London 1877

Secondary sources

Acland, Anne, *A Devon family: the story of the Aclands*, London 1981

Armstrong, Alan, *Farmworkers: a social and economic history, 1770–1980*, London 1988

Ashby, M. K., *Joseph Ashby of Tysoe, 1859–1919: a study of English village life*, Cambridge 1961

Ashton, T. S., *Economic and social investigations in Manchester: a centenary history of the Manchester Statistical Society* (1st edn 1934), Brighton 1977

Bales, Kevin, 'Charles Booth's survey of *Life and labour of the people in London* 1889–1903', in Bulmer and others, *The social survey*, 66–110

———— 'Lives and labours in the emergence of organised social research, 1886–1907', *Journal of Historical Sociology* ix (1996), 113–38

Bellamy, Liz and Tom Williamson (eds), *Life in the Victorian village: the Daily News survey of 1891*, London 1999

Betham-Edwards, M. (ed.), *The autobiography of Arthur Young, with selections from his correspondence*, London 1898

Blunden, Edmund, *Thomas Hardy* (1st edn 1942), London 1967

Boyer, George R. and Timothy J. Hatton, 'Did Joseph Arch raise agricultural wages?', *Economic History Review* 2nd ser. xlvii (1994), 310–34

———— 'Did Joseph Arch raise agricultural wages? A reply', *Economic History Review* 2nd ser. xlix (1996), 370–6

Boyes, Georgina, *The imagined village: culture, ideology and the English folk revival*, Manchester 1993

Bradshaw, Jonathan, 'Preface', to B. Seebohm Rowntree, *Poverty: a study of town life* (1st edn 1901), Bristol 2000, pp. xix–lxxxii

———— and Roy Sainsbury (eds), *Getting the measure of poverty: the early legacy of Seebohm Rowntree*, Aldershot 2000

Briggs, Asa, *Social thought and social action: a study of the work of Seebohm Rowntree*, London 1961

———— 'Seebohm Rowntree's *Poverty: a study of town life* in historical perspective', in Bradshaw and Sainsbury, *Getting the measure of poverty*, 5–22

Brown, John, 'Charles Booth and labour colonies, 1889–1905', *Economic History Review* 2nd ser. xxi (1968), 349–60

Bulmer, Martin, Kevin Bales and K. K. Sklar (eds), *The social survey in historical perspective, 1880–1940*, Cambridge 1991

Burnett, John, *Plenty and want: a social history of diet in England, from 1815 to the present day*, London 1966

———— *A social history of housing, 1815–1985* (1st edn 1978), London 1986

Cartwright, T. J., *Royal commissions and departmental committees in Britain: a case-study in institutional adaptiveness and public participation in government*, London 1975

Chambers, J. D. and G. E. Mingay, *The agricultural revolution, 1750–1880*, London 1966

Charlesworth, Andrew (ed.), *An atlas of rural protest in England and Wales, 1548–1900*, London 1983

Chase, Malcolm, *The people's farm: English radical agrarianism, 1775–1840*, Oxford 1988

———— and Ian Dyck (eds), *Living and learning: essays in honour of J. F. C. Harrison*, Aldershot 1996

Clokie, Hugh McDowall and J. William Robinson, *Royal commissions of inquiry: the significance of investigations in British politics*, London 1937

Cohen, Susan, 'Miss Loane, Florence Nightingale and district nursing in late Victorian Britain', *Nursing History Review* v (1997), 83–103

———— and Clive Fleay, 'Fighters for the poor', *History Today*, January 2000, 36–7

Cole, G. D. H., *The life of William Cobbett*, London 1924

Corrigan, Philip and Derek Sayer, *The great arch: English state formation as cultural revolution*, Oxford 1985

Cruikshank, R. J., *Roaring century, 1846–1946*, London 1946

Cullen, Michael J., *The statistical movement in early Victorian Britain: the foundations of empirical social research*, Hassocks 1975

Davidson, Roger, 'Llewellyn Smith, the Labour Department and government growth, 1886–1909', in Gillian Sutherland (ed.), *Studies in the growth of nineteenth-century government*, London 1972, 227–62

———— *Whitehall and the labour problem in late-Victorian and Edwardian Britain: a study in official statistics and social control*, London 1982

Dentith, Simon, *Society and cultural forms in nineteenth-century England*, Basingstoke 1998

Digby, Anne, 'The rural poor', in Mingay, *Victorian countryside*, ii. 591–602

Douglas, Roy, *Land, people and politics: a history of the land question in the United Kingdom, 1878–1952*, London 1976

Drew, Philip, 'Richard Jefferies and the English countryside', *Victorian Studies* xi (1967), 181–206

Dunbabin, J. P. D., *Rural discontent in nineteenth-century Britain*, London 1974

———— 'Can we tell whether Arch raised wages?', *Economic History Review* 2nd ser. xlix (1996), 362–9

Dyck, Ian, *William Cobbett and rural popular culture*, Cambridge 1992

———— 'The town and country divide in English history', in Chase and Dyck, *Living and learning*, 81–102

Ellis, Peter Berresford, *H. Rider Haggard: a voice from the infinite*, London 1978

Encyclopaedia of the social sciences (1st edn 1930–5), London 1962

Englander, David, 'Comparisons and contrasts: Henry Mayhew and Charles

Booth as social investigators', in Englander and O'Day, *Retrieved riches*, 105–42

———— and Rosemary O'Day (eds), *Retrieved riches: social investigation in Britain, 1840–1914*, Aldershot 1995

Fisher, J. R., *Clare Sewell Read, 1826–1905: a farmers' spokesman of the late nineteenth century*, Hull 1975

Freeman, Mark, 'The agricultural labourer and the Hodge stereotype, c. 1850–1914', *Agricultural History Review* xlix (2001), 172–86

———— ' "Journeys into poverty kingdom": complete participation and the British vagrant, 1866–1914', *History Workshop Journal* lii (2001), 99–121

———— 'Rider Haggard and *Rural England*: methods of social enquiry in the English countryside', *Social History* xxvi (2001), 209–16

———— 'The provincial social survey in Edwardian Britain', *Historical Research* lxxv (2002), 73–89

———— 'Folklore collection and social investigation in late-nineteenth and early-twentieth century England', in David Hopkin (ed.), *Folklore and the historian*, London (forthcoming)

Fussell, G. E., 'English agriculture from Arthur Young to William Cobbett', *Economic History Review* 1st ser. vi (1936), 214–22

Gazley, John G., *The life of Arthur Young, 1741–1820*, Philadelphia 1973

Geertz, Clifford, *Works and lives: the anthropologist as author*, Cambridge 1988

Gervais, David, 'Alive or dead? George Sturt (George Bourne), 1863–1927', *Cambridge Quarterly* xxvii (1988), 397–403

———— 'Late witness: George Sturt and village England', *Cambridge Quarterly* xxx (1991), 21–44

Gilbert, Bentley B., 'David Lloyd George: the reform of British landholding and the budget of 1914', *Historical Journal* xxi (1978), 117–41

———— *David Lloyd George, a political life*, II: *Organizer of victory, 1912–1916*, Columbus, Ohio 1992

Gillie, Alan, 'The origin of the poverty line', *Economic History Review* 2nd ser. xlix (1996), 715–30

Ginswick, J. (ed.), *Labour and the poor in England and Wales, 1849–1851: the letters to the* Morning Chronicle *from the correspondents in the manufacturing and mining districts, the towns of Liverpool and Birmingham, and the rural districts*, London 1983

Gittings, Robert, *Young Thomas Hardy*, London 1975

Glass, D. V., *Numbering the people: the eighteenth-century population controversy and the development of census and vital statistics in Britain*, Farnborough 1973

Glass, Ruth, 'Urban sociology in Great Britain: a trend report', *Current Sociology* iv (1955), 5–76

Goddard, Nicholas, *Harvests of change: the Royal Agricultural Society of England, 1838–1988*, London 1988

Goldman, Lawrence, 'The origins of British "social science": political economy, natural science and statistics, 1830–1835', *Historical Journal* xxvi (1983), 587–616

———— 'A peculiarity of the English? The Social Science Association and the absence of sociology in nineteenth-century Britain', *Past and Present* cxiv (1987), 133–71

———— 'Statistics and the science of society in early Victorian Britain: an intellectual context for the General Register Office', *Social History of Medicine* iv (1991), 415–34

Green, E. H. H., *The crisis of conservatism: the politics, economics and ideology of the British Conservative party, 1880–1914*, London 1995

Groves, Reg, *Sharpen the sickle! The history of the farm workers' union*, London 1949

Halévy, Élie, *The rule of democracy, 1905–1914* (1st French edn 1932), London 1952

Hanser, Charles J., *Guide to decision: the royal commission*, Totowa, NJ 1965

Harris, José, 'Between civic virtue and social Darwinism: the concept of the residuum', in Englander and O'Day, *Retrieved riches*, 67–87

Harrison, Brian, *Peaceable kingdom: stability and change in modern Britain*, Oxford 1982

Heeney, Brian, 'On being a mid-Victorian clergyman', *Journal of Religious History* vii (1973), 208–24

Hennock, E. P., 'Poverty and social theory in England: the experience of the eighteen-eighties', *Social History* i (1976), 67–91

—— 'The measurement of urban poverty: from the metropolis to the nation, 1880–1920', *Economic History Review* 2nd ser. xl (1987), 208–27

—— 'Concepts of poverty in the British social surveys from Charles Booth to Arthur Bowley', in Bulmer and others, *The social survey*, 189–216

Higgs, Edward, 'Disease, febrile poisons, and statistics: the census as a medical survey', *Social History of Medicine* iv (1991), 465–78

—— *A clearer sense of the census: Victorian censuses and historical research*, London 1996

Himmelfarb, Gertrude, *The idea of poverty: England in the early industrial age*, London 1984

—— *Poverty and compassion: the moral imagination of the late Victorians*, New York 1991

Hobsbawm, E. J. and George Rudé, *Captain Swing* (1st edn 1969), Harmondsworth 1973

Holman, Bob, 'Research from the underside', *British Journal of Social Work* xvii (1987), 669–83

Holmes, G. S., 'Gregory King and the social structure of pre-industrial England', *Transactions of the Royal Historical Society* 5th ser. xxvii (1977), 41–68

Horn, Pamela, *Joseph Arch, 1826–1919: the farm workers' leader*, Kineton 1971

Howkins, Alun, *Poor labouring men: rural radicalism in Norfolk, 1870–1923*, London 1985

—— 'The discovery of rural England', in Robert Colls and Philip Dodd (eds), *Englishness: politics and culture, 1880–1920*, Beckenham 1986, 62–88

—— 'Rider Haggard and rural England: an essay in literature and history', in Christopher Shaw and Malcolm Chase (eds), *The imagined past: history and nostalgia*, Manchester 1989, 81–94

—— *Reshaping rural England: a social history, 1850–1925*, London 1991

—— 'From Hodge to Lob: reconstructing the English farm labourer, 1870–1914', in Chase and Dyck, *Living and learning*, 218–35

Humpherys, Anne, *Travels in the poor man's country: the work of Henry Mayhew*, Firle 1977

—— *Henry Mayhew*, Boston, Mass. 1984

Hunt, E. H., *Regional wage variations in Britain, 1850–1914*, Oxford 1973

Jahoda, Marie, Paul F. Lazarsfeld and Hans Zeisel, *Marienthal: the sociography of an unemployed community* (1st German edn 1933), London 1972

Johnson, Paul, *Saving and spending: the working-class economy in Britain, 1870–1939*, Oxford 1985

Jones, David, 'Rural crime and protest', in Mingay, *Victorian countryside*, ii. 566–79

——— 'Thomas Campbell Foster and the rural labourer: incendiarism in East Anglia in the 1840s', *Social History* i (1976), 5–43

——— *Crime, protest, community and police in nineteenth-century Britain*, London 1982

——— *Rebecca's children: a study of rural society, crime and protest*, Oxford 1989

Jones, David Caradog, *Social surveys*, London 1949

Jones, Gareth Stedman, *Outcast London: a study in the relationship between classes in Victorian society* (1st edn 1971), Harmondsworth 1984

Jorgensen, Danny L., *Participant observation: a methodology for human studies*, London 1989

Keating, Peter, *The working classes in Victorian fiction*, London 1971

——— (ed.), *Into unknown England, 1866–1913: selections from the social explorers*, Manchester 1976

Keith, W. J., *Richard Jefferies: a critical study*, London 1965

——— *The rural tradition: William Cobbett, Gilbert White and other non-fiction prose writers of the English countryside*, Toronto 1975

Kent, Raymond A., *A history of British empirical sociology*, Aldershot 1981

Koss, Stephen, *The rise and fall of the political press in Britain*, London 1981

Laslett, Peter, *The world we have lost* (1st edn 1965), London 1971

Lawton, Richard (ed.), *The census and social structure: an interpretative guide to nineteenth-century censuses for England and Wales*, London 1978

Leavis, F. R. and Denys Thompson, *Culture and environment: the training of critical awareness*, London 1930

Lewis, Jane, 'Social facts, social theory and social change: the ideas of Booth in relation to those of Beatrice Webb, Octavia Hill and Helen Bosanquet', in Englander and O'Day, *Retrieved riches*, 49–66

Looker, Samuel J. and Crichton Porteous, *Richard Jefferies, man of the fields: a biography and letters*, London 1965

McKibbin, Ross, *The ideologies of class: social relations in Britain, 1880–1950*, Oxford 1990

MAFF and Department of Agriculture and Fisheries for Scotland, *A century of agricultural statistics: Great Britain, 1866–1966*, London 1968

Manthorpe, Victoria, *Children of the empire: the Victorian Haggards*, London 1996

Marsh, Catherine, *The survey method: the contributions of surveys to sociological explanation*, London 1982

——— 'Informants, respondents and citizens', in Martin Bulmer (ed.), *Essays on the history of British sociological research*, Cambridge 1985, 206–27

Marsh, Jan, *Back to the land: the pastoral impulse in England, from 1880 to 1914*, London 1982

Mathias, Peter, 'The social structure in the eighteenth century: a calculation by Joseph Massie', *Economic History Review* 2nd ser. x (1957), 30–45

Meacham, Standish, *Toynbee Hall and social reform, 1880–1914: the search for community*, New Haven, Conn. 1987

Mills, Dennis, *Lord and peasant in nineteenth-century Britain*, London 1980

Mingay, G. E. (ed.), *Arthur Young and his times*, London 1975

—— (ed.) *The Victorian countryside*, London 1981

Mitchison, Rosalind, 'The old Board of Agriculture, 1793–1822', *English Historical Review* lxxiv (1959), 41–69

—— *Agricultural Sir John: the life of Sir John Sinclair of Ulbster, 1754–1835*, London 1962

Molloy, Pat, *And they blessed Rebecca: an account of the Welsh toll-gate riots, 1839–1844*, Llandysul 1983

Morgan, David Hoseason, *Harvesters and harvesting, 1840–1900: a study of the rural proletariat*, London 1982

Nattrass, Leonora, *William Cobbett: the politics of style*, Cambridge 1995

Neuberg, Victor E., 'The literature of the streets', in H. J. Dyos and Michael Wolff (eds), *The Victorian city: images and realities*, London 1973, ii. 191–209

Newby, Howard, *The deferential worker: a study of farm workers in East Anglia*, London 1977

O'Day, Rosemary, 'Before the Webbs: Beatrice Potter's early investigations for Charles Booth's inquiry', *History* lxxviii (1993), 218–42

—— 'Interviews and investigations: Charles Booth and the making of the religious influences survey', in Englander and O'Day, *Retrieved riches*, 143–63

—— 'Women and social investigation: Clara Collett and Beatrice Potter', in Englander and O'Day, *Retrieved riches*, 165–200

—— and David Englander, *Mr Charles Booth's inquiry*: Life and labour of the people in London *reconsidered*, London 1993

Oddy, D. J., 'Working-class diets in late nineteenth-century Britain', *Economic History Review* 2nd ser. xxiii (1970), 314–23

Offer, Avner, *Property and politics, 1870–1914: landownership, law, ideology and urban development in England*, Cambridge 1981

Osborne, J. D., 'Introduction', to Stephen Reynolds, *A poor man's house* (1st edn 1908), London 1980, pp. vii–xvi

Packer, Ian, *Lloyd George, Liberalism and the land: the land issue in party politics in England, 1906–1914*, Woodbridge 2001

Perry, P. J., 'Edward Girdlestone, 1805–84: a forgotten evangelical', *Journal of Religious History* ix (1977), 292–301

Razzell, P. E. and R. W. Wainwright (eds), *The Victorian working class: selections from letters to the* Morning Chronicle, London 1973

Reay, Barry, *The last rising of the agricultural labourers: rural life and protest in nineteenth-century England*, Oxford 1990

—— *Microhistories: demography, society and culture in rural England, 1800–1930*, Cambridge 1996

Reed, Mick and Roger Wells (eds), *Class, conflict and protest in the English countryside, 1700–1880*, London 1990

Samuel, Raphael (ed.), *Village life and labour* (1st edn 1975), London 1982

Saville, John, *Rural depopulation in England and Wales, 1851–1951*, London 1957

Sayer, Karen, *Women of the fields: representations of rural women in the nineteenth century*, Manchester 1995

Scoble, Christopher, *Fisherman's friend: a life of Stephen Reynolds*, Tiverton 2000

Scotland, Nigel, *Methodism and the revolt of the field: a study of the Methodist contribution to agricultural trade unionism in East Anglia, 1872–1896*, Gloucester 1981
—— 'The National Agricultural Labourers' Union and the demand for a stake in the soil', in Eugenio F. Biagini (ed.), *Citizenship and community: liberals, radicals and collective identities in the British Isles, 1865–1931*, Cambridge 1996, 151–67

Searle, G. R., *The quest for national efficiency: a study in British politics and political thought, 1899–1914* (1st edn 1971), London 1990

Selley, Ernest, *Village trade unions in two centuries*, London 1919

Selvin, Hanan C., 'Durkheim, Booth and Yule: the non-diffusion of an intellectual innovation', *Archives européennes de sociologie* xvii (1976), 39–51

Semmel, Bernard, *Imperialism and social reform: English social-imperial thought, 1895–1914*, London 1960

Sheils, William, 'Church, community and culture in rural England, 1850–1900: J. C. Atkinson and the parish of Danby in Cleveland', in Simon Ditchfield (ed.), *Christianity and community in the west: essays for John Bossy*, Aldershot 2001, 260–77

Simey, T. S. and M. B. Simey, *Charles Booth: social scientist*, London 1960

Smith, F. B., 'Mayhew's convict', *Victorian Studies* xxii (1979), 431–48

Snell, K. D. M., *Annals of the labouring poor: social change and agrarian England, 1660–1900* (1st edn 1985), Cambridge 1987

Spater, George, *William Cobbett: the poor man's friend*, Cambridge 1982

Springall, L. Marion, *Labouring life in Norfolk villages, 1834–1914*, London 1936

Stapleton, Barry (ed.), *Conflict and community in southern England: essays in the social history of rural and urban labour from medieval to modern times*, Stroud 1992

Taithe, Bertrand (ed.), *The essential Mayhew: representing and communicating the poor*, London 1996

Thompson, Denys, 'A cure for amnesia', *Scrutiny* ii (1933), 2–11

Thompson, Dorothy, *The Chartists: popular politics in the industrial revolution* (1st edn 1984), Aldershot 1986

Thompson, E. P. and George Rudé, *Captain Swing* (1st edn 1969), Harmondsworth 1973

Thompson, E. P. and Eileen Yeo (eds), *The unknown Mayhew: selections from the Morning Chronicle, 1849–1850*, London 1971

Thompson, Paul, *The voice of the past: oral history* (1st edn 1978), Oxford 2000

Veit-Wilson, J. H., 'Paradigms of poverty: a rehabilitation of B. S. Rowntree', *Journal of Social Policy* xv (1986), 69–99 (repr. in Englander and O'Day, *Retrieved riches*, 201–37)

Walkowitz, Judith, 'The Indian woman, the flower girl and the Jew: photojournalism in Edwardian London', *Victorian Studies* xlii (1998), 3–46

Waller, P. J., *Town, city and nation: England, 1850–1914*, Oxford 1983

Ward, W. A., 'Poor old Grover!', *Cambridge Quarterly* iii (1967), 86–8

Watson, J. A. Scott, *The history of the Royal Agricultural Society of England, 1839–1939*, London 1939

Wells, A. F., *The local social survey in Great Britain*, London 1935

Williams, David, *The Rebecca riots: a study in agrarian discontent* (1st edn 1955), Cardiff 1968

Williams, Karel, *From pauperism to poverty*, London 1981

Williams, Raymond, *Cobbett*, Oxford 1983

———— *The country and the city* (1st edn 1973), London 1985

Williams, Sarah C., 'The problem of belief: the place of oral history in the study of popular religion', *Oral History* xxiv/2 (1996), 27–34

Wilson, Adrian, 'Foundations of an integrated historiography', in Adrian Wilson (ed.), *Rethinking social history: English society, 1570–1920, and its interpretation*, Manchester 1993, 293–335

Wrigley, Chris, *Lloyd George*, Oxford 1992

Yeo, Eileen Janes, 'The social survey in social perspective', in Bulmer and others, *The social survey*, 49–65

———— *The contest for social science: relations and representations of gender and class*, London 1996

Unpublished theses

Cohen, Susan, 'The life and works of M. Loane', MPhil diss. Middlesex 1997

Fraser, John, 'George Sturt ("George Bourne") and rural labouring life', PhD diss. Minnesota 1961

Freeman, Mark, 'Social investigation in rural England, 1870–1914', PhD diss. Glasgow 1999

Lister, Anthony, 'George Sturt: a study of his development as a writer and his conception of village life', MA diss. Manchester 1961

Osborne, J. D., 'Stephen Reynolds: a biographical and critical study', PhD diss. London 1978

Index